E IN THE NINETIES

Douglas
Camp Neosho

Riverside Drive Was Radiant With the Multi-Colored Headlights of Returning Bicyclers

IN THE
GOLDEN NINETIES

BY
HENRY COLLINS BROWN

VALENTINE'S MANUAL
NUMBER TWELVE, 1928

VALENTINE'S MANUAL, Inc.
HASTINGS-ON-HUDSON
1928

To

A. C. J.

FOREWORD

"Fond Memory brings the light
Of other days around me."

THE last three issues of the Manual, recalling our old city in the closing years of the Nineteenth Century, have been received with a measure of favor much in excess of my expectations. This has been a pleasant experience and one which I duly appreciate.

The "Golden Nineties" proved so rich in material that it could not be contained in one book. So the next number of the Manual will be a continuation of the same period. In it, much to my sorrow, I shall record the final passing of the ancient city of New York. After 1898 the city becomes Greater New York, and the island at the mouth of the Hudson becomes the Borough of Manhattan.

Among the vast changes I have witnessed, the one that seems to stand out apart from all the others is the disappearance of old age. The spectacle of grandfathers and grandmothers dancing on the same floor with their grown-up children was something never seen in my day.

I approve of this change. Perhaps I may yet enjoy cigarette smoking by women. Nothing can surprise me any more.

THE AUTHOR.

ACKNOWLEDGMENTS

MANY of the interesting old pictures in this number are taken from back numbers of *Harper's
Weekly, Harper's Magazine, Century* and *Scribner's.*
The people of the theatre from the Albert B. Davis collection; Brown Bros., Wurtz Bros., Byron, Aimee Dupont and Pach Bros. The decorative posters from the
wonderful private collection owned by Mr. H. L. Sparks
of this city. The old time colored theatrical posters
were supplied by the Strobridge Litho Co. of Cincinnati, the Buffalo Courier Co.; New York Public
Library and New York Historical Society. The Currier
& Ives prints are from Kennedy & Co., Fifth Avenue,
New York.

CONTENTS

CHAPTER I

NEW YORK IN THE GOLDEN NINETIES

CHAPTER II

COMING OF THE SKYSCRAPER

CHAPTER III

THE THEATRE

CONTENTS

CONTENTS

CHAPTER VII
ADVERTISING

CHAPTER VIII
WALL STREET IN THE GOLDEN NINETIES

CHAPTER IX
PASSING OF THE LIVERY STABLE

CHAPTER X
COMING OF THE BIG HOTELS

CHAPTER XI
TROTTING HORSES.—FLEETWOOD PARK
PASSING OF THE CARRIAGE, ETC.

CONTENTS

LIST OF ILLUSTRATIONS

LIST OF ILLUSTRATIONS

LIST OF ILLUSTRATIONS

CORNER PARK AVENUE AND 97TH STREET IN THE 90'S

NEW YORK IN THE GOLDEN NINETIES

CHAPTER I.

I CONFESS to a feeling akin to sadness as the thread of my story reaches the nineties. They record, in one sense, the last days of another Pompeii— the last days of little Old New York. The proud name which she had gallantly borne for three centuries was now to be torn from her grasp. The last link that connected her with her days of romance, her Indians, her Pirates, her valiant struggle for freedom, her Raines Law sandwich was to be a thing of the past. No more was the little seaport at the mouth of the lordly Hudson to be called by the name which navigators, explorers and mariners had made known to the Seven Seas. In order to realize her manifest destiny—to become still greater—it became necessary to ally herself with

Hunter's Point, Far Rockaway, Long Island City and the Bronx! The mantle of her shining greatness fell upon these benighted communities and now the traveller from Brooklyn is no longer ashamed to register from his home town, but gaily and at last truthfully inscribes himself from New York. The Borough of Manhattan may in time come to mean something. For the present it is a mouthing—a cymbal of brass. To the old New Yorker the name New York will always mean the city on Manhattan Island at the mouth of the Hudson River and will never mean anything else. All the consolidations, annexations, combinations, etc., to the contrary notwithstanding.

And now to the burden of my discourse. It is yet the early nineties and I am still in real old New York. Not till almost the closing years of this decade am I obliged to record this lamentable change. So till almost the last page I am speaking of New York and not of the contraption of five upstart Boroughs strutting around in unmerited splendor as part of that ancient and honorable commonwealth, the Empire City, little old New York.

The city had now a population of about one and a half millions. One could see that it was entering upon a larger and more imposing career. It had definitely emerged from its small town atmosphere and was beginning to acquire the mannerisms and customs of a world capital. Hotels had discontinued the neat but necessary sign in the bedrooms adjuring guests not to blow out the gas. The freeborn American servitor no longer regarded a tip as a personal insult. Eatin' tobacco was slowly but surely losing its former high standing in society and the streets were full of "dudes".

"PLUG" HATS AND CELLULOID COLLARS

Ladies no longer muttered curses under their breath when the usher politely requested them to remove their hats in the theatre, and it became an unwritten law among our common or garden citizens to perk up in their manners and cut out a good deal of rough house in their daily contacts. Many were saddened to know that the use of double negatives was decidedly "bad form", an expression just then coming into vogue. Sartorial matters, hitherto an almost exclusively feminine concern, began to be subject of male inquiry. The gentleman in the theatre programme of today, who instructs the raw and untutored occupant of a twelve dollar seat in the arts of dress, had his literary ancestor in the Sunday papers of the Nineties. They discoursed learnedly on the enormity of wearing plug hats with reefers, straw hats with swallow tails, celluloid collars, and made-up neckties. Men began to make a serious study of tying an Ascot. It became a matter of common knowledge that evening dress was not to be worn until after six o'clock. The higher education of the middle classes was accomplished without offense, by the introduction of jokes about the man who never ate peas with a knife because they rolled off, and other pleasantries designed to impart etiquette without the vulgar necessity of constantly yelling that something is wrong with this picture.

The end of the century also saw the blessed ending of an institution that called down the anathema of Tom Hood in his "Song of the Shirt"; I allude to that underpaid, overworked starveling, the seamstress. This pathetic figure was usually the symbol of the "she may have seen better days" legend. In the early days of New York, shirt making, before Helen of Troy entered the industry, the seamstress was largely engaged in that jovial occupation, whereby as much as ninety cents a day of fourteen hours, was earned bending over cambric and fine linen.

In those days, and later, the shops had no such variety of ready-made garments as today. There were no "Slenderforms", "Boyishforms", or other illusions of attenuation. All these subtleties of feminine attire had to be the subject of individual attention and the seamstress was a periodical inmate of every well ordered home where femininity was to be outfitted. Here she was subject to the maddening problems of "making over". She had to make stout "Mama" slender, and poor, peaked "Ethel" plump. She had to perform miracles with odds and ends from the rag-bag, and to turn out a Worth "creation" from an assortment of old petticoats raked out of a "Saratoga" trunk. Nervous prostration was the lot and the reward of such an one, and the industry contributed its full quota to the "cuckoo" ranks.

These dames of the needle were great gossips. They were bound to have some antidote to their deadly vocation. Going from house to house they always had a store of tittle-tattle and back-stairs chatter to entertain their employers, and many of them had the "low down" on family skeletons that were supposed by their custodians, to be safely closeted.

Ladies' bustles began to decline, and in the dawn of Twentieth Century civilization were banished altogether. Likewise a long list of intimate articles, the wearing of which, produced the opposite of a boyish form. The use of the handkerchief was encouraged, and numerous persons were astonished to learn that the

THE FLATIRON ON A WINDY DAY

Prince of Wales never used a toothpick during meals or after them. Women wore enormous leg o' mutton sleeves, "common sense" shoes, and "straight front" corsets, and I remember as if it were but yesterday a small paragraph in the Sun to the effect that Miss Daisy Miller "walked down Broadway after the rain yesterday wearing one of those abbreviated skirts specially designed for wet weather, which she is trying to popularize. The skirt not only clears the ground, but does it by enough inches to expose the wearer's shoe top. The skirt seems practical, although a trifle immodest." In spite of this blatant exposure, the new garment was so obviously a good idea that it rapidly came into fashion. It retained the name suggested by its inventor and was known as the Rainy Daisy skirt. A young lady, however, could easily get herself talked about by wearing this particular skirt on days when it didn't rain.

In these trailing skirt days it was nothing unusual to see a crowd of boys and young men and men not so young, congregate around the sheltered doorways of the Flatiron Building. The gusts that were created by the peculiar position of this particular building were the cause of much embarrassment to the ladies caught unaware in a small-sized hurricane. The resultant effect —sometimes you could actually see a glimpse of hosiery —was the cause of much merriment among the cloistered group in the doorways.

I often wonder what would have been the effect on the young men of the nineties if they were suddenly confronted with the styles of today?

The men wore Prince Albert frock coats at almost any polite function, except formal dinner, where the tailcoat reigned supreme, and high silk toppers with wonderfully curved rims. The present Tuxedo was practically non-existent. Derbies and covert coats with spats, marked the well dressed man downtown. The covert coat was a fawn colored melton or box-cloth not long enough to conceal the tails of a cuta-way, a few inches of which were generally exposed. The coat was cut high in the collar, fitting the neck closely, and a huge Ascot with a diamond horseshoe decorated the tie. Occasionally one would encounter a suit of such extreme cut and pattern as to fairly shriek as it moved along the thoroughfare.

It was about this time, too, that men began to dis-card boiled shirts as hot weather attire. Heretofore "outing" or "tennis" shirts were made of flannel and worn only for sports, or by the hoi polloi at chowder parties, with white duck caps. Then the Madison Square haberdashers began to import "Oxford" weave shirts, which were rather heavy cotton, and improving on these later offered "Zephyr" weaves, of a lighter texture. These were eagerly seized on by the swelter-ing populace, who found in them a new dispensation of Providence. It took quite a time, however, to allure the dandies of the Seventies and Eighties away from the cast-iron "shield" bosom shirt that would deflect a bullet. It opened only at the back and had a tab on it with a button-hole for some mysterious purpose con-nected with underwear.

Once freed from the yoke of this armorial garment we swung to the other extreme and men's shirt waists appeared in the shop windows with no sign of mob vio-lence. The shirt waist brought the belt in place of suspenders and removed this unsightly blot on the landscape, to the further advancement in popularity of the shirt waist.

Tan, or "russet" shoes also made their first appearance on the local stage of fashion. Previously the only alternative to black shoes were canvas "baseball" or "tennis" shoes. Almost all shoes were high, only a small minority wearing "Oxford ties" in summer and in winter not at all.

OLD FIFTH AVENUE

The stateliest street in all our village was then at the peak of her magnificence. Fifth Avenue never again touched the dizzy heights she achieved in the Nineties. Private houses such as kings and potentates might envy were of such common occurrence that they ceased to occasion remark. The hunter was home from the hills. He brought his kill with him. Foreign countries are satisfied with one king. Fifth Avenue had many. Royalty in the shape of Glue Kings, Copper Kings, Railroad Kings, were everywhere. New York was taking no chances. If one dynasty collapsed, there was always plenty left just as good.

There was not as yet beyond 28th Street the slightest intimation of the coming avalanche of tradesmen. Along the street, in many of the "front yards" were pleasant spots of color where flowers grew and grass still suggested a miniature lawn. Brownstone stoops in unbroken company-front formation lined the Avenue on both sides from Washington Square clear up to the Park. Even after the Waldorf was built, the space included in the stoop line was utilized as a flower garden. And a brilliant show it made with its scarlet geraniums, timid violets and yellow tulips. With the brilliant colored awnings above it, the glimpse of well dressed men and women in the dining room plainly visible from the street, this was quite an attractive point in a stroll down the Avenue. Similar charming spots were in front of Delmonico's at 26th Street, the Union League and in front of Avery's Art Galleries. At 37th Street there was a florist whose stock in trade was always a riot of color and added to the joy of living.

But the right to the stoop line turned out to be a right based on custom but not in fact. So when the great rush of business invaded the Avenue and caused a tremendous pressure for more room and still more room, Mr. George McAneny discovered this flaw in the title, claimed the land for the city, and the Avenue was widened fifteen feet on each side and all the front stoops, areaways, gardens, etc., disappeared. Thus does beauty ever suffer when utility rears its ugly head.

The church parade on Sunday had become a ritual and one of the sights of the Metropolis. It was also a gift of manna from Heaven to the growing cloak and suiters. Their most adept designers were among the most devout worshippers and their cleverest copiers were conspicuous for their religious piety. In a few weeks, Chicago, Kansas City and other points West would bristle with cheap imitations of the styles seen in the Easter parades and the department stores in towns as small as Los Angeles or San Francisco would display the latest New York creations at $14.98 marked down from $50 within a month after their appearance on the Avenue.

Around the Reservoir where now stands the Public Library, the crowd was densest. It milled up and down

HOW FIFTH AVENUE LOOKED IN THE 90'S AFTER A SNOW FALL

The figure is dressed in the current last minute fashion.

A Typical Afternoon Costume for the
Well-Dressed Man

A Rain Coat of the Ninetie[s]

FOR A PRIVATE DINNER AT SHERRY'S

This is the manner in which the waiters were dressed

THE TWIN VANDERBILT HOUSES

In Fifth Avenue between 51st and 52nd Streets. Northern twin, demolished 1927

the few blocks north and south and in this section at least, a majority of the strollers were old families who knew each other intimately and their friendly greetings imparted an air of neighborliness strangely missing from a similar gathering to-day. By one o'clock the street would be largely deserted to again resume its crowded condition as the afternoon wore on.

Perhaps the greatest change—at least the one that would excite the most remark today—would be to say that there were no crowds on the Avenue on week days between 34th street and the Park, and men folks were seldom seen on it at all. North of 42nd street there were a number of private schools for young ladies. Detachments from these schools, marching demurely two by two, were frequently seen in this section in the afternoons but beyond that, passersby were few and far between. But for the shining equipages of the many handsome family coaches the Avenue was practically bare of animation.

I remember walking up from Madison Square one evening in December. A light snow had fallen—just enough to deaden the sound of foot falls and soften the crash of the iron shod wheels on the Belgian blocks. As far north as I could see, there was scarcely a person in sight. Away off in the distance, I heard the faint tinkle of the horse car bells on the 42nd street crosstown line, as it passed Governor Morton's house and was lost behind the bleak ramparts of the Reservoir. Occasionally, a handsome carriage with two in livery on the box, would draw up at the curb. At the top of the massive stone steps, a great door would open, throwing a stream of golden light on the whitened street and then all would be dark and silent again.

A "DIRT FARMERS" CLUB

The Metropolitan Club at 60th Street, marking an advance beyond 59th Street, came into existence about this time as a result of a squabble with the Union. In those days, members of the Union Club would post their male children for membership on the day of their birth. Consequently the waiting list had the accent on the wait. Besides, they were rather fussy about other inconsequential details mainly relating to family connections. During the late war, the members of the Union Club astonished the *hoi polloi* by putting up a splendid scrap with some hoodlums who attempted to haul down some of the flags flying from the club house. Broken heads, blackened eyes and sundry other damages were worn by the attackers for days but the injury to their feelings was worst of all; no gentleman's club was ever supposed to have real fighters in it and they could not forgive this flagrant breach of etiquette on the part of the members.

The Metropolitan became known as the "Millionaires' Club" and probably no term was ever more ineptly applied. As a matter of fact most of the members are farmers. You can't get a corporal's guard to attend a meeting unless some dirt farmer is billed to give them a talk on raising chickens by electric light or some other bucolic subject. Their heroes are the persons who compete successfully in hog calling and duck calling contests. The plaintive lone quack of the mallard duck and other duck calls, as exchanged between a woman and her husband on one notable occasion, won them high honors in the club. When the news reached them that these same two quackers had won first prize at a National Quacking Championship Contest out in Illinois, excitement ran high.

"I am willing to quack against the world", was the telegraphed triumphant quack of the champion, announcing his victory. Five other ranking quackers were likewise remembered with suitable gifts and the enthusiasm in the club was so great that all seven quackers narrowly escaped being elected honorary members.

The Metropolitan structure marked what was to be "Farthest North" on the Avenue for Clubland. Beyond that soon stretched a mile of magnificent residences of all shapes and schools of architecture, ending with Carnegie's Castle at 91st street. This whole stretch was supposed to be impregnable against the assaults of business and was dedicated for all time to the sacred purpose of preserving the old homestead. In the Nineties there was not the slightest intimation that this arrangement would ever be called in question buttressed as it was by more than a mile of similar minded persons south of the park. One would have been justified in saying that the permanency of Fifth Avenue was as unalterable as the laws of the Medes and the Persians. It was a noble thoroughfare, impressive beyond description and the most celebrated highway in the Western World. It lasted through the "Golden Nineties" intact. But the new century had hardly opened ere the débâcle began.

The first shot from the enemy's camp appeared in the shape of a woman's specialty shop opened by Franklin Simon at the corner of 38th street. This was in the very heart of the lower residential section and its advent carried consternation into the ranks of the old timers. A general assault all along the line followed and one stronghold after another capitulated. Rockefeller, Vanderbilt and others spent millions in a vain attempt to head off the onrushing hordes but in the end were defeated. Commodore Gerry headed the militants above 59th street. He fought valiantly against the threat of apartment houses. His recent death removes the last of the old guard. The apartment builder has now no more opposition than the business man.

The demolition of the Vanderbilt and Huntington Houses this year removes the last of the old structures that are so indelibly associated with the avenue in its days of glory. There are now no houses left that gave the avenue the regal splendor that was hers in the Golden Nineties.

The Huntington House always held for me a peculiar fascination. It seemed to symbolize the owner's final triumphant gesture over obstacles that would have engulfed a less resolute soul. Many years ago, in San Francisco, I saw the sign *Huntington, Hopkins & Co.,* over a hardware establishment. Yes; it was the identical store in which Huntington and his partners dreamed the dream of an iron band linking this great nation together. I had little difficulty in persuading one of the clerks to re-enact for me the birth of the transcontinental railroad. Some tenpenny kegs, a couple of empty barrels, a little scene-shifting to get them in their old time places, and the stage was set for Act I.

It was quite easy to picture the group—at first mildly indifferent, and gradually, as Huntington enthused, becoming more and more interested. As success seemed less and less chimerical, the leader's heels kicked a swifter and a louder tattoo against the resounding barrel staves.

The iron band had been completed many years before Collis P. Huntington permitted himself the luxury of a castle on the avenue. I wonder—I wonder, if he really enjoyed it as much as lying beneath the shining stars of the Rocky Mountains under a canopy of murmuring pines? He built within the shadow of the Twin Houses and his home eclipsed in splendor even that of Vanderbilt. In the end both were purchased and wrecked by Polish boys who struck the town penniless and friendless less years ago than were spent in building the Pacific and Hudson River Railways.

The twin houses were erected by William H. Vanderbilt, the first in succession to the doughty Commodore— one for himself and the other for Mrs. Sloane. For its day and generation they were considered a marvel. Upon completion of the buildings, Mr. Vanderbilt caused a mighty tome to be printed—several mighty tomes to be exact—each two and a half feet wide by four feet long. There were fifteen of these huge volumes in all, and they weighed about a ton. And from cover to cover they set forth the glories of the new mansions. They were published by a firm in Philadelphia whose chief claim to fame in a literary way was their ability to "trim the suckers", as it was vulgarly expressed.

Beginning with the entrance through the vestibule on the south side of which were two huge bronze doors from the originals in Florence by Ghiberti and which were unostentatiously called "The Gates of Paradise", the various pages were each in turn assigned to a special room. Elaborate etchings, photographs reproduced in the most expensive manner and enormous colored drawings, embellished the book throughout. No expense was spared, and if there was any doubt left as to the exact size and heft of the Vanderbilt fortune these books undoubtedly proved that it was not to be sneezed at, no matter what else you might think. These volumes were presented by Mr. Vanderbilt to his admiring friends at first, though I think, in later years this distinction was reserved for his enemies.

Curiously enough, amidst all this splendor, the room reserved for the personal use of the head of the house is singularly small and homelike. I have taken it for granted that his favorite nook would be a corner of the library. For a bibliophile of such robust taste that is a natural conclusion. So out of all the numerous plates, engravings and lithographs I have chosen to reproduce only the inexpensive line drawing of a corner in the library.

The rocking chair seems to me a trifle delicate in structure, considering the ponderous weight it was supposed to uphold, but it has a Staten Island atmosphere about it which perhaps endeared it to the owner. In no other way can I account for the chenille trimming or the chaste and delicate pattern of the upholstery. The skilled hand of the decorator is strangely missing from the library. All the other rooms show unmistakably the fine practised hand of the professional atelier, and each one would look equally well in a museum. But William H. was vastly pleased with his new possessions and doubtless greatly enjoyed the huge structure which he fondly called home. He did not live to hear his heart's desire called by the ribald crowd "the twin horrors". It was fashionable in his day to live in a dim religious light and exclude all air by massive layers of heavy curtains. He was seldom away from these houses. He undoubtedly enjoyed every minute spent in them, and when he was called to his fathers no doubt his chief regret was, that there couldn't possibly be any Mansion in the Sky that could equal the one he left behind on Fifth Avenue.

This Vanderbilt had a rather erratic career. He was the eldest son of the Commodore, but for some reason or no reason the Commodore made up his mind that William couldn't row his own weight in the boat. So, at first the son had to play the part of the poor relation —very poor—while the Commodore continued to pile up the millions.

But eventually the mantle of Elijah descended upon the shoulders of the despised William Henry. Was he downhearted? Not much. All the pent up energy of a million years seemed to be his. The crushing weight of the vast responsibilities which were now his slipped off his back like water from a duck. Almost every afternoon he let the wind blow through his flamboyant whiskers in a spirited brush behind Maud S. or Goldsmith Maid against Dick Swiveller or Dexter on the way to Hiram Woodruff's or Gabe Case's. Under his able management the New York Central flourished like a green bay tree planted by a river. He was no post prandial speaker as was his friend Chauncey Depew, yet on one memorable occasion he revealed the possession of a gift of eloquence wholly unsuspected.

It is now known in English classics as the "public be damned" speech. It ranks with the best efforts of Cicero or Demosthenes. Incidentally, it almost busted the railroad and despite a prompt disclaimer, the storm did not abate for a long time.

Aside from this little by-play, William H. has little or nothing to his discredit. And the little was more than offset by many other things in the way of valued public services. He came at a time when the fortunes of the Vanderbilt family needed a guiding hand, wise, cautious, and yet progressive. In all these traits William H. Vanderbilt more than met the test.

The custom of publishing expensive volumes exploiting the contents of noted houses seemed quite the proper thing in those days. Mr. Vanderbilt was not alone in his glory. Imposing volumes, though on a lesser scale, describing the residences of Henry Villard, Louis Tiffany, James L. Breese and about twenty others were in circulation. None of the interiors, to my mind, showed any individuality whatever. They were all the product of gifted gasfitters, masquerading as professional decorators. The Elsie de Wolf School had not yet put in an appearance but I have no doubt the sight of these dreary wildernesses of culture, had much to do with lifting this capable artiste from the land of make-believe to the more practical field where her undoubted abilities were sadly needed.

It seems to me that the loss of the Cornelius house was a real public calamity. This building had some architectural beauty. It recalled the amazing cult for everything French in New York, at the time of its erection. While not ranking with such a typical American house as the Wentworth house in Portsmouth or the Schuyler home in Albany, it was, nevertheless, an excellent reproduction of French architecture. Its beautiful grilled iron entrance with its porte cochère was the last of its kind in the city. It was a pity that some public institution did not succeed in acquiring it.

The William K. house on 55th Street was a splendid copy of a famous French Château. It was much

A CORNER IN THE LIBRARY OF WILLIAM H. VANDERBILT I.
In the twin houses, recently torn down. 1885

BALL ROOM IN THE VINCENT ASTOR RESIDENCE

This is the sort of thing that has been ruthlessly destroyed in the demolitions of Fifth Avenue

less pretentious in size and appearance, but it was beautiful. It should have been preserved and re-erected elsewhere. With all these individual buildings gone, the curtain falls on a scene that will not be soon forgotten by the old New Yorker.

Although there has been loud lamentation and much gnashing of teeth over this débâcle of old homes on Fifth Avenue, there has been a silver lining to this otherwise devastating cloud. The Clark mansion has been included in the general destruction.

The Broadway that we know today is not by any means the Broadway of thirty odd years ago. It is more congested, more hectic, but it is not as important relatively to the rest of the city. Its fine shops have departed to other streets. Its theatres lurk in by-ways, its hotels mere commercial caravansaries. In the delectable day we are discussing it was the city's representative highway, its real Main Street. The leisurely found it a pleasant promenade, the busy were unimpeded by the swarms of industrial workers, now in overwhelming numbers. All the world came to Broadway, to shop, to dine, to flirt, to find amusement, and to meet acquaintances, and the legend ran that one standing in the portico of the Fifth Avenue Hotel would one day meet any long sought acquaintance whencesoever he might come. The pen and pencil of the writer and draughtsman always found contrasting types of interest on Broadway and the weeklies gave a little series of portraits by a notable delineator in both arts of the town's celebrities. V. Gribayedoff probably did more free hand sketches of the famous and near famous of the city than any other man who had ever wielded a pencil within its borders. A trenchant master in the graphic art, Gribayedoff often supplemented his drawings with descriptive matter hardly less penetrating. This series of sketches had almost the authenticity of photographs.

First, and most distinguished, is General Fitz-John Porter, attended by his valet. The General was the central figure in a bitter army feud that was periodically aired in courts martial and Federal inquiries. He was charged by General Pope with disobedience of orders at the battle of Warrenton, and the consequent defeat of the Union army at the Second Manasses. Porter spent years in efforts to rehabilitate himself and I believe that the upshot of it all resulted in a sort of vindication of his claims.

Addressing one of his colleagues we see the hero of Lillian Russell's third matrimonial venture, John Perugini, *née* Chatterton, one of the early tenors of the Casino forces. Perugini was one of the company that opened the Casino in 1882 in *"The Queen's Lace Handkerchief"*.

In quite another sphere was Professor Corbitt, "the Shakespeare of the Bowery", reputed to be the inventor of the chicken incubator. An antithesis to this figure in the Broadway throng is Lawrence M. Godkin, the scholarly editor of the *"Evening Post"*, a most trenchant supporter of good government and one of the nation's most distinguished publicists. In his good company we must put Bruce Crane, painter, and Bruce Price, architect, and a notable figure in art circles.

Here we have expounding some altruistic theory on a park bench, George Francis Train, philosopher and eccentric, who, in a white duck suit, was the delight of children, in Madison Square Park whither he repaired in fair weather from his quarters in the old Continental Hotel on Broadway and 20th Street. After a career of extraordinary vicissitudes Train was averse from conversation with adults, and as a gesture of cynicism devoted most of his intercourse to children.

In the shadow of the Fifth Avenue Hotel stands Fred de Belleville, known to all playgoers of a generation ago. Fred was one of the most accomplished actors of his day, his distinguished bearing being always in demand in drawing-room drama. His support of Mrs. Fiske in the charming comedy of *"Divorcons"* was a notable bit of high comedy. He excelled, perhaps, in romantic rôles of the sword-play variety, to which he might be said to have fallen heir. He was a scion of a noble Belgian family, his father and brother being high officers in the army. Young de Belleville would have none of the rigid regimentation of arms, preferring the sock and buskin, to the great chagrin of his relatives. He served his apprenticeship on the classic boards of Sadler's Wells, in London, under that renowned master, Samuel Phelps and came to America, a versatile technician of the drama. His "Henri" to Rose Coghlan's "Countess Zicka" in *"Diplomacy"* and his "Nortier" in James O'Neill's, *"Monte Cristo"* are high lights in a brilliant dramatic career.

We have with us also on this page the celebrated international gambler, "Pat" Sheedy. During his last years Pat became a kind of "Mister Dooley" of the green cloth, and moralized against the wheel and the "layout". Pat had the confidence of the underworld and of the police and was the "go-between" in the return of the famous Gainsborough portrait of the Duchess of Devonshire, cut from its frame in Agnew's

London artrooms. Sheedy was known to gamesters the world over and at one time was a backer of John L. Sullivan.

Less renowned, but a figure entitled to a corner in our gallery is the bushy-haired, fierce mustachiod Leo Von Rosen, the inventor of the modern theatre programme in its booklet form. The old-time programme was a kind of broadside, whose principal artistic feature was a portrait of a toothsome young woman advertising "Sozodont". Von Rosen enlarged the advertising possibilities of the programme and condensed it to a more compact and handy form.

Others whom we find taking the air on Broadway are Charley Reed, gambler and horseman, Winfield Scott, son of the Mexican War leader, Archbishop Corrigan, a popular ecclesiastic, and "Jakey, the Hawk", a street character; a strange assortment but part of the colorful throng that made what was once "Broadway".

Upper Broadway was at this time a fascinating Street then called "The Boulevard". This was one of Bill Tweed's benefactions to the city. It was built while the rage for everything French still controlled the population, had a fine central parkway with splendid trees dividing the roadway, and bordering the sidewalks. Sea-going horse cars in which a ride equalled the sensation obtained on the back of a cantering horse, provided transportation to the leisurely. A few apartment houses had been built up as far as 72nd Street. Above that, the Boulevard was garnished with old mansions, set on rocks in spacious grounds; roadhouses, blacksmith shops and the usual sundries of shantytown. The roadhouses provided an apparatus in which a bicycle might be locked, while the owner was inside

enjoying refreshments. A personage, the successor of
the old time hostler, had this in charge. Building along
the Boulevard was much later than on parallel streets
like Columbus and Amsterdam Avenues, as the owners
of land were holding on for the big prices that Broadway property always commands as the street crawls
northward.

The change from Boulevard to Broadway was largely
due to the efforts of the proprietor of the new Empire
Hotel, Mr. W. Johnson Minn, who discovered that his
advertising in out-of-town papers, bearing the address
"Western Boulevard" led many readers to imagine that
his very accessible situation was, on the contrary, in
some outlying suburb. He, therefore, appealed to that
influential body, the West End Association, to use their
functions in behalf of a generally desirable change of
name. On February 14th, 1899, Mayor Van Wyck
signed the necessary papers officially bestowing the name
of Broadway on this relic of Second Empire nomenclature.

One of these old Broadway mansions deserves particular mention. Along about 1890 saw the last of it—
the famous old Apthorpe Mansion, on the Boulevard
between 78th and 79th Streets. Perched on the rocks
there, hidden from the view of thousands who daily
passed on the elevated road, by a row of modern flats,
this old historic house still stood, a battered, neglected
relic of Revolutionary days with scarcely a trace of its
former splendor. Its original owner, Charles Ward
Apthorpe, was an Englishman who had acquired large
wealth by trading in this country. This house, which
he built about 1757, was then the centre of an imposing
country estate; for Apthorpe had purchased many acres

of land in that neighborhood. He had acquired much prominence in the political and social circles of those days, his strong Tory sympathies making him particularly intimate with Governor Tryon and other English officials, who with the leading social personages of the colony, attended the balls and dinners which he frequently gave for the entertainment of his friends. Doubtless many courtly dames and charming damsels passed into the spacious hall with its painted floor imitating flags of marble. The rooms, to the last, bore signs of early splendor, bits of carving, mahogany panels, and stray pieces of cornice, serving up to the time of its demolition to indicate their past glories. Wandering through the deserted chambers, marred and defaced though they were by the almost sacrilegious uses to which they had been put in their later years, sufficient traces of the Eighteenth Century remained to induce visions of a time when the view of the broad Hudson in the rear was obstructed only by trees, and majestic verdant rocks met the eastward glance.

Although Apthorpe was a Royalist, and had even gone so far as to sign an address to Lord Howe asserting his allegiance to King George, his home sheltered George Washington during the night of September 14th, 1776. After supper he planned there the expedition which Nathan Hale took into the country occupied by the King's troops, and which resulted in Hale's execution as a spy. General Lord Howe supped in the old mansion on the following night, presumably much to the gratification of its owner, who must have been sorely vexed over his enforced hospitality to the Revolutionary leaders. Washington had retreated up the Bloomingdale Road to Colonel Morrison's house on Harlem

Heights, and British soldiers, flushed with their success at the Battle of Long Island, pillaged the hen-roosts of neighboring farmers and camped in the grounds surrounding the Apthorpe house.

Apthorpe contrived to retain his lands after the American Government was firmly established and peace declared, and outlived his Tory notoriety. When in 1789, his only child was married to Hugh Williamson, a member of Congress for North Carolina, the social world of New York participated in the festivities, and the Apthorpe house was crowded with guests as in the days of British supremacy. In 1797 Apthorpe died and his estate passed out of the hands of his family. For many years the Mansion was occupied by Colonel Thorn, but it finally fell into the hands of a German, who built a big shed in the rear, dubbed the grounds Elm Park, and provided accommodation for picnic parties. As a beer-garden it proved very attractive. The shed was filled on summer evenings with thirsty Teutons, and the chief rooms of the house were reserved for the use of "committees". The strains of dance music once more stirred the echoes of the place, but the dancers were of a very different class from the courtly dames and gallants of the Eighteenth century.

At last the erection of houses around it did away with Elm Park and the old house fell into utter ruin. Blasts that upheaved the rocks all around shook its foundations. Building contractors erected cranes and engine houses at its very doors. Italian laborers camped in its desolate rooms, and filled them with dirt and smoke. Huge excavations yawned in front and rear, where once a carriage drive surrounded the grass plots. The few fine old trees—indications of the timber that had once surrounded the house—were felled by Carlo's hands. Finally the house itself was torn to pieces as roughly as if it were but a temporary shed, and soon the rocks on which it stood were yielding to the steam drill and blasting powder. I often wonder what this wreckage would bring in these days of Americana and Colonial antiques; but in 1890 people were only concerned with Italian *baroque* and the Apthorpe pillars and beams probably fed the flames in the stove of a neighboring squatter.

An enormous eruption of bill boards suddenly appeared on these old mansion sites along the Boulevard. It was quite possible to learn the name of almost every kind of condiment, panacea or patent medicine, or other human want, from these bill boards. Already the traffic was important. It was the favorite route of the bicyclists, especially on holidays and Sundays, and the home coming of these merry makers formed a fascinating picture with the vastness of their numbers, the countless colored lights and the never ceasing undulating of the crowd. Toward the end of the craze, this scene on the Boulevard and on Riverside Drive was one of the really great sights of New York. So big and as fine was the parade of vehicles that men and women stood on the street curb hours at a time gazing interestedly at the fascinating spectacle. Excellent entertainment could be had any day studying the different types of things on wheels.

It was the advent of the Bicycle that created the present enormous vogue for athletics amongst women. Of course, there had previously been some ladylike tennis and croquet playing, skating and archery on the distaff side, but it was only by a small minority, in a spirit of

48

THE CORNELIUS VANDERBILT II. MANSION

Extending from 57th to 58th Streets on Fifth Avenue facing the Plaza. The most desirable site in New York. Erected in the 80's. Demolished 1927

THE HUNTINGTON HOUSE

THE J. PIERPONT MORGAN HOUSE

On Madison Avenue and 36th Street. Removed to make room for an extension of his private library which has been given to the city by Mr. J. P. Morgan II.

THE WILLIAM K. VANDERBILT I. HOUSE

On Fifth Avenue corner of 52nd Street. Beautiful reproduction of a French Château.

high adventure, or as an excuse to wear some jaunty, if tight fitting, sporting costumes. The real beginning of swimming the Channel for mommer, popper, the babies on our block, and the Star Spangled Banner; of tennis quarrels, and similar amenities of feminine sport, is found in the great bicycle craze of the Nineties, which put the world awheel. "Daisy Bell" and her bicycle built for two, was the lyric expression of this furore. Bicycles were at first constructed for skirted females. Then some intrepid women revived the bloomer, which had caused so much laughter and indignation way back in the Fifties, and rode men's "bikes" in them. Society took up the fad, and organized the Michaux Club on Broadway near 53rd Street, then still an equine neighborhood. Pictures of society belles in fetching bicycle costumes, including the popular Tyrolean hat, appeared in the Sunday papers, and of course, what Society favored, who could resist? It took only a few months for the fad to make a conquest of the entire population.

During the bicycle craze Governor Smith became an expert rider and was popularly known as "the Coaster King". The New York Athletic Club held these novel contests which consisted in coasting down the hills of Westchester and the Orange Mountains. The Governor was an easy winner.

For a time, it looked as though the bicycle was even going to revolutionize our whole ideas of transportation. It was fondly believed that it would supplant all horse cars and the elevated. To carry out this scheme two fairly wide belts of asphalt adjoining the curb was laid on many streets for the special use of the cycler. He was to use this new method in going to and returning from the chase.

However, the bicycle path, strange to relate, did not justify its existence. Too many trucks, with long wooden tongues swaying wildly in the air; horses and wagons of all kinds, and other impediments made the journey downtown rather hazardous, and painfully slow. The elevated resumed its sway. It was a rather curious example of individual municipal rapid transit, while it lasted, and is now all but forgotten.

Yet the bicycle had a tremendously good effect in the direction of improving the paving of our streets. Miles of the new asphalt were laid down in place of the rough granite blocks that for years had echoed to the roar of iron-shod hoofs and iron-tired wheels. Not alone was it a boon to the rider and driver, but it afforded a new sport to the gamin of the streets. The small boy on roller skates found it a paradise, and spent hours "hitching behind" vehicles of all kinds. Sometimes as many as a dozen urchins were attached like tails of a kite to carts and drays moving along the avenue. The drivers of these would sometimes resort to strategy to dislodge these appendages by steering their course along the cobblestones between the car tracks. This invariably spoiled the fun but the dangerous pastime was persisted in as long as the horse-drawn vehicle was common on the avenue. The bicycle also led to the construction of the Harlem River Speedway for trotting horses. The roads above Central Park became so infested with cyclists that the owners of fast horses could no longer indulge in those impromptu brushes that were at once a diversion of the tired business man and an entertainment of the promenaders along upper Seventh and Lenox Avenues. Thus came the Speedway and it was soon one of the city's noted attractions.

54

'IS GROICE H'ARRESTED FOR SPEEDIN'

It is to be regretted the bicycler of that day suffered from the "scorcher", that idiot with head sunk between bent handle bars just as the motorist suffers today from the speed maniac and it became necessary to apprehend and arrest the offender then, as now. It may be interesting to recall what was probably the most distinguished violator of the local speed ordinances at that time. This was none other than the Duke of Marlborough, the prospective bridegroom of Miss Vanderbilt. It was a genial autumn morning when Policeman Mike Sweeney, ever vigilant and hawkeyed, discovered, seated on a grassy slope, near the Block House in Central Park, a young man with a bicycle lying nearby. At that period in the history of our kaleidoscopic burg the sign "Keep Off of Grass" actually referred to the well known product of Mr. Henderson's catalogue. Central Park was a real park, and not a garbage dump and a local replica of Barren Island. The sight of the figure, therefore, on the verdant slope aforesaid electrified Mr. Sweeney to a condition of active indignation. If Mr. Sweeney had perchance been a member of Her Majesty's Constabulary his reaction to the scene presented to his astonished gaze might have been couched thus: "H'I say!—You cawn't stop there, you really cawn't, you know; h'it's not allowed." But Policeman Sweeney of the Arsenal Station had a rich and sonorous argot of his own and to the reposeful figure on the idyllic bank addressed these words, "Hey! What t'ell yer doin' on dat grass? Don't yer see der sign? G'wan outer here!" His Grace—it was none other—rose regretfully from the grassy knoll, so reminiscent of the park at Blenheim and under the wrathful eye of Mr. Sweeney departed on his wheel. Mr. Sweeney, regarding the incident as closed, continued on his alert and untiring beat. Judge of the petrified astonishment of this admirable, if inflexible officer of the law, to observe, a few moments later, a figure, with its legs across the handle bars of a bicycle, coasting, actually coasting down an incline in the roadway! And furthermore, the perpetrator of this heinous offense was the self-same loller on the grass, so lately the object of official rebuke. Mr. Sweeney could no longer abide this contemptuous disregard of law and order. He was no longer wrathful, but cold, with that icy coldness characteristic of retribution descending on the malefactor. He, therefore, intercepted the miscreant and marched him to the arsenal police-station.

The desk sergeant there, on learning the name of Mr. Sweeney's prisoner, was suitably impressed. Many a germ-carrier had answered his stern catechism, but such a carrier of blue blood, never. The sergeant was a philosopher and a diplomat. He was also a humane man and in the circumstances felt that:

"Kind hearts are more than coronets".

Here was a young man, an emigrant from a foreign clime, friendless, but for the British Minister at Washington and the Vanderbilt family in New York, who had come to the traditional refuge of the oppressed to seek his fortune. There was really nothing as reprehensible in riding a bike, even not under control as there would have been in driving tandem at the ferocious rate of twelve miles an hour, or tooling a four-in-hand imperilling the lives of future Tammany Hall voters. The sergeant looked at Mr. Sweeney and a suspicion that the latter's recent proceedings had not been entirely disinterested, permeated his brain. Had he not all along been cognizant of his prisoner's identity and seized this opportunity of getting his name in the papers? Perhaps he saw himself, at some distant time, a pensioned official, spending a well earned vacation under the ancestral oaks at Blenheim. How, then, would *he* be regarded. He therefore addressed the prisoner in well modulated tones, on the heinousness of bicycle coasting on the Park's roadways and in view of it being his first offense, released him from custody in time for luncheon at the Metropolitan Club.

Another mode of transit, supplementing the pioneer work of the bicycle in carrying people afield, was the trolley. This newly invented vehicle had by this time about wholly superseded the old, slow moving horse car. The greater speed of this new transportation system made it a popular vehicle, especially in these remote sections of Greater (?) New York where lamps were still lighted only in the dark of the moon.

The power that furnished the transit also furnished the light. The small incadescent lamp was perfected by this time and the cheerful brightness of the trolley car at night soon suggested its use for a novel purpose —neighborhood outings. For a trifling expense a car could be illuminated from one end to the other in a perfect blaze of multi-colored lights, producing at once a carnival spirit that was quite irresistible. Many of the companies bedecked these cars at their own expense and found the added patronage adequately justified the cost. In these outlying districts, especially in Brooklyn and the small towns around the city, these trolley parties became quite the fad and all through the summer this delightful pastime was vastly popular and entertained whole communities.

In the city itself this same attraction made itself felt, and encouraged a new class of passengers known as "pleasure-riders", who paid their nickels merely for the sake of the ride and the cooling breezes incidental thereto. This had hitherto been the monopoly of the poorer East Side classes. With the introduction of the new open cars and speedier transit on the West Side lines, this form of enjoyment became the common privilege of all classes. Particularly on Broadway did it flourish, the cars then running without change from Harlem to the Battery. The noisy family parties of the Third Avenue line found an antithesis in the more sedate, and also more varied types, of the Broadway line. Down Columbus Avenue, curving into the "White Light" district, then into the semi-gloom below Madison Square, and the deserted wholesale and financial quarters the cars sped. After a pleasant hour or less it finally disgorged its cooled and gratified passengers into the still delightful precincts of Battery Park, with its view of the bay and the twinkling lights of the moving craft on its dark and romantic waters.

The cable-car innovation on Broadway (afterward changed to underground trolley) also brought a new local term into the city's nomenclature—"Dead Man's Curve". This was the curve in the line at Broadway and 14th Street which occasioned the city's first experience in dodging fast-moving vehicles coming around corners. The old time horse-cars were no source of peril of pedestrians at this point, but the cable-cars were compelled to make the turn at an accelerated speed that was the cause of many casualties and the consequent sinister appellation. Extra policemen were stationed at the curve, and their shouts to the unwary mingled with the hideous clanging of the motorman's bell, and the shrieks of frightened women made the crossing a scene of pandemonium for a long time, until it was recognized as a danger point, and traffic regulations instituted. It was also a prolific source of damage suits against the railway company. Curiously enough all this was finally found to be an engineer's mistake, who thought brakes could not be used in rounding a curve.

There were still a considerable number of horse-cars doing duty in the city all through the Nineties. These were mainly on cross-town lines and their trundling arks were familiar sights at many crossings to the cable-car riders. In fact, one of these lines still exercised its franchise over the cable tracks. This was the famous old "Green Car" line that traversed a tortuous route between the Grand Street and Forty-second Street ferries, and formed a very useful link between the lower East Side and the middle West.

One of the latest sections of the city to respond to the great uptown movement was Central Park West, which in the nineties still retained the aspect of a minor Alps with the festive squatter's goat playing the part of the mountain chamois. Here is a contemporary description of the transportation facilities of this urban wilderness.

"Eighth Avenue has the longest line; from Canal Street to 155th Street. Below 59th Street the service might be called fairly satisfactory; above that line the inhabitants simply call upon heaven for vengeance. Imagine, if you can, in great New York, this condition of affairs. At the park entrance this company maintains a 'waiting room' out of an old car, side-tracked by the curb, as here it is necessary for passengers to change from a red to a yellow car in order to go all the way through, and as the average is about two red cars to one yellow one, the comfort provided for the public can be more easily imagined than described. The 'waiting room' up to midnight has a man in attendance to see that passengers are properly transferred; after that hour the car is *locked* up tight and the public is respectfully requested to stand out on the street in the rain, snow or sleet at least fifteen minutes until the next car arrives."

The popularity of trolley riding was certainly a wholesome and inexpensive mode of recreation and I believe, but for the automobile, would have developed into a permanent institution. It seems to have completely disappeared for the time being, but perhaps it will be revived as an annex to these national roads we are building. A parallel track along the Lincoln Highway would add much to the gayety of a trip across the continent. It would knit together the little scattered townships along the way. But this is such an obviously good suggestion that nothing will ever come of it. The Rolls Royce will continue gaily on its way with two chauffeurs and one passenger; the five passenger Ford will carry nine or ten as usual: so wags the world away.

"The gondola of London", as Disraeli termed the hansom cab, had been an institution in that city years before its advent on New York streets. We find them as far back as John Leech's drawings in "Punch" and later in Charles Keene's, both inimitable draughtsmen and craftsmen. It was not until the early nineties that

THE WILLIAM C. WHITNEY HOUSE

Southwest corner Fifth Avenue and 57th Street. Erected about 1880. Demolished 1924.
Now the Hecksher Building

THE HENRY PHIPPS HOUSE

THE WILLIAM WALDORF ASTOR RESIDENCE
Southwest corner Fifth Avenue and 34th Street. Erected in the
Fifties. Demolished 1895. Now site of Waldorf-Astoria Hotel

WHITNEY WARREN, PETER COOPER HEWITT AND COMPANY AT
A FANCY DRESS BALL

the hansom appeared on our streets in any numbers. Its four-wheeled predecessor in the cab ranks was generically termed a "coupe". The New Yorker of that day was not a cab riding biped. Except on those rare occasions when for some particular reason he desired to create an impression, the street cars served his purpose quite adequately and cheaply. The transfer system then in vogue allowed transfers in all directions and it was even possible for a passenger to ride all day on an original five cent investment.

The coming of the hansom gave a considerable impetus to cab riding here. There was an old maxim among cab patrons—"Never ride in a cab with two men on the box". This harmless observation carried a world of meaning to the initiated; numerous robberies occurred where the warning was disregarded. The lure of driving has always held an irresistible appeal to ex-convicts, ticket of leave men, robbers, etc. Perhaps it is the temporary contact with genteel life that fascinates them. At all events not only in the Nineties but even in our own day this same attraction persists, and the taxi cab bandit is only the legitimate successor of the two men on the box of which we speak.

The hansom had only room for two passengers, and its open front made it very pleasant for sightseeing. It was also much handier to navigate than the old four-wheeler. Ladies, in particular, liked the hansom to see and be seen, and it soon became the most popular form of *de luxe* transit. In fact, the first taxicabs on our streets were built on the hansom pattern.

New York's first "rubber-neck" wagon was the old Fifth Avenue stage which rumbled over the granite stones of that renowned thoroughfare drawn by a pair of dejected steeds that often excited the commiseration of the S. P. C. A. and were the occasion of their official interference. The original stages had not outside accommodation for passengers. In fact, business on the line was not very brisk as it ran parallel with the Madison Avenue cars and public preference for the smooth rails instead of the jolting stones was pronounced. But the strangers and the sightseers all wanted to see the outside of the millionaires' mansions along the 'bus line. The company issued little booklets containing a directory of these fabled domiciles which were faithfully consulted by the passengers interested. The tendency to this form of "rubber necking" became so pronounced that the company installed seats on the roofs of its vehicles and, to the great relief of the general public, also improved their horse power. Business picked up wonderfully, and thus began the present admirable system in vogue.

Another obsolete system of transportation was the Central Park tour by which the visitor was taken around the Park for the mythical price of 25 cents. The vehicles in use were a kind of carryall, and on Sundays and holidays, in pleasant weather, there was always a crowd waiting at the park gates to enjoy the luxury of a drive along the roadways echoing the hoof-beats of equine aristocracy.

The automobile was something one read about but never saw. France was the headquarters for what was then called "the horseless carriage". Hilton, Hughes & Co., predecessors of Wanamaker's, were the first to import them. They had one or two small delivery wagons. When they appeared on the streets they created a tremendous sensation and crowds gathered around them in great numbers when they came to a halt. Their use was not apparently a success as the number was not increased.

In a few years we began to hear of similar machines being made out West in our own country. You entered them by doors in the rear. They were very crude affairs. Among several designs a Mr. Ford seemed to have a rather practical model and quite cheap. But he was said to be infringing a certain patent and although he gave a certificate with each car guaranteeing you against a law suit, nobody knew Ford, nor how good his guarantee was. It was not until John Wanamaker, who became Ford's first agent, and joined Ford in the guarantee, that Ford's cars began to really sell. The public knew Wanamaker and that was enough.

Like the moving picture, the great development of the motor car came in the next decade. So I will leave that subject for another time.

The problem of transportation has always been a serious one for New York. You can read the papers for almost a hundred years back and there is always the same "Pro Bono Publico", "Constant Reader", "Vox Populi" and all the rest of that numerous body of worthy citizens who express their discontent just as regularly and as futilely as the Merchant Associations of today. Conditions do not seem to change. Everybody knows that the population of New York has doubled itself practically every ten years for over a hundred and fifty years, and yet nobody seems to have sense enough to look ahead and provide for this increase. It looks like a simple matter, but apparently it isn't. Even the advent of the skyscraper, which would inevitably complicate this problem, brought no corresponding realizing of the impending change. Not until enough of them were built to seriously challenge the attention of the public, was the Subway started.

The year '95 was remarkable for a notable record of unpublished exports from the United States. I refer to the exports of American heiresses, who became the brides of sundry lordlings of the hereditary nobility of Europe. Three of these marriages made the year a gala one for New York. Paget-Whitney, Castellane-Gould, and Marlborough-Vanderbilt. The last named capped the climax of these international nuptials for the year, and brought the total value of these exports in dollars and cents far above the combined total of all our wheat, corn, cattle and other food stuffs. Great Britain's scheme of having a class of titled nobility, may seem silly to many of us but as a revenue producer for the Empire it raises more money than any other scheme they have yet devised. Even Republican France holds on to her obsolete titles and largely for the same reason. It's a sucker game and our country gets the worst of it every time. There is no return made us for these vast sums that are disposed of in this fashion and the saddest part is that our girls find little or no happiness in their new homes. The exceptions are few and far between. It is strictly a matter of business with these princes, dukes, and lordlings, and there ought to be an export tax on all such expatriated fortunes. Of course the newspapers recorded the minutest details of these fascinating events. The bridegrooms were dogged and the minutest items of their dress and deportment described. The lingerie and other intimate but none the less delightful details of the trousseau were retailed with the most careful feminine accuracy. The weddings were attended by vulgar crowds of the curious, and the police department debated whether it would be necessary to employ the riot squad to keep order.

The furore attending the Marlborough-Vanderbilt wedding was extraordinary even for an event of this kind and had not abated when the newlyweds returned from their honeymoon at *Idle Hour*. When it became known that they would attend the Horse Show, a monster demonstration of the curiosity of the mob was on foot. All the avenues of entrance were choked up by a hustling, frantic mob. The men in the box offices sat fuming, in a sea of greenbacks, which they flung anywhere and everywhere in a crazy effort to make change. The police howled out commands that were disregarded or laughed at. It was almost impossible at eight o'clock to force an entrance from the lobby to the promenade. Women stood a half dozen deep against the walls, imploring their escorts to drag them through the mass.

The vast publicity accorded these events produced a rather curious situation. The public appetite for Society news became insatiable. The objects of this attention also suddenly changed their attitude of indifference and proceeded to install private secretaries galore. These industrious persons were provided with unstinted material for the press. The department allotted to this phase of metropolitan life expanded to such an extent that it almost crowded out news of much greater importance, notably the campaign against spitting in the streets, hotel lobbies and theatre aisles. For the benefit of those who fondly imagine that our present love of cleanliness is a natural attribute let me explain that the army of Virgin Leaf chewers, Climax Plug lovers, etc., was a doughty one. Private pressure made slow progress but gradually public opinion became interested and finally the Board of Health secured the necessary legal authority to suppress it. Not a particularly enviable record but true nevertheless.

That magic entity called "The 400" came to its full bloom and fruition at this time. Mr. McAllister's *haute ton* was now practically the Court of New York, although he, himself, was no longer its Lord Chamberlain. The Court's doings were recorded in minute detail and profuseness. Zealous reporters infested the back-stairs and bribed the servants halls for the tittle-tattle of the great. All the big functions were covered and the costumes described in detail for the delectation of those remaining millions who were not there to see. The stage held the mirror up to its foibles and the soubrette of a musical comedy at Daly's warbled the prevailing sentiment in a ditty with the refrain:

> "Oh, I love Society:
> High Society, Gay Society"

which found an echo both in the stalls and the gallery.

Of course the backbone of all these fine doings was Wall Street, whence the railroad kings and the cotton kings and sundry other monarchs had drawn the wherewithal. But the railroads were all built, the public held the watered stocks, and the brokers whiled away their time pitching pennies in the Stock Exchange. Slowly, but relentlessly, appeared on the windows of Wall Street the ominous legend "To Let" and things began to look very blue indeed. Then came the "Industrials"—the "Pittsburgh Crowd", the miners, the smelters, the iron-masters, the tinsmiths, the tobacconists, the Captains of Industry—all eager for homes on Fifth Avenue and boxes at the Opera and the Horse Show.

Far and away the greatest social sensation of the decade was the Bradley Martin ball held at the Waldorf-Astoria Hotel in the winter of 1897. It is curious to reflect on the different points of view then taken of this spectacular rout. Many of the clergy inveighed against it, foremost among them being Dr. Rainsford of St. George's on Stuyvesant Square. It had its warm defenders, however, who declared it served to give employment to thousands in need, particularly seamstresses. In this connection I am reminded of the passing of that once numerous class in industry. The sewing woman was once a periodical visitor in the home of all who could occasionally afford the luxury of a new dress, but the vast cloak and suit industry that now practically provides the raiment of all the femininity throughout the land, has rendered her obsolete.

The general public, however, preferred to view the Bradley Martin ball in a facetious light, and it became the current butt of the funny man in the papers and on the stage. Oscar Hammerstein produced a burlesque on it, called *"The Bradley-Radley Ball"* at the Olympia, and the lesser comic stages did not neglect it.

There were rumors, nevertheless, of a possible anarchistic outbreak, fomented no doubt by imaginative reporters, and the neighborhood of the Waldorf-Astoria on the night of the ball swarmed with policemen with the strenuous Teddy in charge.

The ball was cleverly described by one of the guests in a parody on the immortal Pepys:

"Alighting near the great Waldorf hostelry, we out

and went into the landlord's own dwelling house and there found all things meet for our coming, but tarried not, but passed thence through a privy passage way to the first upper story of the hostelry, there to divest us of our wrappes and cloakes. And I marveled much to behold so many fine costumes and sweet-smelling flowers and posies, yet the serving men and maydes dressed in the grievous garb of these latter days, a spectacle that shamed me into remembrance how we shall all be arrayed in like sorry fashion on the morrow.

My wife, coming out of one of the dressing chambers, very pretty to behold with her many patches on chin and cheeks, and all the diners assembled, we down the wynding steps to the shining ballroom, while the lackeys did loudly announce our names and the names of them we portrayed.

There stood Mistress Martin, arrayed in black velvet and red brockade an she had stepped from one of Sir Peter Loly's portraitures, with her husband standing by in a quaint costume like unto that of Henri III, the French King. Then did I glut mine eyes on many dazzling dresses of ladies and fine gentlemen, bewildering to behold, and knew of few what was their guise but did comprehend at last many familiar figures. So much rich raiment did I never see, no, not even at the great masque of ten years ago, all wonderfully blended in the great quadrille d'honeur.

So to supper before I had half beheld all to be seen, my wife flushed pink from dancing; and after a proud, noble supper, back to the ball room to see Elisha Dyer, the courtly dancer, lead the so-called German dance, in which were to be seen our Queen of Revels, with Mistresses Fish, De Lanier, Bryce, Lispenard Stewart, and

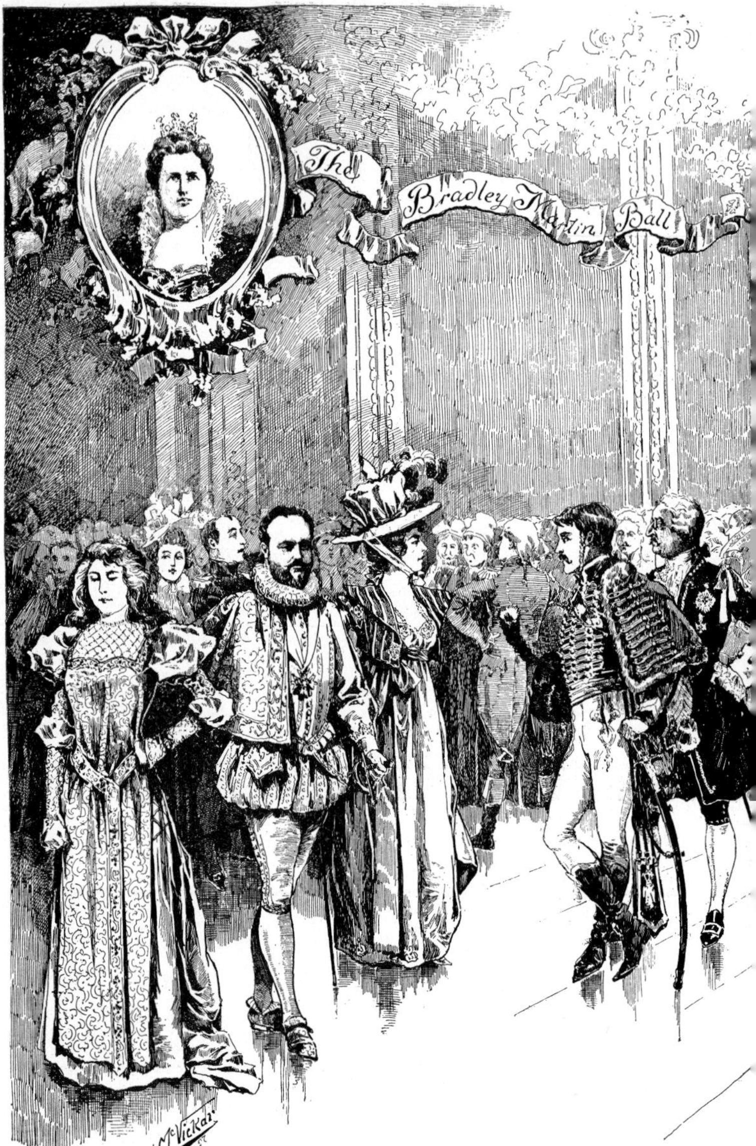
The Bradley Martin Ball
H. McVickar

THE GREAT

MR. BRADLEY LEAVES US FLAT

Spinster Gerry, followed by many Queen Besses, Queens of Scots, with other play Kings and Queens, and famous payntings seemingly come to life.

Whilst I stood there, feasting mine eyes on such noble sights, a lady sneezed backward upon me, but after seeing her to be a very pretty lady, I was not troubled at it at all.

So after some more dances with much frolique and jollity at last away and to bed, but lay long awake discoursing of the many sights of the night and how many noses were thereby put out of joint, I reckoning the cost thereof to be a full hundred thousand pounds sterling."

I may add that the Bradley Martin ball was not a masque *ad lib*. It was required that the costumes assumed should be those of historical characters and many brilliant examples of various periods were consequently in evidence.

One unexpected effect of the ball was to direct the attention of the tax collector to the worldly possessions of Mr. Bradley with the disastrous result of raising his assessment to correspond with his social aspirations. This so enraged Mr. Bradley that he shook the dust of an unappreciative country from his feet and departed for Scotland, where he dressed himself in Kilties and had himself surrounded by gillies in number befitting his rank and financial importance.

Another spectacular performer in the social world was Mr. Harry Lehr who climbed the ladder of immortality by means of a luncheon given in honor of a monkey. It must have been a particularly dull season at Newport that year for this performance was the sensation of the moment, and the celebrity achieved by Mr.

Lehr was of gigantic proportions. For months the newspapers contained numerous references to this simian function and Lehr was regarded in certain circles to have done something equivalent in our day to the feat of Lindbergh crossing the Atlantic in a monoplane. At first the incident was properly regarded as a mischievous prank—perhaps in questionable taste, but a joke, nevertheless. When the papers began to print stuff by the mile about it, public opinion rapidly shifted from one of good natured tolerance to that of decided disgust.

Mr. Lehr fortunately made a matrimonial alliance which precluded the further necessity of keeping himself on the front page and shortly after was submerged in respectable domesticity.

CORNER OF

80TH ST. AND 9TH AVE.

1890

CHAPTER II.

COMING OF THE SKYSCRAPER

THE downtown section gave as yet no sign of the coming of the great Cathedrals of Commerce. The highest building was still the Western Union. Across the street at the noon hour crowds still gaped at the flag pole from which dropped, at the stroke of twelve the famous time ball, one of the City's most cherished institutions. Upon the successful performance of this spectacular number, the audience would consult numerous Waterburys, Ingersolls, and other reliable time pieces, make a mental note that they gained or lost a couple of hours each day and let it go at that. The Equitable Building, a few blocks further down, stood next in the public's affection. The headquarters of the Weather Bureau were in this building and the guiding spirit of this institution was a Mr. Dunn, familiarly known as Farmer Dunn. The subject of the weather was an unfailing topic of interest. Two years before my story opens (1888) Mr. Dunn and the other meteorological prognosticators were somewhat disconcerted by the appearance of a blizzard which was so sadly lacking in the usages of polite society as to give no advance notice of its unparalleled severity. Even the Weather Bureau and Mr. Dunn himself were completely eliminated temporarily during this visit, but his office and his forecasts acquired a new and deeper interest to the public and the Equitable Building shared in this popularity.

So long as the weather bureau remained on top of this building, it shared largely in the day's gossip and as an early example of the value such a building had in an advertising way, the old Equitable was decidedly unique. At that time, the building occupied only half the block on Broadway.

The blizzard to which I refer was the famous one of 1888. Even to this day all other blizzards are compared to this one, which is now designated in history as "The Great." Those of us who lived through it can testify to the justness of this application. Looking back on the half century that has since elapsed, I can truthfully say that nothing in storms, Summer or Winter, has ever approached it. It was unique in the annals of New York and its unsavory reputation will, I fear, ever remain an outstanding feature of one of the most dramatic and tragic experiences of the Elegant Eighties.

TELEPHONE PAY STATIONS ARRIVE

The Post Office in City Hall Park completed the trio of buildings that were nationally as well as locally of wide repute. This unique reputation, however, was soon to disappear. The success of a new school of architecture whereby New York was to go up in the air and not along the ground, soon brought other and more imposing structures for the star gazers. And in a short time the skyscraper lost its novelty and no longer excited remark.

The extended use of the telephone was a marked feature of the decade. Pay stations, which were previously an exotic feature of metropolitan life, located only in the most important situations in the city, now appeared in every corner drug-store and tobacconist's. Deserted most of the day, these stations suddenly became alive around six o'clock with tired business men telephoning the lil' woman they were detained at the office while their grinning companions stood by. There were very few booths at this early extension of telephone activities. Conversation was in the open, at a small desk, and payment was made to the storekeeper, there being no coin machines. Coinciding with the common use of the telephone came the passing of the telegraph messenger boy, that small blue coated mercury, whose propensity for the dime novel was one of the stock gibes of the contemporary humorist. The hasty message now transmitted over the telephone was then intrusted to the care of the "telegraph boy", and on the whole, faithfully transported. His duties were multifarious, including the carriage of bundles, bouquets, etc. One of his accomplishments, the subject of a well known cartoon by C. D. Gibson, was that of chaperone to otherwise unescorted ladies attending the theatre in the evening.

The neatest boy in the office, with the cleanest nose, was delegated as impromptu knight-errant, thus providing an example to his mates of the importance of keeping his silver buttons polished and his hair brushed. Nearly every well appointed residence had a messenger call and our local "commissionaire" was regarded as an important adjunct to its conveniences.

Among the great benefactions of this age in the commercial world, was a new enterprise known as the Towel Supply Service. This provided business offices with clean towels and a small cake of highly odoriferous soap every week. The initial service also included a varnished cupboard, with a mirror and a comb and brush. Before this foray of civilization the roller-towel slowly and stubbornly gave way. It was a time honored institution in the days when there was real democracy, not to mention liberty, equality and fraternity. The roller-towel was a symbol of brotherhood, and while there was a hand's breadth of uncontaminated space upon it, hung undaunted upon the rolling pin behind the office or shop door. Every infant industry had one in the days when the boss of a business sat in his shirt sleeves within easy call of the workshop, ready to lend a hand. When the towel service came in, it was felt that a chasm had opened between capital and labor that no sanitary discourse could bridge.

At this time and for many years after, the safe movers staged an act every once in a while that never failed to provide a thrill and attract a delighted audience of typewriter salesmen, chaps on commission with a weekly drawing account, and other busy personages. Now that the safe hoisting artist is no more, these people spend this time in the movies. The funny part of it was that these onlookers were invariably native New York. They who passed with disdain written all over their features were adopted sons from Keokuk, Kalamazoo, Chicago, St. Louis and all points West, who dreaded lest such a lapse would betray the fact that they were from "hick" towns where such a scene would naturally be front page matter.

All sorts of heavy things were thus hoisted up the outside of buildings. The late George P. Rowell, the original advertising agent in this city, and a man of more than passing culture, once got himself into serious trouble by a comment made on such an occasion. "I see," he wrote in *Printer's Ink,* a journal which he then owned, "signs of so and so going up." A suit for damages immediately resulted, whereupon Mr. Rowell naïvely explained that he merely referred to the fact that two signs belonging to his rivals were being hoisted up the building to their proper location.

Hatchways were still in use and heavy merchandise was constantly being hauled up and constantly falling out of the slings. Skids were in general use throughout the city on all the side streets and you either climbed over them at the imminent danger of a barrel of white lead colliding with you, or waited till the truck was loaded. In the wholesale dry goods district and in the produce section, merchants simply grabbed all the space out to the middle of the street. You threaded your way in and out of the boxes, bundles or barrels or sought some other thoroughfare. The rights of pedestrians were no more respected then, than they are by motor car drivers today. "Life" once printed a cartoon showing two ladies lolling in the soft cushions of a victoria, with a pedestrian in the distance who had apparently just escaped being run over. Fixing her lorgnette she asked her companion, "I wonder if pedestrians have the same feelings we have?" That attitude was altogether too common. We have become a little softer since then but not much.

Now let me make a radical jump from the battle-ground of the homesteader to that quieter and more serene atmosphere—behind his palisades.

I fancy that the Nineties saw about the last of the old family servants that were a part of every well regulated menage among the elite of the city. A pleasant recollection, particularly, are the old negro servitors that were as much fixtures to a house as the very walls themselves. Many years ago wealthy New Yorkers owned negro slaves and long after the Civil War the tradition of negro servants persisted in their houses. An example was in the home of the late Elbridge T. Gerry, where, at one time many of the servants were the descendants of old slaves, and where there was never a nurse who had remained with the family less than twenty years. A survivor, in the Gerry household, into the nineties was William Wood. William's principal avocation was to walk around, examining things with critical eyes, and descant upon the virtues of the servants then employed as compared with those of an earlier time.

The Goelets had an old darky retainer named Jane Smith, who insisted upon cleaning the windows of her own room. For this purpose, she maintained, nothing was so efficacious as gin to give the proper brightness and clearness. The Goelet children were hugely enter-tained by seeing Jane slyly gulp down some gin and then breathe on the window. Not a drop of the pre-

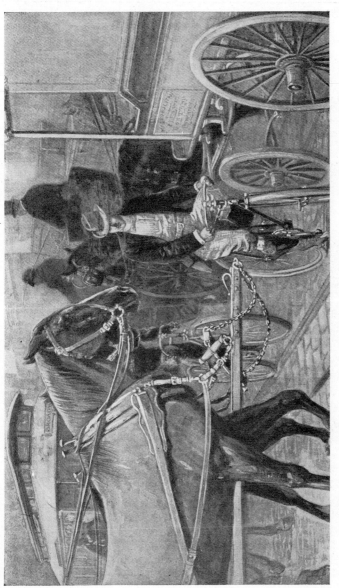

On Account of the Traffic Jam, the Scheme of Going to Business on Your Bicycle Proved Impractical and We All Went Back to the Elevated

"The Century Run." A Favorite Pastime of the Bicyclers

THE ROAD HOG OF THE NINETIES

Laying the Tracks for the Change From Cable to Trolley Car on Broadway, at

cious liquor found its way to the glass but in this roundabout way.

There were many old white servants who remained loyal to their employers for generations. One of the most remarkable of these was Becky Jones, house-keeper for A. Gordon Hamersley. Hamersley's son, Louis C., left an estate of $6,000,000. There was a contest over his will and Becky was called as witness to testify to certain characteristics of the testator. She sat in court, waiting to be called, reading a book entitled "A Christian Secret, or a Happy Life". There was no idea that she would prove a refractory witness but the Surrogates' Court never knew a more obstinate one than Becky Jones. She positively refused to tell anything.

"When Mr. Hamersley was alive", she said, "he would have said to me, 'Becky, keep still', and that's just what I intend to do".

The case was adjourned a number of times in order to induce Becky to change her mind. Society people crowded around her in court, but all to no avail. Finally she was committed to Ludlow Street Jail for contempt of court. She laughed and shook hands with the Surrogate, and even said good-bye to the opposing counsel. She induced the Sheriff to allow her to take her cat and parrot to jail with her, where she received a special room. "When old Mr. Gordon Hamersley was alive", she said to a visitor, "he used to say 'Becky, hold your tongue; don't let it wag about family matters'. 'Yes, sir,' said I, "and I'll keep my word, as I told the Judge, if they put me on the gallows for it."

Becky received a number of checks from strangers who admired her pluck and letters poured into the papers commending her. Finally she got out of jail, and went to London to live on the bounty of the then Duchess of Marlborough, widow of Louis C. Hamersley.

In view of the tremendous change in that vital and important realm of domestic economy—the nursery—I am somewhat amazed to think that any of us ever survived the crucial period of babyhood as practiced in the Nineties. In those days cradles were considered the only proper bed for babies, and no end of popular poems and songs were written around this sainted object. "Rock me to sleep Mother, rock me to sleep," sang Elizabeth Akers, and countless millions echoed her cry. Nowadays if Elizabeth were to attempt any such nonsense with little precious she would have a brick thrown at her head.

Mother no longer hugs baby to her bosom and croons a lullaby to make it sleep. The proper caper is to chuck the kid out on the front porch and let it yell its head off. When exhausted it falls into a natural slumber.

Dear old Mrs. Winslow's soothing syrup and all other poisonous narcotics are now considered bad form, and any six months infant caught using habit-forming drugs is today taboo in good society. Yet in the nineties she was brought up on them.

A mother who made her child sleep alone in a separate room from its parents—there were a few such fiends—was considered heartless or out of her mind. Today Daddy would raise the roof if you merely suggested having the baby in the same room and mother would back him up.

No baby up to its second year was trusted in public without a thick, monogrammed bib to protect its dress against drooling. Toddler's dresses were full floor-length, with untold-of layers of petticoats and underwear beneath them. Baby capes were vogue, with lace edging used profusely. At home the tot always wore a protective slip—sometimes sashed—over its regular clothes. Nighties were cumbersome and night-caps, tying snugly beneath the chin, were common. The publication of Frances Hodgson Burnett's "Little Lord Fauntleroy" in the '90s was responsible for a rage of sashed and tight-fitting colored velvet suits for boys. Large point-lace collars and cuffs and long hair, kept industriously curled by fond mothers, went with the affliction.

And the "Second Summer!" Was there ever such a harrowing time? No matter how well the child might be, it was the "Second Summer" and if nothing serious developed the mother's anguish worked overtime just the same. It was a cheerful period.

And an expectant mother. Do you know what invariably happened to her if she thoughtlessly raised her hands above her head—putting up curtains or such? Why she would inevitably strangle her unborn babe with the navel cord around its neck! Perhaps she doesn't do any curtain hanging these days, but they play golf and swim. And some toy with the tennis racquet.

Little Precious was never taken out for a toddle unless he was enmeshed in a body harness or had leading strings attached. Nowadays he knocks a hole in the ground with his head or cracks the asphalt with the violence of his fall—gets up and starts playing again. Even the babies that make their appearance before they have received their cue today need not necessarily be thrown in the ash heap. They go in the incubator with eggs that will soon reappear as "Day old chicks" and after a brief sojourn are as good as any.

A "pacifier" of yesterday would cause a riot today.

There were other cheerful and delightful folk lore about newly born infants that were accepted by the average mother as gospel truth. If baby was to rise in the world, it must be carried upstairs the day it was born. A sure sign of an incipient Napoleon was to have baby cry at birth and lift one hand. And if it cried on its first birthday it would be unhappy through life.

The ceremony when the infant lost its first milk tooth was solemn and portentous. Standing with the tooth in your hand you cast it backward over the left shoulder, at the same time making a wish. It was absolutely believed that the wish would come true. None of them ever did, which was rather annoying, but it never weakened the faith.

The poor kid had other and equally nonsensical lore reared around it. If you cut its nails before it was a year old it was sure to turn out a thief. This pleasant future, however, was only assured if you cut it with the scissors. If you bit them off with your teeth that was different, so every mother practised this cannibal rite in preference to cutting. Similarly, if baby looked in a mirror before its first birthday it would surely die. Pleasant thought, eh? And if it fell out of bed before it was eleven months old it would turn out to be a fool at maturity. Most of us seem to have fallen out before this time, as far as I can see.

Taking it all in all, baby had a happy time in the nineties. Midwives still officiated at 60 per cent of native born American confinements because up-to-date young mothers of those days considered it too unendurably immodest to have a male physician attend them on such an occasion. The medical profession itself was apparently reluctant to enter this field in the proper spirit and it was some time before the "baby doctor", when such an one appeared, was free from the jibes of his colleagues, and it took some time for the subject to secure the discussion which its importance demanded. In these days of necking parties, knee length skirts and Birth Control magazines, it certainly looks as if we had come a long way since the eighties and nineties.

In one important particular there has been a decided change for the better. When baby wakes up in the middle of the night and proceeds to lift up its prematurely developed voice, daddy no longer utters a snort of rage and buries his head in a pillow. He takes the little one with the abnormal vocal accomplishments tenderly in his arms and walks up and down forty or fifty miles. After a few hours he finds that baby will fall into sweet slumber if daddy doesn't fall dead first.

It was Marion Harland who first brought the discussion of these immodest topics into general circulation. Her magazine "Babyhood" rendered an incalculable service to the mothers of this country. The centuries old fetish of shrouding all diagnosis and treatment under a veil of pompous mystery began to give way under the enlightened position taken by Mrs. Harland and the enormous, largely unnecessary rate of infant mortality was no longer regarded as natural. Soon after, the profession took up a study of the question in earnest and with remarkable results. Strange to relate, one of the editors associated with Mrs. Harland in "Babyhood" was none other than our old friend, Sylvanus Cobb, Jr., author of the *Gun Maker of Moscow* and countless other favorites of Old Cap Collier's dime novels. One topic was doubtless used to relieve the tedium of the other.

The craze for amateur photography which existed in a mild way more or less over the country began to assume imposing dimensions in the nineties. Mr. Eastman's slogan, "You press the button; we do the rest," stared at you from almost every printed page. The bicyclists were perhaps the most rabid; the many beauty spots which they saw awheel came in for faithful recording, and although it was not exactly the most inexpensive fad in the world there were few of us without a Kodak.

It was sometime before the business of developing these little snap shots was generally practiced by the local dealer and most of our films were sent to Rochester. The delay of from two to three weeks which ensued was accepted philosophically but was never very popular. When the small stores throughout the country began to cater for developing work the situation improved and the popularity of the craze increased. There were sometimes very amusing scenes when these films came home; the picture of father lying on the lawn showed only a huge pair of feet in the foreground and nothing else. A family group was sometimes worse than a Chinese puzzle and occasionally a whole reel of films would turn out perfectly blank—the result of some slight carelessness at time of exposure.

In some instances amateur photography was practiced on a very impressive scale by well known men and women. Several names socially prominent were known to be highly proficient in the art and their collections, made largely of foreign travel, were of imposing dimensions

94

and not without great interest. Col. E. H. Green, son of Hetty Green, was a particular enthusiast, and his photographic appointments were on an elaborate scale. The names of scores who were equally proficient will no doubt occur to many of my readers.

The use of Mr. Eastman's handy little Kodaks may have become less spectacular and their existence largely taken for granted these days. But in the time of which I speak the achievements of the amateur was the subject of widespread comment and general discussion. The newspapers and magazines teemed with articles on the subject and the paragrapher never lacked for a popular squib when he poked fun at the omnipresent Kodaker.

Out of Mr. Eastman's modest spool of film, was destined to come what has proved to be not only a great industry but one of the greatest forces in modern civilization of this or any age—the moving picture.

I have elsewhere in these pages recorded the first appearance of moving pictures as having occurred at Koster & Bials as part of a regular paid performance. Several other claimants for this honor have since appeared —notably Mr. Holaman of the Eden Musee—all of them more or less fortified with impregnable evidence.

At that time they were known as Kinetoscopes. That was the name used by Edison in an article in the *Century* illustrating the new invention and which was the first public mention of the coming art. Long before the Kinetoscope appeared there used to be sold what was known as a Wheel of Life. It was a drum-like tin cylinder with narrow slits or openings down the side which revolved like a top. Placed along the sides were long strips of various pictures or scenes. A horse race was one I specially remember. When the drum was rotating rapidly the horses, seen through these narrow openings, suddenly came to life and galloped madly down the home stretch. Many of my readers will doubtless recall this amusing contraption, and like me, have often wondered how much this curious toy had to do with the introduction of moving pictures.

Great inventions, however, rarely appear until all conditions are ripe for their introduction. Nothing but glass plates had ever been seriously thought of in connection with photography and not until George Eastman's film came along could moving pictures have been possible.

In this connection it is strange to note that not one firm then in the photographic business—Rockwood, Bogardus, Brown Bros., Falk, Kurtz, Aimee Dupont, Pach, Marceau, Sarony—ever profited or saw any possibilities in this wealthy and powerful newcomer in their business. They did not ever hand her a chair and ask her to sit down. It was left for total strangers to bid her welcome and introduce her to the folks at home. For this little act of civility she made them all rich beyond the dreams of avarice. The fortunes made and lost in these early hectic days of the movies; the staggering effect of the piled up millions suddenly poured into the lap of the starving prospector, afford colorful material for a book all by itself and I must not attempt it here.

There still exist in many attics old time albums in which repose the *carte de visite* family portraits popular long before the "cabinets." Tin-types were always a feature of those collections and usually recalled some pleasant outdoor memory. If it were at the seashore, the tin type always had a rousing surf as a background, while if it were in the country a peaceful and bucolic

Mrs. Stuyvesant Fish

WHEN BONI MADE A TEN STRIKE
The Castellane-Gould Wedding

PLUCKING A LEMON IN THE GARDEN OF LOVE

The Vanderbilt-Marlborough Wedding. Bridal procession
returning from the chancel at Saint Thomas's Church

THE FIRST HORSELESS CARRIAGE TO BE SEEN IN NEW YORK
Hilton, Hughes & Co., delivery wagon

THE FIRST SUBMARINE

The "Holland" lying at her dock at Perth Amboy. Bought by the government for use in the Spanish-American War. This was the forerunner of all the undersea boats. It carried a crew of six men

atmosphere was imparted by the representation of a lake and a row boat. These tin types were ghastly affairs as a rule, but their popularity was undoubted and they chimed in very appropriately with the Turkish Corner, painted coal scuttles, pyrograph work, burnt leather pillows and the gilded rolling pin, without which no home with any pretensions to culture was complete.

To this period also belongs the introduction of open plumbing. Previously man's natural enemy, the plumber, before sending his helper back to the shop for more tools, had to batter down a protective armor of mahogany or French walnut, before disclosing the defective pipes. These enclosures were the result of the general intelligence brought to bear on the construction of houses after the Civil War. They belong to the period of brown-stone and tin cornices. Also that of tin bathtubs. How the water would roar when it struck the tin! Porcelain bathtubs came in during our blessed period, and when they did, some genius with a flair for economy hit upon the idea of painting tin bathtubs white. This was almost as clever as the hand-painted coal-scuttle, it being only necessary for the bather to use a little turpentine after his immersion to remove the enamel from his skin. I think that the porcelain tub was a great encouragement for bathing. The old tin tub always had the appearance of being a small boy's penalty for mud-pies; but it was considered a great luxury by those whose hebdomadal ablutions had been previously performed in the laundry tubs.

To our period also belongs the rise of that curious anomaly the "interior decorator". This term was originally the title of swanky house painters and wall-paperers who wished to lift their profession out of the ranks of the humble "coon kalsominer" class. As the hardy frontiersman, the iron puddler and the copper miner began to acquire opulence and settle in town, a new class developed among the "interior decorators", many of them ladies who had failed in running boarding-houses, but who now felt an unconquerable "urge" for destroying Victorian relics and substituting "Art Nouveau" for them. This was the time when American walnut was consigned to the wood pile as being incompatible with the "period". Oak was going out and the "decorator" wrought havoc with fine old examples because they weren't mahogany.

There were certain creature comforts ushered in during this period that were boons to the suffering myriads condemned to city life in the summer. Prominent among these benefits was the electric fan, which began to be used wherever there was electric current. This was still only to be found in places of business, large hotels, and theatres. The average home used gas, and the gas lighter with the long wax taper, used to reach chandeliers, was still a common household appurtenance. The early electric fan buzzed so loudly that it was used in theatres only between the acts. There were no oscillating fans, or other gyratory specimens.

In winter, steam heat was by no means the general necessity it has since become. Medium priced flats had no central heating plant and either depended on parlor coal stoves or gas stoves, which were just beginning to emerge from kitchen functions to service as general heaters. Even in the kitchen the gas stove was, prior to the Nineties, a mere auxiliary to the coal range. There were no gas ovens, and a two burner affair was considered a housewives' boon.

PYROGRAPHY—BURNT LEATHER

The craze for "pyrography" also is contemporaneous with this time. This was the burnt leather and burnt wood fad that filled homes with whiskbroom holders, match boxes, umbrella stands, screens and a pandemonium of "what-nots" all decorated by scorching. Who can forget the "Souvenir of Niagara", "Greetings from the Mammoth Cave", "Atlantic City", "Yale", "Amherst", burnt by relentless hands on the ghastly paraphernalia of that awful fad.

Along with these domestic improvements came a public clamor for clean streets. Before the Civil War the peregrinating pig had been the chief functionary in this municipal department. Afterwards a sort of hit and miss contract system had prevailed to the intense satisfaction of the politicians. The reform administration under Mayor Strong held the unique view that cleaning the streets of a great city was a scientific function, and appointed a noted sanitary engineer, Col. Geo. F. Waring, as Commissioner of Street Cleaning. One of his first official acts was to put an army of men with hand-brushes on the streets during daylight in lieu of the horse-drawn cylindrical brushes that had cleaned the surface of the Belgian blocks and left the dirt in the crevices during the night. This army Waring garbed in white duck uniforms and helmets as a sanitary symbol. The public was delighted, but the Tammany politicians set up a howl of derision at the "White Wings" and declared it an outrage that the hard working men of the pavements should be humiliated by a badge of servitude, like a mere policeman or street car conductor. It was soon apparent, however, that public sentiment would never permit a return to the erstwhile ragamuffin attire, and as the streets acquired an unprecedented neatness, it was agreed that white duck was the primary cause of this municipal miracle, and it has ever since been indispensable in the city's service.

Colonel Waring's services to the city cannot be over-estimated. He succeeded in imparting dignity to a calling that was formerly among the most despised of all in the gamut of human industry. He showed us that streets could be made clean and kept clean. He afterwards took up the fight against cholera in Havana and fell a victim to his efforts to eradicate this plague. His was a noble end.

In consonance with the vast improvement in street cleaning, the Department of Highways and that of other public works began to show the results of a competent administration. There was a wide extension of asphalt paving, due, as I have said, to the introduction of the safety bicycle, and the universal adoption of that vehicle by the general public. New York began to emerge from the condition described by a noted essayist as a "backwoods Paris" into some semblance of a more civilized metropolitanism.

FRANCIS WILSON

CHAPTER III.

THE THEATRE

A PECULIARITY of the theatre in those days was the adoration of the matinee girl for her favorite on the stage. During the run of *The Little Minister,* the stage entrance of the Empire was thronged with violet-laden devotees who stood patiently waiting for Maude Adams to come out to her hansom hoping that, as she hurried by, she might accept one of the bouquets held out to her or perhaps by some lucky chance drop a glove or a handkerchief. These would be snatched up and carried off to some school-girl sanctum. Ethel Barrymore's admirers were about evenly divided between the young bloods of the day who wanted to marry her and the matinee girls who tried to copy her delightful, seductive throaty voice and mobbed her after performances in the hope that the haughty Ethel would glance their way which she rarely did. Mary Mannering likewise had her quota of stage-door followers who imitated the Janice Meredith curl which the actress made famous during the run of that play. Unlike the shy Ethel and the mystery enshrouded Maude Adams, Mary Mannering rewarded her devotees with a dazzling smile and always some warm-hearted expression of appreciation of their devotion so that when she married Hackett, it seemed a right and fitting climax to the many romantic love scenes they had seen these two enact.

In those days we said it with flowers to our stage favorites right out in front of everybody, usually at the end of the first act when the hurried tramp of the ushers' feet as they rushed the huge floral offerings to the stage and handed them over the footlights to riotous applause, was as much a part of the *entr' acte* as the selections by the orchestra. Nor did the audience wait until the end of an act, either, to show its appreciation of some particularly thrilling or charming bit of acting. A heroic speech, a rescue of the leading lady in the nick of time, and bouquets which a moment before had ornamented the bosoms of the well-dressed feminine theatregoers were torn loose from their moorings and hurled at the stage, sometimes with disastrous results. It must also be confessed that the behavior of the audience was frequently embarrassing to the players since they often insisted that the dead or fainting thespian arise, take the flowers and bow, before the action was allowed to proceed.

Out in the lobby, before the performance, these floral

tributes were on display so that all who looked might see which members of the cast received the greatest number; but alas for this most charming custom, it was whispered by some old meanies that many of the five-foot floral offerings were purchased by the actors themselves and sent to the theatre with fictitious names attached; of course there was no truth in this, but the rush of the flower-laden ushers down the aisles was found to be a serious interference with the carefully selected *entr' acte* program. Some hardboiled conductors were even said to have objected strenuously to being hit on the head with the flying bouquets. Followed a managerial pronouncement and one more prerogative of the audience passed into history along with the wearing of hats by the ladies.

No account of the theatre in New York in the Golden Nineties would be complete without a record of the histrionic achievements of the Right Honorable gentleman who occupies the Executive Mansion in Albany, Governor Alfred E. Smith.

The time of the first appearance of our amiable friend was on the evening of November 15th, 1897, and the place, St. James Hall. On this occasion the play was that fine old Union Square success *"Hazel Kirke"*. Despite his unquestioned democracy, the Hon. Alfred appeared as *Arthur Carringford* (*Lord Travers*). As the noble British Lord, Mr. Smith acquitted himself admirably, and the historic setting of the play in an old baronial mansion found him quite to the manner born. *Lady Travers* was played by Miss Helene L. Perry and *Hazel Kirke* by Miss Marie McNamara. The drawing room in the villa at Fairy Grove and the kitchen scene in Blackburn Mill were handled with equal skill.

His next appearance was in Billy Florence's famous play *"The Mighty Dollar"*, in which he assumed the character of the Hon. Bardwell Slote. He was evidently more at home in this rôle as we find that the numerous speeches of the voluble member of Congress from Kohosh were received with much applause and great laughter. By this time Mr. Smith was the leading man in the brilliant company of young amateurs who were achieving a great reputation for the St. James Lyceum.

The Governor also played the leads in *"May Blossom"*, *"The Confederate Spy"*, and the *"Long Strike"*. He received an offer to join the Frohman stock company but decided he would stick to politics.

The Governor has acted many parts since, and we hope to see him the star in a new play now in rehearsal entitled "Four Years in Washington".

At about this time a most interesting and radical change in theatrical practice began to make itself manifest. The star system was about to be staged. The introduction of this novel departure created no end of piquant gossip and the name of Charles Frohman, who was credited with being its instigator, was on every tongue. It was a large, vibrant and dramatic moment in the development of the American stage. The never-to-be-forgotten stock companies of Union Square, Wallacks and Madison Square theatres were already part of local history. Their successors, Dalys and the Lyceum were about to follow suit. For twenty years the former company occupied the premier place in New York's theatrical affections, but early in the nineties it began to disintegrate, first in the passing of "Jimmie" Lewis and then in the resignation of John Drew to go a-starring with a young actress named Maude Adams in sup-

COLONEL GEORGE F. WARING
Who revolutionized street cleaning in New York

First Street Parade of Colonel Waring's Famous "White Wings"

Two thousand uniformed men, seven hundred and fifty horses and carts in line. 1895

Specimens of Colonel Waring's splendid work in street cleaning, before and after he began. 1893–1895

"ROLL CALL OF STREET CLEANERS."

port. The fleeting years had already somewhat dimmed the lustre of this renowned company and competition began to make itself seriously felt. The Lyceum stock had established a clientele of the socially elect in its snug, intimate playhouse on Fourth Avenue mainly in the production of the brilliant comedies of Pinero— *"Sweet Lavender", "Lady Bountiful", "The Princess and the Butterfly", "Trelawney of the Wells", "The Charity Ball", "The Moth and the Flame"*, and others —not to mention plays by Jerome K. Jerome and Henry Arthur Jones. Daly floundered from old time London melodrama to the new school of musical comedy such as *"The Messenger Boy", "The Geisha", "San Toy"*, etc., all very clever of their kind, but not the sort of thing to give employment to the supreme talents of an Ada Rehan, or the delicate comedy of a Sidney Herbert. The opening of the Empire Theatre, with its excellent stock company under Charles Frohman, also tended to divide the clientele devoted to the polite drama. The premier playhouse of New York for over twenty years, felt this competition keenly and to the great regret of its many admirers finally closed its doors early in the present century.

The death of Daly shortly afterwards produced a melancholy effect on his old time playmate Ada Rehan. The theatrical business seems to create a peculiar bond between managers and stars. Maude Adams and Mrs. Leslie Carter seemed to go into eclipse also after a similar experience. There must be a different set of nerves in professional life than in business; like children, they seem to be helpless when the guiding hand is removed.

The Star system thus inaugurated, seems a permanent fixture. Mrs. Fiske's objection to a return to the Stock company does not appeal to me, though her staunch friend and supporter, Alexander Woollcott, tells me it is now economically impossible. Perhaps he is right. Yet the enthusiastic audiences which greeted the revival of *"Trelawney of the Wells"* would indicate that a repertoire of these old plays would easily keep a stock company successfully engaged during the short season in New York.

The Star system has some very silly provisions in its contracts as witness the experience of Miss Eagles in *"The Cardboard Lover."* The audience plainly desired to show its approval of a certain other actor in the cast —Leslie Howard. They made no bones about their wishes, even going to the extreme of calling him by name. The only response they got was more appearances of Miss Eagles. The critics next day conceded that Howard had run away with the show and laughed at the silly treatment accorded him. However, it seems that according to the star system, all the honors are the star's. She alone must take the curtain calls; she alone must be featured in big type in the program; and she alone must be credited in the advertisements with the success of the performance. Perhaps we blame Miss Eagles unjustly. The whole thing was disgusting and did her a lot of harm.

Under the same system we have endured some other equally trying experiences—cheap support is one. Even Booth employed such awful duds that his plays were sometimes perilously near a joke. When he allied himself with Bangs, Barrett and Davenport, for one trial season, the result was an enormous success for the actors financially and an equally great success on the part of the play goer, who finally got something for his money. Yet for some reason or no reason the experiment was never made permanent.

The numerous "little" and "community" theatres that now dot the city had their prototype about thirty years ago when "Mrs. Osborne's Theatre" began business. This was a tiny playhouse in the Berkeley Lyceum on West 44th Street near Fifth Avenue. Mrs. Osborne's idea was a playhouse for the intelligensia, who were, in those unsophisticated days, known by the less euphemistic title of "nuts". Here came the then novel species, short-haired women and long-haired men. Here gathered parlor socialists, people with "missions" and sundry hazy humanitarians, not without a goodly leaven of real people, to listen to the drama of revolt and to indulge in that new perennial indoor sport, "elevating the stage."

It was here that Ibsen had his first hearings before audiences that were "hip to the snow", and I may say that the Scandinavian philosopher may well have exclaimed "Save me from my friends"; every one of them had his own conception of the "symbols" which these dramas portrayed. Ibsen societies sprang up, like the Browning clubs of an earlier day, to study pathological types, "rat women", and other odd fish of the new drama. William Winter, that nineteenth century oracle of the "Tribune", had so little respect for Ibsen that he declared that most of his followers were in need of pathological suspension. He was regarded as a reactionary by the idolators of the Norwegian master. The lapse of time, if it has not entirely vindicated him, has proven that the Scandinavian drama is still caviar to the general. Mrs. Osborne, in the meantime, conducted a highly successful dressmaking concern as a side line.

The "problem play" absorbed the attention of theatre-goers in our decade. Prior to this there had been no problems in the drama. The villains were clean cut rapscallions, the adventuresses beautiful but baleful, the ingenues naïve and adorable, and the "comic relief" an enormous gamut ranging from butlers, housemaids, yokels, street boys, jockeys, etc., in the lower orders, to pernickety old maids, fussy bankers, heavy swells, etc., in the upper—not to mention dialect comedians of the genus Chinaman, Dutchman, Mick and Hayseed, all parts of those mosaics of the Comedy-Drama, Society-Drama, and Melodrama of the popular stage. The problem play broke up this chess-board arrangement of dramatic characters. Its chief protagonist was the lady "with a past", but who has a first-class forensic argument for her defection. *"Mrs. Dane's Defense"*, *"The Notorious Mrs. Ebbsmith"*, *"The Second Mrs. Tanquery"*, *"Mrs. Warren's Profession"* make up a quartette of eloquent assailants of the *status quo* who received the respectful attention of tired business men who were dragged to these melancholy invectives by advanced consorts anxious to convey the lesson that what was sauce for the goose was specially well thickened for the gander.

The nineties also saw a great influx from abroad not only of the stars of vaudeville, but also of the luminaries of the legitimate stage. Henry Irving and Ellen Terry came over and opened Abbey's Theatre (now the Knickerbocker), with *"Becket"* in 1893. This house, for a number of years thereafter, became the favored of most of the noted French and English stars of the day.

116

Bernhardt played her repertoire there; Mme. Rejane appeared there as *"Mme. Sans Gêne"* and in other Gallic comedies; John Hare, dry, and cameo-like in style, played the "Duke of St. Olpherts" in *"The Notorious Mrs. Ebbsmith"*, "Eccles" in *"Caste"* and the delightful "Benjamin Bulfinch" in *"A Pair of Spectacles"* with its ever to be remembered tag "It is better to trust and be deceived than to suspect and be mistaken". Then there was Beerbohm Tree's "Falstaff" in the *"Merry Wives"*, his "Gringoire" in *"The Ballad Monger"* and, best of all, his leading rôle in *"A Bunch of Violets"*. Of his Svengali I have already spoken. Mounet-Sully, the eminent French tragedian, also played there in a repertoire of classic Conservatoire plays. Mr. and Mrs. Kendal, purer than Ivory Soap, were welcomed for several seasons in drawing-room plays like *"White Lies"*, *"The Queen's Shilling"* and *"The Elder Miss Blossom"*. Then there were seasons of George Edwarde's *"Gaiety Girls"*, and other musical pieces like *"The Toreador"*, *"Cinderella"*, etc.

Irving made some splendid reproductions of his Lyceum successes at this house, including *"Macbeth"*, *"Merchant of Venice"*, *"Much Ado About Nothing"*, *"King Arthur"*, *"Faust"*, *"Don Quixote"*, *"The Bells"*, *"Robespierre"*, *"A Story of Waterloo"*, and *"The Lyons' Mail,"* the last named a most thrilling melodrama of a superior kind, in which Irving's rendering of a dual rôle was one of the finest of his representations. But the most delightful of all Irving's plays was undoubtedly *"Olivia"*, in which Miss Terry shone resplendently.

Richard Mansfield was another luminous name among players in that golden day of the drama. When he took control of what is now the Garrick Theatre, then Harrigan's, it held high promise of becoming an epochal seat of the drama. Mansfield here produced Bernard Shaw's *"Devil's Disciple"*. It was Mansfield, and not Arnold Daly, as has been recently noted in the press, who was the first producer of Shaw in this country. This was with *"Arms and the Man"* at the Herald Square Theatre. Mansfield was a son of Mme. Rudersdorf, of some renown on the operatic stage fifty years ago. His own career began in comic opera in which he continued until an engagement in *"A Parisian Romance"* as "Baron Chevrial" catapulted him into fame as a serious actor. His versatility led him into all departments of the drama, but he excelled in the weird and horrible, and as a graceful comedian. His *"Doctor Jekyll and Mr. Hyde"* was an example of the first, and his *"Prince Karl"* and *"Beau Brummel"* examples of the latter. His weakness as a producer lay in his surrounding company of mediocrities, a fault he shared with others as part of the star system, and one of the prime drawbacks to the advancement of the dramatic art. His personal eccentricities were many and gave him a reputation for surliness that like most stage reputations was probably exaggerated. But withal he was a brilliant figure on the stage of his time and a most intelligent and sincere protagonist of its improvement. His loss was an irreparable one to the American stage.

"The Old Homestead" was one of those institutions of the drama like *"Uncle Tom's Cabin"* and *"Rip Van Winkle"* that was a sure fire hit amongst the great mass of patrons of the theatre. Denman Thompson traversed the length and breadth of the land with it for years and

played the "Opery House" in Kickapoo Centre and the Academy of Music in New York with equal assurance. He made and lost several fortunes with it—lost them because old "Josh Whitcomb" (a synonym for his own name) was an inveterate gambler. It would have astonished most of the auditors of that famous bucolic drama *"The Old Homestead"* to see its chief exponent, the guileless New Hampshire rustic "Josh Whitcomb" —the hayseed—the hick—this bumpkin who might possibly be pictured making a two-dollar bet on a County fair race—ascend the steps of the country's greatest gambling hell to go up against the wheel or the faro bank. Yet this is just what Denman Thompson did, oft and many a time.

The green table did not break him. *"The Old Homestead"*, true to its implications weathered the storms that assailed it. Thompson might have retired a millionaire but for his fatal penchant, and Swansey, New Hampshire, might have become a shrine to the homely, sturdy sentiments of that vast majority of playgoers who enjoy whatever is redolent of the soil. The first scene of *"The Old Homestead"* purported to be a faithful reproduction of Thompson's farm in Swansey and was regarded by his audiences as an ideal picture of rural domesticity.

In Bronson Howard's *"Aristocracy"* was attempted a satire on international marriages, a rather stilted affair, in which all the titled foreigners were villains of the deepest dye, and the Americans guileless victims of their machinations. Another parody, though in a different and far more boisterous vein, was Harrigan's *"Reilly and the 400"* with its "tough girl" and epidemic song "Maggie Murphy's Home."

SACRED (?) CONCERTS

The society play opened the door to a highly artificial
school of the drama, that in which Oscar Wilde was the
acknowledged master. The dialogue bristled with epigrams and "wise-cracks" such as would be impossible
in any real life conversation. The plots of the plays
were mere vehicles upon which to hang cynical and
decadent observations on life, love, marriage and divorce. This was the school of *"Lady Windermere's
Fan"*, *"The Importance of Being Ernest"*. A number
of flabby local imitators of this class of play arose, and
their dialogue is singularly vapid when read today,
and leads one to the reflection of how our modern so-
called epigrams will sound after an equal lapse of time.
The question of Sunday night theatrical performances
began at this time to be agitated. Even to this day we
have declined to follow the Sunday evening performance, an almost universal custom in our Western cities.
The entertainments given at a few houses were disguised under the euphemism of "Sacred Concert".
Then there were "Benefits" for various more or less
laudable purposes, on Sunday nights at the regular dramatic playhouses, which contained on their programmes
the names of numerous stars, who never appeared and
were seldom apologized for. These subterfuges were
employed for many years, until the high state of
respectability now enjoyed by vaudeville was established.

Even the dime museums gave "Sacred Concerts",
when the freaks took a day off, and the beer gardens
of the East Side also had slap-stick artists and "vocal-
ists" to enhance their sanctimonious proceedings. The
excise laws were evaded or entirely flouted by the
saloons where "the boys in the back room" held carni-

Frederic Remington
after photograph

RICHARD MANSFIELD AS RICHARD THE THIRD

Mme. Calvé as Anita in "La Navarraise"

MRS. FISKE, THE SUPERB

MAURICE BARRYMORE AND ROSE COGHLAN IN A "WOMAN OF NO IMPORTANCE"

val. Many restaurants used to serve beer to their patrons, but having no license to sell, had to send a waiter for it to the nearest barroom. Some of the restaurants that adjoined licensed premises cut a hole in the wall through which drinks were passed. These were rapidly capturing the trade of those eating houses not favored by this ideal situation, when the latter protested to the authorities against the unfair advantage, with the result that the hole in the wall was sealed up, much to the disgust of the patrons whose beverages were no longer to be so conveniently acquired.

As far back as the nineties the first rumblings of the Eighteenth Amendment were audible. Transcontinental travelers were loud in their complaints when refused alcoholic drinks when passing through "dry" States. Loud and deep were the lamentations and dirty remarks were made concerning a certain free (?) country.

In New York no such restrictions existed. Along with the dog wood, the pussy willow and other harbingers of Spring came the highly-colored Bock Beer Sign with its rampant goat. Whether there was any real difference between Bock and the usual run of beer I never knew. Probably not. Simply an excuse to start the season I imagine, though no excuse was really needed.

Somewhere in these pages I mentioned "Peacock Alley" in the old Waldorf. That was of sufficient fame, I believe, to warrant a word or two of description.

A long passage-way extended through the section from the office to the ladies' waiting room adjoining what was known as the Turkish Room. Persons seated along the chairs in this lobby could easily be seen by almost every person in the hotel, so popular was this particular part of the hotel. It became a natural rendezvous. There was rarely a vacant seat and all were occupied by women elaborately gowned and fair of face. Many were sent by leading modistes merely to show off their handsome clothes. It speedily became known as one of the most attractive and interesing places in New York, and Peacock Row was thronged with people who came to see and to be seen. It was a brilliant scene at night, especially, and many a stroller down the row was there for the single purpose of looking over the glittering throng.

Upon that sad, sad day when Captain Churchill finally threw up the sponge in favor of prohibition and gave over his famous eating place to the wreckers, there was scarcely a dry eye or a sober breath among those of us who had had the now inestimable privilege of having once been recognized and bowed to a preferred after-theatre table by the genial Captain himself. How our stiffly-starched bosoms swelled with pride as we trod the softly carpeted floor, the ladies of our party, properly impressed by our importance, trailing their long silken gowns in our wake down the aisle of tables until, with just the right adjustment of their draperies, a dainty pat to their daring elbow-length sleeves and a final pulling off of the sixteen-button gloves, they smiled happily at us under the rose-tinted table lights as the string orchestra struck into *"Violets"*.

Of the supper itself it is scarcely possible to speak without emotion. Cocktails to begin; oysters with all the trimmings, followed by one of the justly-famous Churchill planked steaks; wine, salad, more wine; ices, champagne, the demi-tasse, the final cordial. Then, the regal exit of yourself and party to the entrance where it was either "Home, James," with your own coupe and pair of high-steppers or one of the waiting hansoms and a whirl through the Park (if you were a real devil), before turning your latchkey at, maybe, one o'clock in the morning. All this, for less than the price of a ringside seat at one of the modern night clubs where it takes a high-priced hostess, an acrobatic jazz band and a whole company of hired performers to make you forget that you haven't had anything to eat and that you must make love to your supper partner under the influence of nothing stronger than white rock.

This little domestic picture, however, applies only to those solid citizens of the nineties who took their wives or fiancees and went in parties. The other and more celebrated side of New York's after-theatre night life was the bird and bottle supper with the musical comedy stars and chorus beauties as guests of the Broadway spenders.

The witching hour at these parties was eleven thirty, when the show girls began to drift in from the various Broadway successes. It was a sight for the gods to watch their majestic progress down the room. The famous beauties, whose pictures were in the lobbies and whose names were in the feature stories, knew just the right moment for their entrance into the crowded restaurants. The wise orchestra leader knew his cue and, as a headliner appeared at the door with her escort, he gave the signal to his men and the strains of her song hit greeted her. She was always just so surprised; fluttered nervously with the great bouquets of violets or orchids which her well-repaid admirer carried for her and finally, with every eye upon her, walked slowly to their reserved table. Her costly pearl dog collar was well displayed upon her shapely neck; her beautiful arms bare to the shoulder, her tightly-laced waist throwing into bold relief the rounded bosom and the swelling hips, swathed in the most clinging of satin skirts that swept the floor in a long, billowing train.

Each talked-about-beauty, whether show girl, high-priced star or member of the chorus, had her similar entrance; drew her own little crowd of devotees and provided ample thrills and excitement for the crowd without the slightest effort. True, these abandoned creatures did not smoke in those days—for well they knew that an outraged proprietor would have had them unceremoniously escorted to the door, at such an open affront to public decency. However, there were compensations. Hundred dollar bills and diamond necklaces were frequently tucked into the bunches of flowers that the flower girls sold from high-heaped trays; champagne flowed like water; it did not need Texas Guinan in those rosy days to plead: "Give this little girl a hand." The little girl of the Nineties didn't need a bit of help.

These recollections of other and younger days brings back also the unalloyed delight with which I watched the bill poster cover the fence around the empty lots near my house with the most exciting, thrilling, blood-curdling pictures that ever were on land or sea. I remember, as if it were but yesterday, Augustin Daly's first play *"Under the Gaslight"*. The hero was tied to the railroad track and the headlights of the express rounding the curve were throwing their beams upon him, so close was the impending doom. Of course the heroine breaks down the door of the cabin that confined her and cuts her lover loose just in time. Then there was that pure young soul in *"Only a Working Girl"* smarting under the insults of the proud and haughty daughter of the rich. Then there was *"The Silver King"* returning to his snow-laden cottage, just in time to save it from the ruthless extortioner about to fore-close the inevitable mortgage. I can see the hero of the *"Still Alarm"* driving his white horses and fire engine to the rescue of the maiden in the burning mansion. I can see the boat race in the *"Dark Secret"*, rowed in I don't know how many thousand gallons of real water. This was the first tank drama. I can see Bettina Girard riding the winner in *"Old Kentucky"* and Leonard Boyne, in *"The Prodigal Daughter"*. I can see any number of bodies lashed to the rails of *"The Limited Mail"*, *"The Pay Train"*, *"The Fast Express"*, or lashed to the plank in *"Blue Jeans"*. I can see the duel in the snow of *"The Corsican Brothers"*, and *"Monte Cristo"* on the wave-lashed rock shrieking "The World Is Mine!" I can see the human bridge over which the heroine of *"Hands Across the Sea"* crosses the chasm in escaping from her pursuers. An unforgotten scene is that of the troupe of exiles in *"Siberia"* on their way to that airy region, under the lashes of the Cossacks. I think it was in this play that the phrase "Back to the Mines!" had its origin. Other Arctic pictures that cross my mind while my feet are on the fender and I watch my twenty dollars a ton coals go to blazes, are those of *"The Land of the Midnight Sun"*, *"The Sea of Ice"* with which Kate Claxton followed *"The Two Orphans"*, and *"Storm-Beaten"*. The great raft scene in *"The World"* was a crackerjack and *"Davy Crockett"* thrusting his arm through the hasps of the cabin door is a classic, as is also Eliza Crossing the Ice in *"Uncle Tom's Cabin"*. So were scenes in *"The World Against Her"*, *"The Black Flag"*, and *"The Danger Signal"*. Fascinating too, were the scenes from the *"Sporting Dutchess"*, *"The White Heather"*, *"The Fatal Card"* and *"The Power of the Press,"* while the pictures of that first and best of "crook" plays, *"Jim the Penman"* riveted the passerby. The perennial Barnum came with the flowers that bloom in the spring and brought an art gallery to the small boy that not all the Metropolitans, Louvres and Salons can ever obliterate.

Among the posters which I have reproduced is one to which I would call special attention as it has unusual historic significance—that of *"Pudd'nhead Wilson"*. It was played at the Herald Square Theatre, by Frank Mayo, also of *"Davy Crockett"* fame. The action of the play hinges upon an identification by means of the thumb prints of two persons, the scientific study of which had been Pudd'nhead's hobby. This identification brings his enemies to confusion, and the play to a triumphant close. Although Galton's thumbprint theory was not unknown to local criminologists, it was the striking exemplification of its use in this play that directed the special attention of the New York police officials to it and led to its adoption by the department.

At the close of the play Frank Mayo was called upon for a speech. He read the following dispatch from Mark Twain: "Cable me the jury's verdict". The audience cried in answer, "A success".

A long time after Al Woods, one of the high lights in the 90s, had become a prominent figure on Broadway, he still clung to some of his old Bowery customs. One of these was to sit in a wooden chair tilted back

against the wall and sink a wicked wad of Virgin Leaf
back of his tongue and shout " 'lo Sam", " 'lo Bill",
"How do Mis' Smith", to the passing throngs. The
atmosphere of a general country store has always been
like a letter from home to Al, and the big thing he
misses in this crowded city of ours is the smell of the
old livery stable with the little sign of T. J. Smith,
Veterinary, in the window. Anyone can get a rise out
of Al by making a noise like a tree-toad and handing
him a bunch of pussywillows. And if you can smell
like a load of new mown hay he is yours for life.

The New York stage in the Nineties was a glittering
spectacle. Many of us think it was then at the highest
point of its artistic and cultural life. Certainly the
men who directed it were less commercial than their
immediate successors. That Daly and Frohman died
practically penniless was no reflection on their artistic
abilities no matter how much of a reproach it may
have been to their business side. The blood of the
martyr is the seed of the church, and in the sacrifices
demanded of these managers, succeeding generations
reaped the benefit. The Stage as a whole was immensely enriched by their efforts.

A whole chapter in these memoirs might be given
to Mrs. Fiske alone; *there* is a colorful figure if ever
there was one. For some fool reason or other she is
not seen often enough in New York. Yet as Woollcott
says: it is pleasant to know that she passed this way.

Then again there are a lot of delightful personages
whom we would all like to see take one more curtain
call. Ada Rehan, Maude Adams, Margaret Illington,
Blanche Bates, Lillian Russell, Edna May, Maxine
Elliot, May Mannering, Edith Kingdon, Viola Allen,

JOHN DREW, JIM LEWIS, JOHN GILBERT

Maud Brunscombe, Fanny Ward, Mary Boland, Billie Burke, Virginia Harned, Annie Russell, Fanny Davenport, Frankie Bailey, May Irwin, Rose Coghlan, Fay Templeton, Mrs. Leslie Carter, Mrs. Whiffen, Mrs. Gilbert, Mrs. John Drew, Ethel Barrymore, Kate Claxton, Clara Morris, Ellen Terry, Mary Anderson and a heavenly host of others. What a glorious galaxy they would make spread across the stage!

With them should be John Drew, Jimmie Lewis, John Gilbert, Maurice Barrymore, Lionel Barrymore, Sydney Herbert, Frederick de Belleville, Kyrle Bellew, John McCullough, C. W. Couldock, Lester Wallack, Frank S. Chanfrau, W. H. Crane, C. E. Robson, Ed. Harrigan, Tony Hart, Johnny Wilde, E. M. Holland, Sidney Drew, James K. Hackett, Walker Whiteside, Richard Mansfield, William Faversham, Augustus Thomas, Walter Hampden, Henry Irving, Lew Fields, Joe Webber, Pete Daily, Wilton Lackaye, Henry E. Dixey, De Wolf Hopper, George M. Cohan, Honey Boy Evans, George Primrose, Billy West, the four Mortons, the four Cohans, Eva Tanguay, Jim and Bonnie Thornton, Willie Collier, Williams and Walker, Eddie Foy, and Murphy and Nichols, whose skit called "From Zaza to Uncle Tom" would still bring out the S. R. O. sign at any vaudeville theater, if they could be lured from retirement to play it once again.

And for all my sins of omission and commission may heaven forefend me!

The amalgamation of all the gold in the nineties was most spectacularly represented in the Golden Horseshoe of the Metropolitan Opera House. The opera in those days was a far more important society function than in these times. It was this importance that was the salva-

MAUDE ADAMS IN THE "MASKED BALL"

THE LAST PHOTOGRAPH TAKEN OF CHARLES FROHMAN BEFORE
THE SINKING OF THE "LUSITANIA"

1. THE FOUR COHANS
2. LILLIAN RUSSELL IN THE DUCHESS
3. MRS. FISKE AS BECKY SHARP

ABOVE MR. HARRIGAN AS THE MAJOR

Miss Ada Lewis in her famous impersonation of the "tough girl" and Harrigan as Waddy Googan

tion of opera in New York, for the stockholders were invariably called upon to foot the deficit that accrued at the end of each season. By the aid of prize fights, wrestling matches, shady French balls, flower shows and other revenue producers, the management sought to reduce this deficit to the lowest possible common denominator. But it always seemed to me that this was lowering the dignity of the Metropolitan far below ordinary decency.

Opera as presented then was a relatively much more expensive undertaking than now. Henry E. Abbey, the foremost impressario of his day, suffered disastrous losses when he first opened the Opera House. In the nineties the firm of Abbey, Shoeffel and Grau conducted opera on a more profitable basis, although they, and later Grau, independently, assembled the most glamorous aggregation of songbirds that local opera has ever known. Their companies in the decade in which they flourished included the brothers De Reszke, Maurel, Tamagno, Van Dyck, Lasalle, Plançon, Ancona, Campanari, Carbone, Scotti, and among the prima-donnas, Melba, Eames, Nordica, Lehman, Scalchi, Homer, Mantelli, Calve, Sanderson, Van Zandt, and lesser lights.

The boxholders of the resplendent horseshoe were all noted on the programmes with an explanatory chart showing the location of their loges according to number. This was a great aid to the sightseer who was thus able on occasion to identify some social celebrity with the assistance of an opera glass, or at least thought the identification made. All visiting dignitaries were taken to the opera, including the dukes, lords, and sundry nobility spending their pre-nuptial periods in the city.

"CRANK'S ALLEY"

These were always a source of great interest to a vast number of people whose only concern at the opera was to wear evening dress and bask in the reflected light of these ineffable luminaries.

Of course this highly magnified operatic situation brought the artists of the company into great prominence, and the adulation with which they were showered was almost hysterical at times. The celebrated "crank's alley" as the aisles nearest the stage were called, crammed with excited idolators, anxious for a nod, a smile, or best of all, a rose leaf tossed among them, was a phenomenon of the times. There is a quaint story among H. C. Bunner's *"Short Sixes"*, named *"The Tenor"*, which throws an amusing sidelight on the situation. A daintily bred young daughter of a Washington Square family takes service as a housemaid in the apartment of a noted tenor in order to be near the object of her infatuation. What happens there to tumble this idol from its pedestal is told in Bunner's best vein, though a bit rough on Fausts and Lohengrins, off duty.

Ever since the days of David Garrick and Nance Oldfield, the "mash note" has been a by-product of the player's art. The screen idol of today is no longer a "matinee idol". The "matinee girl" passed out in the nineties, when it was something of an adventure for unchaperoned maidens to attend evening performances. In those days matinees were predominantly feminine. Today one finds a large male attendance at these functions, including cake-eaters, lounge-lizards, and unemployed gentlemen in general.

What bonfires could have been made of the "matinee girl's" effusions to John Drew, Ed. Sothern, James K.

Hackett, Henry Woodruff, Alexander Salvini, Robert
Mantell, "Bob" Hilliard and other exponents of the
romantic drama! At least their worshippers saw them
in the flesh, and not merely as fleeting pictures on a
screen.

The term "vaudeville" was an imported one, unknown
to the New York theatregoer of a prior age to our
period. Some idea of its social atmosphere may be
gleaned from the fact that the principal local playhouses concerned with it were Tony Pastor's, The London Theatre, Harry Miner's Bowery, and Eighth
Avenue Theatres, and one or two others. These were
augmented by Dime Museum shows, and numerous
beer-gardens convenient to the foreign colonies. Tony
Pastor's was the most famous of this type of resort,
some of his alumni later gracing more elevated boards.
Lillian Russell was one of them, and her earliest appearance at his old Broadway house was marked by a
rendition of a classic ballad entitled "Kiss Me, Mother,
Ere I Die".

These performances were of such a roughneck character that when in the early Nineties there came an
infusion of higher talent from the Cafés Chantant of
Paris and the 'alls of London it was felt that some
more "swankey" description was required for the new
dispensation. Koster & Bial's, whose resort on Twenty-
third Street was *suis generis* among the town's amuse-
ments, inaugurated the term vaudeville, I think, in
presenting such attractions as "Maudi the lightning
calculator", Carmencita, Sandow and other stars of
magnitude.

The lesser playhouses quickly took up the term, and

as if to emphasize the improved morale billed their shows as "Refined Vaudeville". This marked the beginning of the huge Keith and Proctor interests in the amusement world, an event of the first importance in its relation to the less expensive theatrical performance.

It was to Benjamin F. Keith that the world owes clean performances on the variety stage. Before his time, the stuff that was depended upon to get a laugh was monstrously indecent. It is needless to recall the individual offenders in this particular as their names will readily recur to those of my readers who can hark back to the old days. Swear words, "blue" lines as they were called, and innuendoes of questionable character were all banished from the theatres controlled by him. In his successor, E. F. Albee, the same policy has been maintained and if anything improved. As purveyor to a tremendously large clientele this attitude of the Keiths at a time when it threatened the box office cannot be too highly commended. The success which attended his efforts was richly deserved.

Indicative of the heightened social status of this new vogue of entertainment, after this housecleaning by Keith, the Vaudeville Club was organized in 1893, with quarters in the assembly rooms of the Metropolitan Opera House. This was practically New York's first night club. It followed more or less closely the lines of the then celebrated "New Club" of London. It was designed to furnish members, each evening, a stage performance to begin late, and last long after the theatres closed. Reginald De Koven was president, and among the directors were such social magnates as Elisha Dyer, Jr., Theodore Frelinghuysen, Prescott Lawrence,

Stanford White, P. Lorillard Ronalds, Jr., Peter Cooper Hewitt, J. A. Harriman, and others of prominence. Notwithstanding this formidable roster the Vaudeville Club did not long flourish, after its special functions began to be the common property of the playgoer at the regular theatres.

THE WIDOW BEDOTT

CHAPTER IV.

ENTER THE MOVIES

THERE used to be a low circular brick building on the northeast corner of Seventh Avenue and Fifty-fifth Street known as Tattersalls, which, as its name implies, was intended primarily for horse auctions but which at various periods was given over to amusement purposes. Here at one time were shown the cycloramas of "The Battle of Vicksburg" and "The Battle of the Monitor and Merrimac." During the Chicago World's Fair one of the most popular attractions of the Midway was Hagenback's Animal Show, conducted by the famed Hamburg wild beast collectors. This, on its homeward trek gave a season's performances at Tattersalls of really remarkable feats of animal training. Lions and tigers were put through their paces as if they were so many cats and dogs. Seals revealed an almost human sagacity, and the entire show was conducted on a basis that was almost a scientific demonstration.

In this connection I am reminded of the Shaefer Family of sharpshooters who also were a World's Fair attraction. These people appeared here at the Metropolitan Opera House in Kiralfy's great spectacle *"America"* which had packed the Chicago Auditorium during the previous summer. *"America"* did not repeat this success in New York, but the wonderful marksmanship of the Shaefers will not be forgotten by those who witnessed their sensational if squeamish feats with the rifle. I believe certain hazardous feats they accomplished are now quite properly prohibited by law.

Public taste in those days seemed to demand the spectacular and dangerous—or at least the managers of these troops imagined they did, which was the same thing. And of course competition tended to make the acts more and more risky until at last the bounds of reasonable safety were lost sight of completely.

There was a good deal of a thrill in some of these acts we will admit, all due to the ever present and imminent danger of a ghastly tragedy. This was bound to happen sooner or later and always did. And while it does not seem proper to say that the spectators were attracted by this contingency, a good many undoubtedly got most of their pleasure out of this possibility. After one or two fatal accidents, the law stepped in and now the thrillers at the Circus and elsewhere are comparatively harmless.

With the improvement in the type of performances in the vaudeville theatres came a corresponding betterment in the theatre buildings themselves. For years the great music halls of London, like the Empire and Alhambra, had no counterparts in elegance of appointments in New York, and high priced imported acts seemed out of place in the shabby precincts of Tony Pastor's or the old Koster & Bials. Early in the Nineties, however, Oscar Hammerstein, who had previously exercised his 'prentice hand in building theatres in Harlem, invaded the very centre of New York theatredom by erecting the Manhattan Opera House on 34th Street, just west of Broadway, on a site now covered by Macy's. His venture as an impresario failing here, he was fain to take into partnership the firm of Koster & Bial, who now found 23rd Street too far downtown to attract their quondam audiences. Here began the first comparable analogy to the great Leicester Square houses that were the centre of London's night life—minus the notorious promenade so long the object of attacks by London reformers. Salaries here were the highest heretofore paid to vaudeville artists in America. The best known stars of Europe, including Albert Chevalier, Carmencita, Otero, Cleo de Meròde, Marie Lloyd, Cissie Loftus, Belle Bellwood, Charmion, Martinette, pantomimists played here. Here, on April 27, 1896, was the first important showing of the movies when they were added to the regular bill. The movies revealed Annabelle in a serpentine dance, and, as something entirely new, a special film showing waves rolling against a pier at Manhattan Beach.

No more modest appearance was ever made of a great

NED HARRIGAN

Author of the famous Harrigan and Hart plays accorded high
place in the American stage as depicting local East side life
in New York in the Seventies

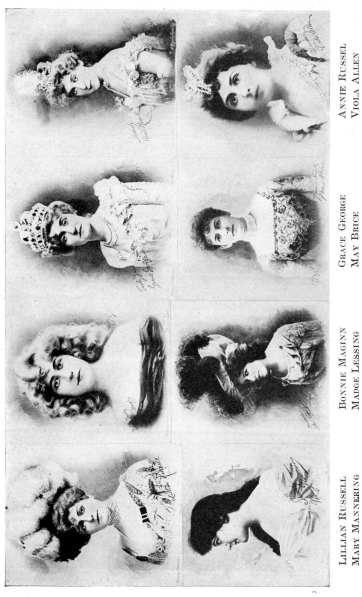

ANNIE RUSSEL
VIOLA ALLEN

GRACE GEORGE
MAY BRICE

BONNIE MAGINN
MADGE LESSING

LILLIAN RUSSELL
MARY MANNERING

SOME OLD TIME SONG BIRDS

Miss Emma Eames, Mlle. Marie Van Zandt, Mlle. Guilla
Ravogli, Mlle. Sofia Ravogli, Mr. Edward de Reske, M. Jean
de Reske

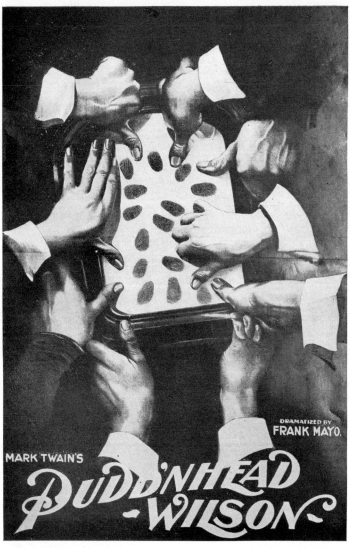

THE IDENTIFICATION OF A CRIMINAL BY MEANS OF THUMB-
PRINTS IN THIS PLAY, LED TO THE ADOPTION OF THIS SYSTEM
BY THE NEW YORK POLICE

event than this unheralded showing of the first movie.
Perhaps this was due to the fact that already movies
had appeared in several advertising signs along Broadway. The future of this industry seemed to be along
such commonplace lines and it was not expected that
anyone would ever pay to see such a feature as part of
a regular performance. The showing at Koster & Bial's
caused no particular excitement, the act was received
merely as one of a dozen, and Carmencita was considered vastly more important.

Of all the attractions offered at Koster & Bial's, perhaps the most eagerly awaited and largely attended was
the noted Albert Chevalier, the London coster singer.
The coster, despite his frequent appearance in the
comic drawings of Phil May, familiar to American
readers, was a rather mysterious individual to our
natives. He was generally classed as on a par with the
New York "tough". W. S. Gilbert had sung of him:

> "When the coster's finished jumping on his mother
> He loves to lie a-basking in the sun,"

and that was the general local idea.

Chevalier presented the coster in his more human
and sentimental aspect. He was rollicking of course in
his "Knocked 'em in the Old Kent Road", but he was
also quizzical in:

> "Oh, 'Liza, dear 'Liza, if yer dies an old maid
> You have only yerself to blime
> Oh, 'Liza, dear 'Liza, 'Ow'd yer fawncy 'Awkins
> For yer h'other nime."

While in "My Old Dutch" he touched the pathetic and
sentimental:

CARMENCITA

"We've been together over forty year
And it don't seem a day too much
There's not a lidy livin' in the land,
As I'd swap for my dear Old Dutch."

Long before Chevalier came to America, his songs had been sung here by imitators, but no one had the real cockney unction that he, alone, could impart.

Carmencita, who has been immortalized on canvas by Sargent and Chase, as Miss Farren was by Reynolds, made her first great hit at Koster & Bial's. She had been a ballet-dancer in Spain at $20 a week. Kiralfy saw her in London, where she earned £8, and brought her to New York at $100 a week. She opened at Niblo's the scene of the old "Black Crook" triumphs, but created no sensation. On February 5, 1890, she came to Koster & Bial's, where she had a proper *milieu,* and soon became the toast of the town.

Unquestionably, she was the most remarkable dancer who has appeared in New York since the days of Taglione and Ellsler. It was Carmencita who really started the vogue of ladies attending vaudeville shows. There used to be a row of curtained boxes on the balcony of Koster & Bial's old place on 23rd Street, and in these, ladies consumed with curiosity to see the latest craze of the hour, would defy the proprieties, and it eventually became the smart thing in society to get up a party to see Carmencita from the half draped boxes. "If the fad keeps up," said the *Sun,* "it will not be long before the number will be so large that they will not make any bones about their going."

What Carmencita would have thought of the modern gyrations of the dance hall we need not enquire. She thought dancing ennobling. She told interviewers that

150

dancing looked at in the right way touches the higher emotions. Delsartè, the famous expounder of physical culture had laid down certain rules for graceful posturing, and when asked if she had studied them Carmencita laughed and replied that in that respect she was a law unto herself. "When I go upon the stage," she said, "I carry with me simply an idea, a motive for the entire dance. I do not know what precise steps I shall take from moment to moment, I let my own mood and the temper of those watching me influence and control the successive steps. Much of the music that is played for me is of my own composition or suggestion and I know what liberties it permits me to take. Practise? No, I never practise. I dance when I go from here; I dance in the morning. It is my amusement, it is my relaxation."

Another celebrity at this house was the *café chanteuse* Marie Vanoni, who was probably the first to introduce the now shop-worn device of making endearing remarks to persons on the lay side of the footlights. Anna Held was one of her successors in this type of performance. It led to the now familiar runway from the stage to the aisles, down which painted damsels cavort to the intense edification of prominent butter and egg men, and less prominent bond-salesmen.

Vanoni's particular *tour de force* was a song called "Georgie" which, after singing several French songs, she gave in English in the same piquant manner. Her verses told a story of burning love unrequited, and the object of it was the bass-viol player, who stood at his instrument just below her. She explains that she fell in love with him much against her will, but he will not take his eyes from his music. Then she draws an invisible bow over imaginary strings and imitates the viol's tones. In the chorus to each stanza she makes violent love to the player. The singer was plump, pretty and mistress of all the arts of stage expression best described as "Frenchy". The lines of each chorus called upon her lover by some pet name and in singing them she had a different inflection for each one, expressing a variation in the intensity of her feeling. The first "Georgie" was pronounced as if the singer thought he would look up on hearing his name; the second a bit imperiously, and so on with increasing emphasis, until at last she was vexed to tears. Failing again, she lost all control of her temper and passed into a reproachful and angry tirade. There was naturally a craning of necks to see the object of so warm and violent an infatuation, and while all ears were attendant upon the singer, every eye was upon the viol-player, who neglectful of the imploring one above him nonchalantly sawed away on his instrument with a bored indifference to both singer and audience, no doubt arising from the reflection that with all this unwonted celebrity his wages were no bigger than before.

The following is the ditty addressed to that basest of bass-violinists by the adoring cantatrice:

"Tonight I am not very gay, the reason I will tell to you,
  I fell in love the other day, my little heart is burst in
        two;
  My own sweetheart is sitting there, the big bass fiddle
        he does play
  Alas! for me he does not care, but practices like this,
        all day.

Chorus
(Imitation of bass viol)

152

OSCAR HAMMERSTEIN

Georgie! Georgie! Devotedly I love you;
My own baby, your music I adore;
Georgie! Georgie! One kiss for her above you,
You won't? Then don't! I'll love you all the more.

No, Georgie, with your double bass, you are not worthy
    such as I,
To some one else I'll turn my face, and to attract his
    love I'll try;
I see a handsome fellow here, who looks as if he yearned
    for me,
And yet—and yet—Oh, Georgie dear, why will you so
    provoking be?

Chorus

Now Georgie, I am mad with you—not mad in love as
    you suppose,
But full of ire and hatred too, for him who dares my
    will oppose;
Henceforth our paths are not the same, we'll never speak
    as we pass by.
What's this? I thought you called my name, or did you
    wink the other eye?

Chorus

The policy of high salaries, however, worked the undoing of Koster & Bial's and the house was closed.
It was later reopened as a regular theatre and after a
season or two, despite its modern construction and
sumptuous fittings, torn down to make way for the
great department store now on its site.

Despite the vicissitudes of this house, its builder,
Oscar Hammerstein, determined to continue his policy
of building extraordinary amusement palaces and in
1897 opened his grandiose Olympia on Long Acre
Square. This establishment was the forerunner of
every species of amusement of the present Great White

Way, and was the apotheosis of that earlier galaxy that extended as far south as 23rd Street. When the Olympia was built it broke ground in what was, to the average New Yorker, untrodden ways. It had a music hall, regular theatre, concert hall, roof garden, billiard rooms, etc., all accessible for the one admission—50 cents. It was gorgeously decorated, and as a whole, eclipsed anything ever known in the world of the theatre. Its opening night, which occurred before the paint was dry on its walls, drew together one of the most heterogeneous crowds ever seen in the city. Dames and matrons of the 400 rubbed elbows with women of the Tenderloin. Clubmen, stock-brokers and merchants jostled racktrack touts, sport and stage celebrities. Décolleté and claw hammers ruled sartorially and the *éclat* surpassed anything the town had known since the opening of the Madison Square Garden in 1890.

There are many who imagine that the revues which are the mainstay of today's light musical stage are a very recent phenomenon of that kaleidoscopic institution, dating, perhaps, back to the first "Follies" of a decade or so ago. The fact is, the daddy of them all— at least on the New York stage—was "The Passing Show", produced at the Casino as far back as 1894. There had been, of course, many burlesques of current events on the stage and off, introduced in early extravaganzas—Dixey's parody on Irving comes to mind—but they were only incidental to the play as a whole. "The Passing Show" was just what its name indicates, a continuous reflection of the contemporary stage and the town in general. One of the most amusing take-offs in "The Passing Show" was the chorus of "Hot Tamale" venders, who were just then a feature of local life. A group of white garbed tamale dispensers came on singing to a catchy tune:

"We are the boys of the hot tamale".

The hot tamale was introduced to the city by a firm called The Mexican Food Corporation, which hoped to rival the popularity of hot corn on the streets, with its exotic condiment. Scores of venders in white duck invaded the highways and for a time the novelty of the thing presaged success. Finally the cheap restaurants began to sell the tamales and also that more abiding dish, "chili con carne" and the rivals of Colonel Waring's "White Wings" disappeared from public view.

Another Casino success of a piece with "The Passing Show" was "The Merry World". One of its songs satirized the "Trilby" craze as follows:

"Now let all the stage swells clamber into their shells,
And all fads disappear from your gaze;
For the whole blooming town just at present bows down
To "yours truly" the popular craze.
Tho' you madly rejoice in De Reszke's grand voice
Or some artist from over the sea,
If you'd be right in line you must curvate your spine
In a graceful obeisance to me.

Chorus

I am Trilby O'Ferroll, Du Maurier's bright idea,
I used to pose in scanty apparel in gay Paree,
My past is a little more shady than most of the pasts
　　　you meet
But all the same I've jumped into fame with both my
　　　feet.

155

TRILBY

When I came to town I was coldly turned down,
For the publishers thought, to a man,
That my chances were slight, and I first saw the light
On the monthly installment plan.
The insanity then took the form of a book
Then dramatists pottered* with me;
Now on everything new from a yacht to a shoe,
My familiar cognomen you see."

Nor did the vogue of "Trilby" stop in New York. There was a town in Florida that dated its prosperity from the time it assumed that name. Founded by Henry B. Plant, the millionaire railroad builder, it was formerly known as Macon, Florida. It was only a station under that name, and when the grade was cut down it was left standing high up on a cliff. It was torn down and the name Macon went with it. Being rebuilt as a nucleus for a new settlement, a new name was required. President Plant was just at the time deeply interested in Du Maurier's book, and when one of the railroad magnate's officials came to him and asked what the new station should be called Mr. Plant looked up with a twinkle in his eye and said, "We will name it 'Trilby' "—and "Trilby" it became.

That was enough. Trilby began at once to grow. A place which had never been heard of so long as it was called Macon became known in a jiffy, to all the world as Trilby. Ever-alert realtors took hold, winter tourists on the west coast of Florida craned their necks out of Pullman windows to see Trilby, and went home to talk about it; newspapers wrote about it, and it shared the general fame of all its cognomen. The streets were named after characters in the book. Ap-

---

*Paul M. Potter dramatized Trilby.

"TRILBY"

Du Maurier's great play as presented by Wilton Lackaye, Virginia Harned, Burr McIntosh, Leo Dietrichstein and others

GREAT SOCIETY FAD OF THE NINETIES

Visiting Sandow the Strong Man in one of his private levees
at Koster and Bial's where he gave a short lecture and allowed
ladies to feel his abnormal muscles

THE COMEDY DRAMA SUCCESS

ONLY A SHOP GIRL

BY MARIE WELLESLEY STERLING

HULDA: "YOU ARE ONLY A LOW SHOP GIRL!" EVE: "AN HONEST SHOP GIRL AS FAR ABOVE A FASHIONABLE IDLER AS HEAVEN IS ABOVE EARTH!"

A BOWERY CLASSIC OF THE NINETIES

EFFIE SHANNON   JULIA MARLOWE
MAXINE ELLIOTT   ISABEL IRVING
HILDA SPONG   ETHEL BARRYMORE

propriately enough, there was a Svengali Square with a network of railroad tracks in the centre, presenting the fanciful spider web which was the emblem of the book. There was also a Little Billee Street, a Taffy Street, and a Laird Lane.

Worthy of note was the improved social status of the actor and actress which was part of the movement to elevate the stage during this decade. It had always been regarded as a fall from caste for any one of any real social standing to go on the stage or to form an alliance there. The stage was regarded as a thing apart —a sort of social no man's land—to which divorcees and prodigals drifted as a means of livelihood.

The tendencies of the time, not only in this country but abroad, brought the stage and its people into better repute. It was beginning to be recognized that the theatre might have an educational value. The melo-dramatic and the romantic began to give way to a type of drama that carried a sermon with it. Preachers who had previously inveighed against the theatre, now began to commend certain plays as salutary lessons. There was a good deal of talk current about the reconciliation of the church and stage. Actors began to give their views on social problems and it was not long before they began to hob-nob over the teacups on Fifth Avenue. This was looked on askance by the old time barn-stormer, who between rehearsals and a new part every week, had never found time, had he ever had the oppor-tunity, to bask in the upholstery of the social elect.

Musical comedy was high in public favor in the Nineties. The spectacular success of the *Belle of New York* with Edna May; *Floradora* with its now his-toric sextette; the *Geisha;* De Wolf Hopper's *Wang* with Della Fox and her famous curl; *La Poupee* which owed its long run to Anna Held's much imitated song, *"I Just Can't Make My Eyes Behave,"* these and many other tuneful and eye-filling musical shows not only created new stellar favorites but unloosed upon the Broadway night life a host of chorus beauties who, with their proud escorts, graced the tables of Rector's, Martin's and Shanley's for the after-theatre supper without which no self-respecting male would think of winding up an evening at the play.

The Casino was also the birthplace of "The Belle of New York", which was the first American Musical Comedy to make a hit abroad. This amusing farrago was also the making of Edna May, whose demure Salvation Army lassie so captured British aristocracy that Miss May became a figure in Mayfair drawing-rooms. "The Belle of New York" was Miss May's outstanding theatrical success, and after a few later ventures on the stage, she retired to private life in London.

The Casino girls of this time had no little success in the eligible "catches" they made in the enhanced glamor of the footlights. The "Floradora" sextette became the shining example of what the $15 a week chorus-girl could accomplish when she set her mind to it, as common report had it that they had all been allied to a corresponding sextette of honest-to-goodnss millionaires—not the stage kind. One of the notables among this class of Casino girls was Mabel Gilman Corey, who took into camp no less a personage than William E. Corey. This little excursion however cost him his job as President of the United States Steel Corporation and eventually Mabel herself gave him the blue envelope.

THE RESPECTABLE WOIKIN' GOIL

The Nineties were already beginning to spoof the "beautiful cloak models" and "woiking goils" that later on became such prolific sources of burlesque humor. Here is a song by one of the last of the Victorians, sung to an audience of Broadway sophisticates:

I keep a manicurin' shop in London on the Strand
Where I toike a little bit off the top of the best nails in
    the land
Sometimes the swells are bloomin' fresh and act in an
    awful way
And that's when you'll hear Sophie 'ere get on her ear
    and say

Chorus

I'm a respectable workin' girl and I've no time to dally,
I'm none of your flirtin' actresses or loidies of the ballet;
I'll give you a smack if you are an earl, if you don't leave
    me go
For I'm a respectable workin' girl I'd 'ave you know.

One evenin' I went out to dine with a gent I thought was
    grand
But he orders everything in words I couldn't understand;
I thought it queer but let it pass till he says when no
    one's by,
Suppose we 'ave a demitasse? Then I says to him, says I:

Chorus

I'm a respectable workin' girl, while you're of the upper
    classes
But you can't come none of your games on me, with wine
    and demitasses
I could 'ave sworn you was a gent as would never treat
    me so
For I'm a respectable workin' girl, I'd 'ave you know.

Another gent, one night, takes me grand opera to 'ear
I loikes it so I never see the loidies sitting near,

"BROKE THE BANK AT MONTE CARLO"

But when I toikes a look about, I gets up in my wrath
And says to my young man, come hout, we're in a Turkish
bath!

Chorus

I'm a respectable workin' girl, and I like your Trovytory
It's decent enough, but the audience is quite another story,
If I wanted to study anatomy, it's not with a man I'd go
For I'm a respectable workin' girl, I'd 'ave you know.

Many old New York playgoers will remember the
team of Evans and Hoey in that most amusing of
Hoyt's farces "A Parlor Match", with which they
struck fire for many seasons. "Old Hoss" Hoey, a natural born fun maker, used to enact bombastic rôles of
"The man who broke the bank of Monte Carlo" type.
It was just the time when a good many apocryphal
stories were current about breaking the renowned financial institution on the Riviera that he sang this song:

"I've just got here through Paris, from the sunny southern
shore
I, to Monte Carlo went, just to raise my winter's rent.
Dame Fortune smiled upon me as she never did before
And I've now such lots of money I'm a gent,
Yes, I've now such lots of money I'm a gent.

Chorus

As I walk along the Bois Boo-long with an independent
air
You can hear the girls declare, 'He must be a million-
aire!'
You can hear them sigh and wish to lie,
You can see them wink the other eye
At the man who broke the bank at Monte Carlo.

I stay indoors till after lunch and then my daily walk
To the great Triumphal Arch is one triumphal march;
Observed by each observer with the keenness of a hawk
I'm a mass of money, linen, silk and starch,
I'm a mass of money, linen, silk and starch.

RUSH TO THE KLONDIKE

Chorus

I patronized the tables at the Monte Carlo hell
Till they hadn't got a sou for a Christian or a Jew;
So I quickly went to Paris for the charms of mad'moiselle
Who's the loadstone of my heart—what can I do
When with twenty tongues she swears that she'll be
     true."

Chorus

Something analogous to the California gold rush of
'49 took place in the middle Nineties, when gold was
discovered in the Klondike. The usual ill-advised rush
of adventurous counterjumpers, bookkeepers, barbers
and sundry rugged argonauts ensued. The route was
to Seattle, thence by steamer to Nome, where the real
hardships began. The Forty-niners had no such cli-
matic conditions to contend with as the Klondikers,
when winter set in. The irrepressible poet of the period
smote his bloomin' lyre in the following Odyssey of one
who lost all to gain gold.

"One day I saw a gallant ship departing
  Friends and sweethearts waved a good bye from the
      shore
  But the merry scene it bore a tinge of sadness
  For 'mong the throng there's one we'll see no more.
  In the crowd there stood a woman lone and lonely
  For against her will her boy had taken flight
  Tempted by the wealth untold to a land that's decked
      with gold
  He is sleeping in the Klondike vale to-night.

                    Chorus

  In far away Alaska, where the Yukon river flows
  Where the mighty boulders stand 'mid wealth and might
  With fortune there untold in a grave that's decked with
      gold
  He is sleeping in the Klondike vale to-night.

TIN PAN ALLEY

The great onrush of industrialism which gave a new complexion to business everywhere throughout the country was also manifested strongly in at least one department of art, and that was among the popular song producers. Songs, which were once the result of inspiration, now became products of industry, like trousers, or cloaks and suits. "Tin Pan Alley", then on Twenty-eighth Street, came into notice as the headquarters of this new branch of commerce. A new school of composers also arose to supply this voracious market with "melodies". These were men, utterly ignorant of music, who had concealed somewhere in their cerebellums a reminiscence of some long forgotten operatic tune which they thought their own. This was transmitted by whistling to some erudite hack who put it in musical form harnessed some claptrap rhyme. Hence the "popular song", the "lyric" writer, and other phenomena of the local jazz school.

The jazz song, the "blues" and "barber shop chords" may be traced with considerable certainty to the "nineties". Before that time nearly all the old negro melodies (which meant the burnt cork minstrel songs) had a pietistic note, *vide* such overwhelming favorites of an earlier day as *"Climbin' Up de Golden Stairs"*, *"Golden Slippers"* or *"In de Morning by de Bright Light"*. As the negro became a part of the country's industrial system and was drawn from the plantations into the city slums his balladry underwent a change and his interpreters drew from a new fount. Now the cry was *"What Yo' Gwine Do When de Rent Comes Roun'"*, *"If Yo' Ain't Got No Money Yo' Needn't Come Roun'"*, *"Yo' Don't Handle Nuff Money fo' Me"*, and other lyrics of an economic trend.

166

"COON SONGS"

It was no longer the "darky melody" but the "coon song". A ribald school of "babies", "honies", mercenary wenches, belligerent swains and sundry "no account niggers". A representative of this school is entitled *"Since I'se Got Money in de Bank"*:

"De odder day, while strollin' down a' Seventh Avenoo,
  I saw a comin' toward me dat ah fickle wench Lulu,
  She smiled at me and sweetly said, I always loved yer
    true;
  Jus' take me back, I'll give the snake to Hank,
  I gave dat gal de glassy eye, likewise de marble heart,
  And said, Nay, nay, mah honey gal from you I'se got to
    part;
  I'se got important business, so excuse me if I start,
  I'm gwine to draw some money from de bank."

A supplementary lyric is:

"Now I'se got another baby and he's all right,
  He spends his money like a Vanderbilt;
  He's eighteen caret, not a bit of gilt,
  Take a look at mah new baby he's out of sight,
  He's de coon dat was made for me."

And for utterly callous self-interest, mingled with apprehension, commend us to the following:

"I'm afraid dis snap is mos' too good to last,
      An' I'm nursin' it good and hard.
  Dis is a mos' too easy task
      I'm saltin' by de yard.
  Dat man thinks he's got money in de bank apilin' up so
    fast,
  But jus' de same it's in mah name;
  He's up against a losin' game,
  I'm afraid dis snap is mos' too good to last."

Among the popular songs of the period, without trace of miscegenation were *"Annie Rooney"*, *"After the Ball"*,

167

"Maggie Murphy's Home", "Comrades", "Daisy Bell", *"Just One Girl," "Oh What a Difference in the Morn-* *ing", "Sunshine of Paradise Alley", "Annie Moore",* *"Tell Them That You Saw Me", "The Band Played* *On", "She May Have Seen Better Days", "My Mother* *Was a Lady", "She Was Bred in Old Kentucky", "On* *the Banks of the Wabash", "Mary and John", "He* *Never Cares to Wander From His Own Fireside", "Two* *Little Girls in Blue", "You Can't Play in Our Yard",* *"Sweet Marie"* and *"Ta-ra-ra-Boom-de-ay",* to name only a handful.

Perhaps the most popular of such lyrics for pur- poses of what is now known as "close harmony" was Harry Kennedy's *"Say Au Revoir, But Not Goodby",* which ran Foster's plantation melodies a close second as a quartette number. It afforded brilliant opportuni- ties for ground and lofty vocal tumbling in this wise:

> "Say au revoir—(piping tenor)
> Say au revoir—(gruff bass)
> But not good by—(first base)
> But not good by—(first bass)
> The past is dead—(lachrymose tenor)
> The past is dead—(lachrymose bass)
> Love cannot die—(anguished tenor)
> Love cannot die"—(doleful bass)

And so on until a final burst of agonized appeal from the entire assemblage to *"Say Au Revoir, But Not Good-* *by."*

One of the very first, and by far the most conspicu- ous of this new school of sable song, was that sung by May Irwin entitled *"If You Ain't Got No Money,* *You Needn't Come Roun'",* which became a byword of the language:

An Illustration by C. S. Reinhart in Harper's Weekly.

A Welsh

theatre

"HULLO! MAH BABY!"

"I'se had hard luck, worst ever struck
  Oh, I'se been up against it good an' hard.
  Shot craps last night, got cleaned up right,
  For dey won mah money by de yard.
  Went down to tell mah culled belle
  How I was broke and didn't have a red;
  Her chin dropped down, she gave a frown,
  Den dat orn'ry nigger gal she said."

Chorus

If you ain't got no money, you needn't come roun',
Ef you is broke, Mister Nigger, I'll throw you down.
De only coon dat I can see, is de one dat blows his dough
    on me;
So, when you bring de stuff Mister Nigger I's to be foun'.
But when you ain't got no money, why you needn't come
    roun',
For you ain't de only poodle in de poun';
So if mah baby you wants to be, you gotter have dough
    and spread it on me,
When you ain't got no money, you needn't come roun'.

A more amorous and less calculating warble is:

"I'd leave mah happy home for you, oo, oo, oo, oo,
  You're de nicest man I ever knew, oo, oo, oo, oo,
  If you would take me, and just break me in de business
    too,
  I'd leave mah happy home for you, oo, oo, oo, oo."

This was a widely popular ditty, as was:

"Hello! mah baby, hello! mah honey, hello! mah rag-time
    gal
  Send me a kiss by wire, baby, mah heart's on fire,
  If you refuse me, honey you'll lose me,
  Then you'll be left alone;
  Oh, baby, telephone and tell me I's your own.
  Hello! hello! there.

The telephone was just then beginning to invade the

173

homes of the "common people" and this song is a contemporary witness of the fact. A prior mode of communication is also celebrated in George M. Cohan's:

"I guess I'll have to telegraph mah baby,
  I need the money bad, indeed I do,
  For Lucy is a very gen'rous lady
  I can always touch her for a few.
  I find the Western Union a convenience,
  No matter where I roam;
  I'll telegraph mah baby, she'll send ten or twenty maybe
  Then I won't have to walk back home."

Other darky songs of wide currencey were *"All Coons Look Alike to Me"*, *"Coon, Coon, Coon"*, and *"I Wish My Color Would Fade"*. But there was literally no end to the almost mechanical output of this type of ditty.

The Spanish-American War found the bards of Tin Pan Alley working overtime. Their themes were the sinking of the Maine, Dewey's victory at Manila, the Rough Riders and other high lights of that almost farcical combat. Well adapted to sentimental stanzas was the response of the South to the call to arms, and the passing of sectional feeling thus manifested. General Joe Wheeler, the ex-Confederate cavalry leader, proffered his sword and was perhaps the most popular figure in the army. The bards exploited the situation with:

"He laid away a suit of gray to wear the Union blue,
  He said we'll show that Dixie's sons will to the flag
    prove true;
  His father's sword he girded on, resolved to dare and do,
  So he laid away a suit of gray to wear the Union blue."

THE BLUE AND THE GRAY

Another epic that had a medley of national songs as an accompaniment was:

"One lies down in Santiago, many miles away,
The other rests in Chickamauga in his suit of gray."

A gem of contemporary song was the following:

"In sixty-five the boys returned, the blue had been
    victorious,
The saddest war in history at last was at an end;
'Twas our fathers who were fighting then, who said
    our cause was glorious;
Their sons now rally round the flag and call each
    other friends.
Forgotten is the bitter past the North and South
    united,
Can throw a challenge to the world without the least
    discovery;
And so we strike for liberty, and Cuba now benighted,
They're fighting side by side, the blue and gray."

The arm-chair patriots who compose the stirring ballads that fire martial ardor, especially when the carnage is at a distance, found, in the sinking of the Maine, a made-to-order theme, as in the following:

"Down with the foes that slew our heroes,
Down with the spies of treach'rous Spain,
Down with their ships in shell and fire,
Let's avenge our gallant Maine.
Though we die upon the field of battle,
Let our courage never lag;
And strike in Freedom's name, lads,
For the honor of our country and our flag."

This cordial invitation was responded to later by an echoing bard with:

"We have remembered the Maine, wiped out the old flag's
     stain,
And proudly once more, as in days of yore,
It floats on the breeze again.
Peacefully sleeping tonight are the loved ones so cruelly
     slain,
Forgotten them, nay, avenged now are they.
We have remembered the Maine."

While this choice effusion was another's:

"Let other nations brag about their well trained soldier
     boys,
And those who fight upon the deep blue sea.
But we have shown the whole world that 'tis not with
     pets or toys
That we drive back all foes of liberty.
Our volunteers have proven that in nerve they far
     outclass
The foreign soldiers drilled just for parade;
And on the mighty ocean not an enemy could pass
The fighting ships and guns by Yankees made."

Even after the war the martial ballad persisted and
perhaps its more popular contemporary number *"Good
Bye, Dolly Gray"* did not gain currency until some time
after peace was restored. The return of Dewey and the
great parade in his honor brought the sailor into the
limelight and he was celebrated in:

"Strike up the band, here comes a sailor;
 Cash in his hand, just off a whaler.
 Stand in a row, don't let him go,
 Jack's a cinch, but every inch a sailor."

The "whaler", in the second line, is a mere euphemism to afford a rhyme.

Of ballads dealing with current events there was a
never-ending stream. *"The Hotel Windsor Fire", "The*

TABLEAUX ON THE BOWERY

Homestead Strike", "Father Was Killed by the Pinker-ton Man", "The Brooklyn Car Strike", "The Pullman Strike", in fact every newspaper scare head furnished matter for the bard. Of course the sophisticates of today are far superior to this sort of banality and it is only on special occasions that they wallow in *"They Needed a Song-bird in Heaven, So God Called Caruso Away"* and *"There's a New Star in Heaven Tonight",* and others of similar character.

Years ago *tableaux* were a staple form of public amusement, not to speak of their private employment as "parlor entertainments". All the "moral shows" of all the ages leading up to the "Age of Innocence" had them. Then art struck the old Bowery and the cellar "free and easies" of old Broadway, and the *tableaux* assumed a wider latitude, in fact so wide that the "leatherheads" (now "cops") used to make periodical descents on them, very much in the same manner as they do today with reference to the unabashed drama, proving that things haven't changed so much after all. The *tableaux* were part of all the old calcium lit spectacles and burlesques and brought down the curtain amid tumultuous applause.

Finally this naïve entertainment passed out with the Crystal Palace school of art and the "Black Crook" coryphees and for many a long day the motionless human figure was unknown to the stage. The nineties, however, saw a recrudescence, or rather a variation of it in the "Living Pictures" which after creating some stir abroad came to New York to advance local education in art. The "Living Pictures" were simply more or less faithful reproductions of celebrated paintings and sculptures by the human model. They were repre-

sented in a gilt frame under a powerful light behind a
red plush curtain which was closed to afford the necessary changes. Some of the pictures were very like the
originals, others required imagination. "Paul and
Virginia" flying from the storm were quite good if
they were not kept too long standing each on one leg.
The "Dying Gladiator" was often the victim of a con-
queror who lacked biceps, and there were other lapses
from strict realism observable to the captious. The
reproductions of the nude were prime favorites in an
age that considered "flesh colored" tights the very mini-
mum of public attire, although most of the "Venuses"
and the "Springs" and "Summers" were generally
wanting in that desirable pulchritude necessary to
classical allegory.

In Europe these pictures were presented without the
protection of even flesh colored tights and persistent
rumors were kept in circulation that the same idea
would be followed here. But that old "Roundsman of
the Lord," Anthony Comstock, was on the alert and
such an exhibition would have been pie for him.
Enough was attempted however to create tremendous
interest in the scheme with the gratifying result of
crowded houses at every performance.

When an exhibition of classic statuary was held in
Cincinnati at about the time Living Pictures were
rampant, the good ladies of that virtuous town decided
that it would only be a wise precaution to have all the
figures draped in clothing before the young people were
admitted, Powers' Greek Slave was accordingly arrayed
in a dainty little calico blouse and a pair of canton
flannel drawers reaching, as was then fashionable, to
her ankles. The others were tastefully arrayed in

panties of dotted swiss, dimities and other popular fabrics of the hour.

The other day I had a call from Rich Holaman, the old Eden Musee man. He recalled many interesting details regarding this famous show place. In the twenty-five years of its existence more than thirteen million persons clicked through its turnstiles. The largest attendance was on Dewey Day, when more than thirteen thousand visitors registered and the smallest was March 12th, 1888, the day of the Big Blizzard, when only seven appeared.

Perhaps the greatest single attraction among the many novelties displayed within was Ajeeb the chess-playing Automaton. This was a genuine sensation for many years. It was supposed to be a machine which worked automatically. As a matter of fact Henry Pillsbury, one of the most skillful chess players of the day, was concealed inside the multitudinous clockwork. The figure was huge and was made to represent an arab sheik. At all events he produced an uncanny effect with his ponderous iron arms and hand when it came to his move. Some of the most brilliant players in the world essayed to beat Ajeeb, but all were defeated and retired in disgust. One of them in particular, a champion at the time, was so completely upset by the swiftness and regularity with which an apparent machine checkmated his moves that he fled in dismay long before the match was finished.

It was a funny old institution, the Eden Musee, and it ought never to have gone out of business. It was originally built by a group of titled Frenchmen, with the idea of duplicating Mme. Tussaud's Wax Works in London, and for many years they were successful. The change in the shopping district caused their demise.

The plague of Little Lord Fauntleroys at this time was something of stupendous proportions and besides Wallace Eddinger, many another boy inwardly swore at his doting mama who rigged him up in the now well known costume immortalized by Reginald Birch in his famous illustrations of Mrs. Frances Hodgson Burnett's story then running serially in *St. Nicholas.* While it would not be true to say that Mrs. Burnett's story could not have scored the success it did without them, here was one case at least where the illustrations really helped and Birch's interpretation of the Little Lord became second in popularity only to the story itself. A whole generation of boys would have been glad to see Birch hung, drawn and quartered. The "Little Lord Fauntleroy" suit with its insipid sash and wide "sissy" collar peered from every shop window in the land and the streets were filled with quandom Fauntleroys.

VIRGINIA HARNED   MARGARET ANGLIN
MRS. LESLIE CARTER   BLANCHE BATES
MRS. FISKE   JULIA OPP

"COSACK & CO.BUFFALO N.Y."   "WOLVES! What can save us?" | "The strong arm of a Backwoodsman."

FRANK CHANFRAU IN "DAVY CROCKETT." A THRILLER OF THE NINETIES

New York Coaching Club Meet

Leaving Claremont after luncheon

BOWLING IN THE NINETIES. ROLLING FOR A TEN STRIKE

98TH STREET AND THIRD AVENUE, 1883

CHAPTER V.

WRITERS AND ILLUSTRATORS IN THE DAYS OF CENTURY, HARPER'S, SCRIBNER'S

NOW that I have touched upon the publishing business I would like to say that I am greatly puzzled by the vast difference in the position occupied by the illustrator today compared with his exalted standing forty years ago. The golden age of the *Century, Harper's* and *Scribner's* has passed and names that were as well known as the proverbial household word, whatever that was, no longer sparkle in the public eye. Some, it is true, have become painters of good repute, but most of them have passed away and apparently left no successors. There was a time, however, when the names of F. Hopkinson Smith, Thure de Thulstrup, W. T. Smedley, Charley Reinhart, A. B. Frost, Howard Pyle, Maxfield Parrish, Charles C. Curran, Irving Wiles, Palmer Cox, Peter Newell, C. J. Taylor, W. L. Metcalf, E. H. Blashfield, Harry McVickar, Edwin A. Abbey, Winslow Homer, Charley Graham, E. Swain

185

Gifford, Chas. Dana Gibson; to mention only a few—
were as widely known to the public as is Gloria Swan-
son, Sinclair Lewis or Charlie Chaplin today. They
were prominent in the literary circles of their day and
an important section of the cultural life of their time.
Their work was notable and gave to American art and
letters a distinction all its own. Of all these names,
and half a hundred more, there remain today only
a few who maintain their old time prominence in the
day's doings. Gibson realized the one ambition of his
career when he purchased "Life", a periodical which in
the early days, he had done so much to bring to fame.
He was the Du Maurier of America and the brilliant
double page cartoons which appeared each week with
unfailing regularity exceeded in style and vigor even the
best work of his prototype. In J. A. Mitchell, owner of
"Life" and himself an artist of no mean accomplishment, Gibson had a wonderful counsellor and guide.
Between these two, the pages of "Life" fairly scintil-
lated with brilliancy and the weekly appearance of Mr.
Gibson's cartoon was eagerly awaited. In them were
keenly satirized all the foibles of society. The ambitions
of the newly rich, the struggles of their wives and
daughters to crash the gates of that mysterious world
known as Society, were appealingly and laughably de-
picted. Mr. Phipps' travels abroad in search of culture
was a series that kept the whole town laughing for
months. The Gibson girl was, of course, of international fame and her clothes, her hats, her walk and her
indescribable chic were at once the envy and despair
of her admirers who were legion.

But Gibson's work had a serious side at times. His
cartoons on the question of Sunday opening of the

Metropolitan Museum undoubtedly had much to do with the final decision of that admirable institution to be of genuine practical use to the community by opening on that day. It was a long and bitter struggle and the final decision of the Trustees to accede to this unquestioned public need was one which I feel sure they have never regretted. In those days, with a lot of blue noses on the Board, who threatened to revoke sundry and divers valuable bequests, this concession was not secured without great diplomacy on the part of the managers. Their action, therefore, was more public spirited than I think was realized at the time. It was Mr. Mitchell's idea originally, but Gibson's powerful pen provided the deadly ammunition.

Another series that made a profound impression was the attack on the attitude of the Episcopal Church on Divorce. In many of these pictures the portly bishops were flayed severely. The ridiculousness and inconsistency of the Church were scathingly exposed and hugely enjoyed by those familiar with the true situation. "Life's" constituency was largely among what we then knew as "The Four Hundred". And the Four Hundred was largely members of this Church and also the source of supply for a large percentage of the candidates for divorce. The immense popularity of Bishop Potter in New York and Bishop Brooks of Massachusetts, both of whom were alive in those days and very influential, who upheld the tenets of the Church on this question, were sufficient to prevent any change or alteration in the slightest degree. But the cartoons undoubtedly made possible a spirit of greater tolerance toward those who were the innocent victims of the narrow policy of the Church.

WINSLOW HOMER AND EDWIN A. ABBEY

Many of the illustrations in the last three numbers of the *Manual* portray the work of the artists I have just mentioned. Most of them appeared in *Harper's Weekly,* a journal of extraordinary power and influence in the closing years of the last Century. It is of absorbing interest to run across some early drawings of Edwin A. Abbey, like "Ringing the Fog Bell for East River Ferryboats" and know that they were made in response to an assignment by Mr. Parsons, head of the Art Department. Or the now very quaint and interesting view of the Fire Tower that stood on the corner of Varick and Macdougall Streets till about the 80's, which was the result of a similar assignment given to no less a world renowned artist than Winslow Homer. Homer at that time, like Abbey, was a 'prentice boy at Harper's. The pages of the old *Weekly* are filled with his amateur efforts, even at that time showing great merit. Curiously enough, all the more ambitious ones portray some incident along the New England Coast. They are not the dramatic, awe-inspiring seascapes with which we were afterwards to become so familiar, but already they show the attraction of the sea. They were evidently made during his vacation, and showed the fascination which the sea was to exert and greatly expand in after years.

From these fugitive news sketches, Homer as well as Abbey rapidly advanced. Abbey developed a surpassing skill in the delineation of old English characters of the fifteenth and sixteenth centuries. The comedies of Shakespeare gave the first intimation of the consummate talent possessed by this young man and a series of illustrations in the *Monthly* which soon appeared, revealed a talent so unmistakable and extraordinary that it was plainly apparent that another star had arisen in the artistic firmament. Presently appeared a special edition of Shakespeare's plays, wholly illustrated by Abbey. The drawings for this edition were the most superb, I think, that ever adorned such a work either here or abroad. This accomplishment established Mr. Abbey's reputation for all time and on a higher plane than had yet been reached by any American artist. In due time Mr. Abbey went to London, where he was the idol of the British public for years. He secured the high honor of being selected to paint the Coronation picture of King Edward VII. He was also chosen by the Boston Public Library to paint the Holy Grail— that magnificent series of mural decorations now in that building and which have become so celebrated.

Mr. Abbey, in defiance of an old superstition, bought an old house in the little village of Broadway, England. It had been formerly occupied by Seymour Haden, the artist. The legend regarding the old house was to the effect that if you bought the house you would die within the year. Haden only leased the premises but on his death Abbey purchased the place outright. Strange to relate Abbey died within the time limit set by the legend. Seymour Haden paid a visit to this country about this time and was the guest of Frederick Keppel, the famous art dealer, whose home in Yonkers commanded a superb view of the Hudson River and the Palisades from the porch. His first view of this magnificent panorama, than whom none could appreciate better than he, brought forth an assumed note of inquiry, "Why Keppel", he said, "you never told me you had a view like this!" On the local trains to New York, Haden was wont to loudly berate the other commuters because they wouldn't rave over the scenery all the way down, but kept their noses buried in their newspapers.

The collection of ancient costumes, armor, etc., gathered by Mr. Abbey were left by him to the London Museum. It is said to be the most complete and valuable one of its kind so far assembled.

As a painter, Homer now stands in the front rank of American artists. "In the Gulf Stream" is probably one of his best known subjects. It hangs in the Metropolitan Museum of Art. Others are in the hands of private collections and public institutions throughout the country. A wonderful ending for two 'prentice boys on Harper's!

F. Hopkinson Smith achieved fame in no less than four different fields. He was a popular writer of stories, an excellent illustrator, a good painter and a first class civil engineer. As a builder of lighthouses and other Government works Mr. Smith was an eminent figure in the world of practical affairs as well as in the artistic.

Writing and illustrating are not infrequently combined in the one person—Robt. W. Chambers is another example, though the list could easily be prolonged—but the apparently antagonistic gift of civil engineering or any other strictly utilitarian gift is not so frequent. Smith was an anomaly in this respect.

Many of his summers he spent in Venice. Upon his return he exhibited in the old Aldine Club in Lafayette Place, the fruit of his summer's toil. He was very fond of French grey board on which his scenes of gondoliers, bridges, houses and the characteristic Venetian mast stood out with startling effectiveness. These sketches, though light and inconsequential, sold with commendable promptness. There was always a mast in the foreground, with its shaky reflection shown in the water.

On one occasion, his friend, A. B. Frost, also an artist of rare genius and what is more remarkable in an artist, possessor of a huge fund of humor, made a burlesque of Smith's Venetian exhibit for the delectation of the club members. The inevitable mast, of course, came in for special attention. In some peculiar manner, Frost managed to impart an almost lifelike aspect to these masts and with a few deft strokes the result seemed to resemble nothing so much as a very tall man trying to get home with what was known in these vulgar days as a "bun". The effect was indescribably ludicrous and the burlesque show outdid in popularity the genuine. Smith, I am sorry to say, did not quite appreciate the humor of his contemporary and I am afraid with rather good reason. One could never again contemplate one of Smith's Venetian pictures without a recollection of the inebriated caricature and I am afraid the net result did not stimulate the sale of the pictures. There was so little real work on them that they were easy money and I never blamed Smith for failing to appreciate the joke.

A. B. Frost was, in my opinion, one of the funniest artists that ever put pen to paper. His great forte was rural scenes in which the farmer and his hired man played the principal parts. His technique was superb. No man seeing one of Frost's farmers or his tramps but recognized at once a type with which he was absolutely familiar.

Frost, in appearance, was very much like a farmer himself. Unusually tall, with reddish hair, he had the typical appearance of the b'gosh type of stage yokel portrayed with such success in the Old Homestead. He was diffident and shy of conversation. Yet once the topic aroused his interest his comments were highly humorous and quaintly expressed.

Frost married a well to do girl whose father was broken hearted over what he termed the mesalliance. His idea was one of these bond salesmen or a vice-president of the go-getter school. Being a prosperous man and a patron of the arts, it was a cruel blow to his pride when the apple of his eye married one of these darned artists. If he had been a sign painter or even a bill board artist he could have seen that, but a comic artist—impossible. So he cut her off without a cent.

Frost's work commanded a high price in these days— a premium, in fact—and his services were in constant demand. The lack of financial assistance from daddy-in-law worried him not at all. The sequel came when quite a number of Frost's more serious works were hung on the line at the Pennsylvania Art Association (of which our hero was one of the sugar daddies) and were loudly praised. Our eminent hay, feed and grain merchant suddenly found that his only excuse for being tolerated was that he was the father-in-law of the most popular artist in the exhibition.

Frost, like Gibson and Du Maurier, was never a colorist. His oils in black and white, depicting American bird hunting scenes, bid fair to become Americana of the first rank. Similar subjects in the awful Currier & Ives products have lately attained astonishing values. Frost's work is vastly superior and I advise any one owning an original to treasure it among his most precious possessions.

Frost's work is found in the leading magazines and

"THE SIDEWALKS OF NEW YORK"

Dancing to the music of the organ grinder. A common sight
in the Nineties

WHEN THE HOUSEWIFE DID HER OWN MARKETING

Gansevoort Market in the early morning, 1890

First Suggestion of Mass Production Among the Italians. Mulberry Bend in the Nineties

An Accident in Central Park. "Way for the Ambulance"

other periodicals of his time. His principal work appeared in the big four, Harper's Weekly, Harper's Magazine, the Century and Scribner's. They are as fresh and vital today as they were forty years ago.

The magazines at this time were at their highest peak of material and artistic prosperity. In the field of illustrative art they were the peers of any in the world. Under the stimulus of Roswell Smith and Theodore L. De Vinne, American printing attained the dignity of an art. No European production approached the mere physical perfection of American printing. And the lavish expenditure for illustrations brought this department of publishing into extraordinary eminence. Not only were the leading American artists steadily employed but the best men in London and Paris were frequently drawn upon. Albert Lynch, Madeleine Le Maire, Myrbach, Caran d'Ach are only a few from Paris I could mention, while R. Caton Woodville, F. C. Burnand, Edwin Lord Weeks and A. Castaigne are merely suggestions from London.

Timothy Cole, a wood engraver of superlative skill, was sent to Europe to copy direct the famous old Italian Masters. His blocks, in this now forgotten medium, were exquisite. They remain to this day the very symbol of perfection. His work appeared exclusively in the *Century*. It was the Golden Age of authors, artists and publishers.

But, as usually happens, when everything seems secure and the outlook is without a flaw, certain influences were at work to disturb this idealic condition and to ultimately produce a cataclysm. Before the end of these changes, of which I shall speak later, was reached, the whole magazine field had changed. And today, of these former powerful influences in American letters, scarce a trace remains. Harper has completely abandoned illustration. Scribner uses them sparingly and the Century is no longer the tender object of the two men who burned incense at its feet and worshipped the very presses which brought it forth. The old order changeth, and our pictures must no longer gaze at us motionless from the page but must prance and walk as in real life.

An incident occurred about this time which has ever since remained a profound mystery. That was the peculiar disappearance of S. S. Conant, at that time editor of *Harper's Weekly*. He was, naturally, widely known and it would seem impossible that he could vanish, leaving no trace. Yet that is exactly what happened. He walked out of his office in Franklin Square one afternoon and was never again seen or heard from. It was as if the earth had opened and swallowed him up.

The matter was the subject of wide comment. His prominence as head of so important a publication caused the story to be printed all over the country but no response of any kind resulted. His affairs were in nowise involved and his home life was happy. It is to this day as deep a mystery as on the day of its occurrence.

CHAPTER VI.

PHOTO ENGRAVING BEGINS.—THE TEN-CENT MAGAZINE

PHOTO-ENGRAVING, the new invention supplanting the work of the wood engravers, began at this time to be a commercial success. It was a marvellous advance in the graphic arts and its use rapidly expanded. I think Stephen H. Horgan had as much to do as anyone with placing it on a practical basis. At all events, he equipped the first newspaper office, the *World,* with a plant for their own work. Pulitzer had been the first to make use of illustrations in daily newspaper work and he rapidly extended this new ally in every direction. The Electro Light Engraving Company, owned today by one of the original proprietors, Ben Wilson, was the main source of supply for the other papers. This concern operated its cameras by means of the newly invented electric light.

It was the latter concern who first perfected the half-tone. In a short time, numerous other firms entered the field—the Galvanotype, Stevens & Morris, Henry C. Jones, Charles L. Wright, and myself. I think that would include all that might be called the pioneers in this field. Henry L. Walker, of the Walker Engraving Company, now perhaps the leading organization, learned his trade in my shop. He formed a partnership with Edward Epstean, who was with the Hopkins Electrotype Company. They opened a shop at 25th Street, where they have ever since remained, prospering mightily. Jones, who had the finest business of them all in those days, deliberately put it on the scrap heap by stupidly going into all sorts of outside will-o'-the-wisps. He did, however, produce a quality of half-tone work in those days that was the despair and envy of his competitors. And he ought to get credit for the vast sums he spent in the experimental days of color work.

Wright developed amazing skill in the more difficult subjects such as Abbey's Shakespeare drawings. The fine lines of this artist were exceedingly difficult to retain in the photograph and even more difficult in the etching bath. Wright succeeded in both.

Kurtz, the old photographer on the south side of Madison Square, was the first martyr to the cause of half-tone color work. He succeeded in reproducing some bird subjects from the stuffed models in their natural colors. Whether the brilliant plumage of the birds was specially sympathetic to the new process or not I do not know. At all events these subjects were highly successful and did much to encourage further and more costly research. Color used in painting did not, for a time, yield the same result as from natural objects in color. Before this difficulty was overcome many exasperating failures were encountered and vast sums expended in developing the art. I think Kurtz may be included among the martyrs. He died long before the process was the great commercial success it is today. If I remember correctly Neltje Blatchan's *Bird Neighbors,* the first book to be issued at a popular price containing so many plates in color, was printed from the experimental plates made by Kurtz and was the first practical demonstration of what might ultimately be expected from this new color process when it was eventually perfected. The new process produced in four printings all the beauty and detail that formerly required from eight to ten printings by lithography. It was an exciting development in the printing craft and seemed to the old timers a ridiculous idea at first. Yet the process was soon perfected and today we accept the result as nothing at all to talk about.

Concerning the great poster craze which raged in the Nineties, my friend, Mr. H. L. Sparks, of the National Park Bank, sends me the following [Mr. Sparks has the most complete collection of these interesting items extant, including not only American artists but foreign as well, and the specimens I have reproduced were kindly loaned by him]:

The interest in artistic posters in New York reverts back as far as 1889 when the first *exhibition d'affiches* was given at the Grolier Club. Of course the inspiration to make advertisements things of beauty came from France. Cherét was the first man who realized the artistic possibilities of the poster and under his leadership a group of Frenchmen began making the art their special study with important results, for anything which is on view, so to speak, publicly, day in and out throughout the year, must have an important influence on the thousands who see it daily, even though they are unconscious of it. Heretofore the poster had been regarded as *declassé* in France, and Grassét, Willette, Ibels, Steinlen, Guillaume, Lautrec were all unknown names until their work in this genre made them famous. In England Beardsley sprang into fame, as did Dudley Hardy, whose "Gaiety Girl" poster was well known in New York, and also Greiffenhagen.

I may mention that one of Cherét's first successes in this new art was a poster of *La Loie Fuller,* who has recently again attracted the public eye in connection with the visit of the Queen of Roumania.

The poster craze in America developed in the early Nineties and in so far as this country is concerned it may be said that Edward Penfield fathered it. Penfield was Art Director for Harper and Brothers at the time, and having become inspired by the fine posters which had been issued in France in 1890, 1891 and 1892, and which were by such men as Chéret, Steinlen, Grassét, Mucha and Toulouse Lautrec, he induced Harpers to permit him to design and issue each month a small poster to be used to advertise Harper's Magazine, then in its prime.

There had been some commonplace posters put out for the magazine before this, but these had attracted no particular attention. There were, however, two exceptions. These were two small and decorative posters designed by Eugene Grassét who, for some reason, was called upon for these special things, probably because of his great popularity abroad.

The first Penfield poster for the magazine was issued

for the April, 1893, number and from this time on these attractive little advertisements continued to appear monthly for over five years and during that period Penfield only twice missed getting out a poster for each month.

Then the deluge began, for every publisher and prominent advertiser followed suit and hundreds of posters, good, bad and indifferent, advertising periodicals, books, newspapers, bicycles, toilet articles, etc., were issued each month and this flood continued for four or five years and then gradually fell off.

The fact of the matter is it was greatly overdone and this doomed it, but the affair was most amusing while it lasted, and because of the many attractive designs published, collectors, both American and European, put in their appearance and posters were preserved, exchanged, bought, sold and dealt in just like rare postage stamps. Eighteen ninety-five and six may be said to have been the years in which the craze was at its peak and the demand for better posters by advertisers had induced many good artists to enlist in the service.

Some of Penfield's contemporaries in these early days were: Will Bradley, Louis Rhead, Ethel Reed, J. C. Leyendecker, Will Carqueville, Frank Hazenflug, Claude Bragdon and Elisha Bird, all of whom were popular, and in 1896, as the result of a poster competition given by The Century Company, Maxfield Parrish came into prominence as a prize winner and also entered the game. New poster artists continued to appear and carry on with the others as long as their services were in demand in this day, but Penfield was one of the very few who, having gone into it in the beginning, stuck almost exclusively until his death, which occurred a comparatively short time ago. This means that he designed posters and covers (the latter a kindred activity) for over thirty years and consistently kept up his standards during the whole period—a remarkable record!

The increasing importance of New York in the Nineties as a publishing centre began to attract in larger numbers than ever the men who produced the books that were then among the best sellers. The supremacy of Boston in this respect had slowly but surely been undermined. The Golden Age of Longfellow, Hawthorne, Holmes, the Alcotts, Aldrich, Howells, and a host of others had ended. Howells alone survived and he came to New York to join the Harpers. He signalized his advent by a noval "A Hazard of New Fortunes", which was in a measure an extenuation and a defense of his abandonment of the Sacred City of the Cod. Aldrich became rich through a benefaction of his patron, Pierce the Baker chocolate man, and the Muse was hence to know him no more. He spent his time in leisurely foreign travel and the delightful outpourings of his charming genius were an irreparable loss. Seldom, indeed, has the beneficent intentions of a kindly spirit mitigated so severely against the world of art and letters. No amount of money is compensation for the loss of Marjorie Daws and the Stories of Bad Boys. Aldrich, of all men, should have remained poor—and busy.

The Nineties were notable for the two distinguished foreign authors who were turning out some of their best work on this side—Stevenson and Kipling, and for the great vogue of another Britisher, Du Maurier, whose "Trilby" swept the country from one end to the

An Illustration by W. T. Smedley in Harper's Weekly.

A THANKSGIVING DINNER IN NEW YORK, 1891

Collection of Mr. H. L. Sparks.

THE GREAT POSTER CRAZE OF THE NINETIES

Some characteristic specimens by Louis J. Rhead, Maxfield
Parrish and Edward Penfield

Do You Remember When We Went Joy Riding in Trolley Cars All Lighted Up With Electricity and a Band in the Front Seats?

GRADE CROSSING ACCIDENTS WERE JUST AS COMMON THEN AS NOW ONLY MORE SO

other very much as Main Street did in our day. The "Trilby" craze reached America at just about the time when the word "Bohemian" began to connote something else besides a Second Avenue cigarmaker. There was no Greenwich Village as we know it today. The Tenth Street Studio, it is true, housed a small colony of Impressionists besides a few old Academicians, and there were a few sparse litterateurs seeking inspiration in the crooked old streets to the west, but nothing in the way of a local *Quartier* yet existed.

It was Du Maurier's pencil more than his pen that brought a new frenzy to our hospitable hearths. The "chappie" of the period began to study the Pall Mall garb of "Taffy", "The Laird" and "Little Billie". In fact, if one would know the fashions of the last two decades of the nineteenth century, it is to Du Maurier's sketches in "Punch" and in book illustrations, that one should go, instead of to the costume plates of the tailors and milliners. I would add in passing, a word of caution to the sophisticates who in their smug complacency, jeer the Late Victorian garb. It doesn't look half so funny in Du Maurier's pages, as the short skirts, the high heels and, the "Kollege Klothes" of the present, will look to posterity in 1960.

A new slang phrase came on the wave of this craze in the term "Trilbies", as a synonym for pedal extremities, a term that has taken a permanent place in the language. Another very curious turn to this furore was the revival of the old song of *"Ben Bolt"* which was made so much of in the story. *"Ben Bolt"* had been forgotten and "Sweet Alice" had given way to "Sweet Violets" and "Sweet Marie" for many a long day, when Trilby's contralto once more brought back the old echoes. "Ben Bolt" resumed its half-century faded garland and became once more a best seller in the music stores. Concurrently the historians became busy, and it was suddenly discovered that Thomas Dunn English, the aged author of the song, was living, "in a corner obscure and alone", over in Englewood, long forgotten by the world of letters he had edified in the days of long ago. The newspapers took up the story and the ancient poet was made much of, but not to the extent of sharing in the prodigious profits garnered by the flood of "Ben Bolt" sheet music turned out by Tin Pan Alley on Twenty-eighth Street.

A great dinner was given, at which English was the guest of honor. The rafters rang with the music of the old song and it is doubtful if any dinner that season ever gave more genuine enjoyment to its guests. Toasts were drank to the memory of Sweet Alice, Ben Bolt, The Laird, Taffee, Little Billie, Du Maurier, and last, but not least, Thomas Dunn English. The enthusiasm at this point reached the breaking point and English received such royal recognition that it must have heartened the old man to the day of his death.

Trilby's enormous vogue gave the name to a legion of objects besides boots and shoes, from yachts to cocktails, particularly to the commodities associated with the nether extremities. Socks and stockings, corn cures and bunion eradicators, garters and shoestrings, and no doubt if arch-supports had been on the market they, too, would have been honored. Trilby was dramatized by Paul Potter and had a long run at the Garden Theatre, where Wilton Lackaye's brilliant performance of the sinister "Svengali" was almost as great a hit as Richard Mansfield's "Baron Chevrial".

R. L. STEVENSON IN NEW YORK

Beerhohm Tree played "Svengali", a season or two later, in New York, but with nothing like the sensational effect produced by Lackaye. Perhaps he toned down the rôle to suit his more subdued method. He belonged to the home naturalistic school. Trilby also gave to our language that curious phrase "the altogether", denoting the utter lack of clothing worn by models in certain poses.

Of the first appearance of Stevenson, in New York, Mr. W. W. Ellsworth, for more than thirty years secretary of the old Century Company, told me how his firm missed being his first publisher. They were still at 743 Broadway, a much less pretentious place than the beautiful offices partly designed by Stanford White which they afterwards occupied in Union Square, and the arrangements for greeting visitors distinguished or otherwise was not very impressive. One day a stranger called and asked the young man behind the counter if any stories were wanted. He was a rough looking customer who had just come off an emigrant ship. The clerk followed the usual routine and told him that anything he cared to leave would be handed to the editors. The stranger turned and went out; the Century had lost Robert Louis Stevenson!

Years after, when it had won him back, Stevenson told Gilder of this call, and looking at him sharply from head to foot, said, "I don't know but it was *you* I saw. Yes, I think it *was,* now that I look at you." But Gilder wasn't the man, though he was properly frightened by Stevenson's well-feigned recognition. He proved an alibi, for he was in Europe at the time, but he said afterward that he would have made the same answer to Stevenson that the clerk made.

RUDYARD KIPLING

Scribner occupied the ground floor of the same building and probably Stevenson went there next though the Scribners always claimed that he came to them through Will Low.

In the early nineties a very bristling and extremely aggressive young man was frequently in and out of the Century's office on Union Square. Our hero was none other than Rudyard Kipling, whose picturesque language in those days was something of a trial in that somewhat religious atmosphere. Mr. Smith was a devout church going man and always opened the business meetings of the Company with prayer. Kipling naturally jarred a little. I often wondered why this whole-souled, red-blooded Englishman, hating all things American as he does, should have picked out a Yankee wife. That seems to have come about in a very pretty and romantic way.

In London, Kipling had made the acquaintance of a young American to whom he subsequently became deeply attached—Wolcott Balestier. His genuine affection for him was evident from the beautiful dedication he wrote for the edition of *Barrack Room Ballads,* published shortly after Balestier's untimely death. It begins:

"Beyond the path of the outmost sun through utter
darkness hurled
Further than ever comet flared or vagrant star dust
swirled
Sit such as fought and sailed and ruled and loved and
made our world."

Wolcott Balestier as a young man started with John W. Lovell, who published Lovell's Library. Then he started a magazine *Time* which didn't last long, followed by two or three novels and a book of short stories which were published by the Century Company. Then he went to London where he established the publishing firm of Heineman & Balestier, now Heinemans, which Doubleday, Page & Company recently took over.

It was while living in London that Balestier met Kipling and they became close friends. It was at this time that they collaborated in writing *"The Naulahka"* which ran as a continued story in the *Century*. It was then that Kipling first met Carrie Balestier who was keeping house for her brother. No doubt Wolcott's sudden and untimely death in a foreign land (he was only thirty) served to draw him and his friend's sister closer together. In any case, they were married shortly after, and came to America. It was at this time that he turned up at the Century's office. Part of some land on a country place owned by the elder Balestier in Brattleboro, Vermont, was given to Kipling's wife and on it they built their home which they called "Naulahka". This explains his selection of a residence so far from town. Their first child, Josephine, was born here.

The Balestiers were an old New York family originally from France, coming here about the close of the Revolution. One of the uncles of Mrs. Kipling was married to a daughter of Paul Revere. This uncle lived at the corner of Varick and Beach Streets. When the old house was torn down fifty years ago an oak tree planted by Lafayette was cut down too. Lafayette visited the uncle bringing two oak trees from Napoleon's Tomb, one of which survived; they had been friends in France.

Kipling's return to England was not prompted by trouble with his in-laws as has been frequently stated.

The children were growing up and the Kiplings preferred to have them educated in England. His business affairs were also growing in importance on the other side.

It was on one of these friendly visits to the Century offices that Kipling told some rambling stories of life in the Indian Jungle to Mrs. Mary Mapes Dodge, with whom he was talking at the time. Mrs. Dodge was one of the most capable editors of the day and immediately sensed a story for St. Nicholas. Kipling had never written anything for children but agreed to try. The result was the famous "Jungle Book".

In the nineties Kipling was taken seriously ill in New York and for weeks his life hung in the balance. His daughter, Josephine, died at about the same time. Mr. and Mrs. Frank N. Doubleday were unremitting in their care of the Kiplings at this time, which perhaps may have influenced Kipling later in his change of American publishers. Upon his convalescence he returned to England, where he has resided ever since, and where farm wagons bearing the name "R. Kipling" are frequently encountered.

There were other best sellers, yet candor compels me to admit that American literature was still in its adolescence. "Barriers Burned Away", "Opening of a Chestnut Burr" and the Elsie Books were among the best sellers. Ian Maclaren's *"Beside the Bonny Briarbush"* had a wonderful vogue. *"Janice Meredith"*, by Paul Leicester Ford had an amazing sale running neck and neck with *"Hugh Wynne, Free Quaker"*, by Dr. Weir Mitchell. Ford, by the way, was the first man to write about the human frailties of Washington. Both Rupert Hughes and Woodward are merely thrash-

ing out old stuff. But at the time Ford's book came out
the public were not yet ready to have the aureole
stripped from their hero's brow. The spirit of good Dr.
Holland was still all powerful in the editorial councils
of the Century and the recollection of his rejection of
"Jim Bludso", was still a vivid memory. Here is the
last verse which made the good doctor take the count.

> "He weren't no saint, but at Jedgment
>   I'd run my chance with Jim
> 'Long side some pious gentlemen
>   That wouldn't shook hands with him.
> He seen his duty—a dead sure thing—
>   And he went for it thar and then;
> And Christ ain't a-goin to be too hard
>   On a man that died for men."

That was altogether too unorthodox. In similar
fashion Gilder balked at one of H. C. Bunner's stories
where the hero, who was momentarily stunned, was
proffered "a dozen flasks". Gilder thought the number
should be reduced; but Bunner stood firm and received
the plaudits of the liberals the country over. In these
days of the equally good Volstead, I am afraid the
number of flasks available would be considerably more
than a dozen.

It was that narrow spirit which gave a mawkish
tinge to our native literature at that time for you must
bear in mind that Gilder and Johnson were the court of
last resort for American writers of that day.

"Ben Hur" was one of the best sellers in these days.
How narrowly it escaped being no seller at all has often
been told by J. Henry Harper, his publisher. The manuscript was returned by the reader, George Ripley,
damned with faint promise.

"If it were the production of a new and unknown writer", wrote Mr. Ripley, *"I could not bring myself to recommend its publication;* but with the prestige of the author and his really uncommon gifts of invention and illustration I think it might be well to accept the manuscript."

And this of a book that proved to be the outstanding novel of the century! I know of no other work of fiction by an American author that anywhere near approached the sale of *Ben Hur*. It is now well over two million copies. The number of persons who have seen it in the play or the movie, would bring this total ten times beyond two million.

And yet if this had been written by an unknown author! *Ben Hur* came about as the result of a casual meeting on a train between General Wallace and Colonel Ingersoll, the noted atheist, and a subsequent discussion on the subject of the divinity of Christ. He was unable to follow Ingersoll as far as the non-divinity was concerned, but was disposed to give the question serious study.

As a result he decided to write a history of Christ so that he could examine the pros and cons of both sides. For six years he worked assiduously on his task till he finally produced *Ben Hur*. General Wallace wound up his story with the trenchant statement that the result of his labors was the absolute conviction that Jesus of Nazareth was not only a Christ and the Christ, but that He was also his Christ, his Savior, and his Redeemer.

To offset the discouragement of beginners who may conclude from this experience that only established

Another Smedley drawing in Harper's Weekly.

A Lu

writers have a chance, let me relate the experience of Edward Noyes Westcott, an obscure clerk in a bank in Syracuse. He had never written a book. As a matter of fact didn't know how to write one in a workmanlike manner. Yet he was the author of *David Harum,* next to *Ben Hur* the best seller of the nineties.

The manuscript was a foot high when it first reached the publisher, and but for the keenness of the reader, Ripley Hitchcock, the book, in all probability, would have died abornin'. It had already been declined by several firms.

Hitchcock saw something in the story. It was badly constructed. The famous "hoss tradin'" chapter was nowhere in sight. Hitchcock took it out of its submerged position and made it open the story. With other alterations the novel began to look like something. When finally published it was a tremendous seller.

The author was absolutely unknown. It was his first attempt. So despite the fact that *Ben Hur* was saved on account of the author's previous reputation, the exact opposite is the case in *David Harum.* So the untried novice need not lose heart.

A few excerpts from the "Elsie" school will further illustrate my view. We have arrived at the point where the hero comes home from Annapolis to spend vacation with his parents.

"Father, may I ride over the grounds before alighting?" asked Max's voice in eager tones, just at that moment.

"If you wish, my son," the captain answered pleasantly. "But suppose you delay a little and let some of us accompany you?"

"Yes, sir; that will be better," was the prompt cheerful rejoinder.

"Ah, I see you have been making some changes and improvements here, father," he said, glancing as he entered the hall door.

"Yes, and in other parts of the house," said Violet. "Perhaps you might as well go over it before visiting the grounds."

"I am at liberty to go everywhere, as of old?" he returned, half in assertion, half enquiringly and turning from her to his father.

"Certainly, my son; it is as truly your father's house, therefore open in every part to you, as it was before you left its shelter for Uncle Sam's Naval Academy," replied the captain, regarding the lad with mingled fatherly affection, pride, and amusement.

"Thank you, sir," returned Max heartily. "Ah, Christine!" as the housekeeper, whom something had detained in another part of the house at the moment of their arrival, now appeared among them, "I'm pleased to see you again; looking so well, too. I really don't think you have changed in the least in all the time I have been away," shaking her hand warmly as he spoke.

"Ah, Master Max, sir, I can't say the same to you," she returned with a pleasant smile into the bright young face. "You are growing up fast and looking more than ever like your father."

"I think you must have forgotten how long I have been away, papa," laughed Max as they finished the circuit of the rooms on that floor, "for I have come upon a good many new things."

"Ah! well, they have been added so gradually that I did not realize how numerous they were," returned his father, adding, "Now you may as well go on to the upper rooms and tarry long enough in your own to make yourself neat for the tea table."

"Yes, sir;" and the lad hurried up the stairs, the captain, Lulu, and Grace following.

"Hurrah!" he cried joyously as he reached the open door of his own room. "Why, this is lovely! prettier than

222

ever, and it was like a room in a palace before compared
to the one I share with Hunt at the Academy."

"Suppose you walk in and take a nearer view," said
his father, and Max obeyed with alacrity, the others following.

"Your mamma and I have made some changes, improvements, as we thought," the captain said in gratified and
affectionate tones, "hoping you would be pleased with
them; and I rather think you are."

"Pleased, papa? I'm delighted!" cried Max. "The only
drawback to my pleasure is the thought of the very short
time I can stay to enjoy all this beauty and luxury."

"Yet, I am sure my boy does not want to settle down
here to a life of inglorious ease," remarked the captain in
a tone of mingled assertion and enquiry. "I rejoice in the
firm conviction that his great desire is to serve God and
his country to the best of his ability."

"Yes, father, it is," said Max earnestly. "But," he added
with a smile, "if you don't want me to love to be with you
in this sweet home you should not make it so attractive
and be so very kind and affectionate to me."

E. P. Roe was built upon the same general plan only
a little more mature. His heroines blushed furiously
when any one happened to say leg in place of limb
and if you wanted the low down on the villain all you
needed to know was that he once drank a cocktail and
was frequently out of bed as late as ten thirty. Roe's
books sold tremendously for his day—equal to Harold
Bell Wright's in our time.

And here is a curious coincidence. Both Roe and
Wright came from the same little Hudson River town
—Cornwall—and both were country preachers. Roe's
original idea in offering his stories to Dodd Mead was
to raise a little money to help pay for a new parsonage
the church wished to build. Fortunately the profits

paid not only for the parsonage but left the good dominie a little patrimony for himself as well.

Wright worked in a small drug store in the same village tending the soda fountain counter. This was of course many years later. He went West and became an itinerant preacher. He thought he could reach a wider audience through books—and he did. Wright may have acted independently but there is a curious parallel in the two lives and a tremendous similarity in the brand of literature each produced.

The state of literature of the nineties therefore showed the two extremes very much as it does today. Elsie and E. P. Roe were flanked by Jack London, Marion Crawford and Mark Twain while we have Dorothy Dainty, Sinclair Lewis and Anita Loos. On the whole our present day output is a great deal less hide-bound than in the days of Gilder, Alden and Burlingame. Alden blazed the way when he published "Trilby". Few today realize exactly how much courage that required. The "young person" was a portentous ogre, and lorded over every editorial office in the city. Yet even in that day and despite their alleged innocence, they often knew more than their elders.

Among the forgotten names of the purveyors of entertainment and amusement of yore that of Archibald Clavering Gunter is an example of meteoric success and extinction. Gunter was the author of that amazingly popular "yellow back" novel, *Mr. Barnes of New York*. He was also known in theatrical circles as the author of *Prince Karl,* which Mansfield included in his repertoire for many years. He began his career as a dramatic author and acquired some renown with his *Bandits of Wall Street, Fresh, The American,* and other dimly recalled ephemera. In drifting into novelistic fiction, Gunter carried his stagecraft with him and his books were practically novelized scenarios. All the familiar tricks of the footlights were there, and the result was a highly exciting product that sold into the hundred thousands. *Barnes of New York* sold all over the world, and there was probably not a railway bookstall on the globe that lacked a copy at the height of its success. It was an ingenious piece of carpentry. All the lay figures of melodrama were in it, and it cannot be denied that they were shifted with no inconsiderable skill throughout its mechanism. The plot was excellent and might have served Dumas, who would have peopled it with living figures. However, its stock puppets served Gunter's purpose to such a degree that he followed it up with *Mr. Porter of Texas, That Frenchman, Miss Nobody of Nowhere* and *A Florida Enchantment,* all more or less creaking trailers to his original comet, and all sharing a proportionate success.

Marie Corelli, an English writer of exotic romances —The Sorrows of Satan, etc., was also immensely popular. She was a great favorite with Queen Victoria and this fact gave her great vogue in England which was duplicated here. No critic of any standing would admit that Marie was anything but a fearful misfit, yet she outsold all her contemporaries and replied in kind to her adversaries. *"Robert Elsmere"* and *"John Ward Preacher,"* also by women, were on everybody's tongue. Although they attacked religion it was by no means in the Sinclair Lewis manner. I rather imagine that *"Elmer Gantry"* would have instantly fallen foul of Anthony Comstock.

Jerome K. Jerome was selling well but perhaps the leader of them all was Rider Haggard's *"She"*. This was everywhere. It was followed by *"King Solomon's Mines"*—another wowser. Amelia Barr, Marion Crawford, Agnes Repplier, Owen Wister, Dr. S. Weir Mitchell, Frank Stockton, and about a dozen others worthily upheld the American end of literature, and while the bulk of the sales went to the foreigner there was much left for local talent.

It was about this time that Poultney Bigelow began his articles in the *Century* on *The German Struggle for Liberty*. This of itself is not of special importance; other writers began articles as well. The difference being that these other articles did not, as a rule, cause their authors to lose the friendship of perhaps the most powerful figure in the world at that time—the German Emperor.

Poultney Bigelow is the son of John Bigelow, Minister of France under Lincoln and sometimes called the father of our Public Library. It was from Paris that Poultney went to Berlin to grow up with the Kaiser's sons.

In his delightful book, *Prussian Memoirs,* Mr. Bigelow recalled these boyhood days at Sans Souci. He described the American game of Indians which he had introduced to the German Princes and played on rainy days. Behind empty barrels lay Wilhelm and Henry in "ambush," pouncing out with tomahawk and knife to "scalp" the unsuspecting wayfarer—Bigelow. The principal attraction of this border warfare was the blood-curdling war whoops emitted by the savages. However, as the scene of the ambuscade was in the garret of the old Palace of Frederick the Great, the boys howled to their heart's content.

For more than twenty years Bigelow was the most intimate personal friend of the Kaiser. They grew up together. As students they wandered over Germany afoot and were not infrequently jostled off the sidewalk by unsuspecting villagers. For years they were inseparable. At manœvres Bigelow sometimes used the same mount as the war lord himself. There was occasionally unexpected commotion in some of the camps at the sudden appearance of the Kaiser's horse. When it turned out to be only Poultney instead of the Kaiser, there was generally a sigh of relief. These visits were generally the result of Bigelow's wandering away from the monotony of the manœvres and losing his way

The publication of the *German Struggle for Liberty* brought the first rift in the life-long friendship. The growing tendency of Wilhelm to enlarge on his divine rights to rule widened the breach, and long before the World War began the estrangement was complete. Upon the appearance of *Prussian Memories* the Kaiser peremptorially ordered Bigelow's name stricken from the membership of the Kiel Yacht Club, much to the delight of Bigelow.

At Bigelow's old family homestead at Malden-on-the-Hudson the walls are still decorated with many fascinating photographs of these bye-gone romantic days. The pictures of Wilhelm and his consort taken the year they ascended the throne, with personal messages of intimate regard, in the Kaiser's own handwriting; views of old towns through which Wilhelm and Poultney wandered in school-boy days; endless scenes of army manœuvres—all combined to recall a picturesque period in the life of an old New Yorker vibrant and colorful as the present days are dull and commonplace.

Bigelow is now rarely in the public eye. I saw him last at the funeral services of his old friend Edward P. Mitchell, of the *Sun*.

The rise of the great firm of Doubleday, Page & Company who supplied a great Ambassador to the Court of St. James during the World War, began at this time. An unknown figure in the success of that firm, and from my prejudiced point of view, the greatest factor in its success bar none, was the gifted wife of the senior partner, Mrs. F. N. Doubleday. Her famous books *"Bird Neighbors"*, written under the pseudonym of "Neltje Blatchan" were among their first important best sellers. But it was her skill in securing the necessary capital to expand the business wherein her great business talent showed.

This firm was also fortunate in selecting an unoccupied field—country life—as the chief market for the output of their wares. The fame achieved by Walter Page as Ambassador, did no harm to their magazine *World's Work*. And "Effendi's" warm friendship with Roosevelt resulted in a perfectly natural though unconscious exhibition of working both ends against the middle. Mr. Doubleday came from *Scribner's* originally, as did Mr. Bok of the *Ladies Home Journal*.

Vast changes in the publishing world have taken place in the last thirty odd years. Of the great magazine that flourished then both the ten cent ones and the more expensive as I have already noted have encountered almost complete eclipse. As I write the daily

Going Home on the Ferryboat

HUNTING IN THE ADIRONDACKS

Do you remember the old Currier & Ives chromos that were in every "best room"? They have now become real "Americana"

RUDYARD KIPLING AT ABOUT THE TIME OF HIS MARRIAGE TO
MISS BALESTIER

WOLCOTT BALESTIER

newspaper field seems on the edge of a cataclysm. The "tabloids", as they are called, threaten the existence of the old time newspaper. Their circulation figures are amazing. How to meet this growing competition is one of the great problems of the hour for the erstwhile leaders in journalism.

Of the first men to sense the real importance of advertising, Cyrus Curtis, of the *Ladies Home Journal,* and George H. Hazen, of the *Century,* may be mentioned. Mr. Curtis was also the first to institute censorship of his advertising columns and to put the ban on patent medicine copy. Hazen organized the Quoin Club which undertook to regulate a lot of abuses existing among advertising agents and put in operation a plan to separate the sheep from the goats and otherwise elevate the business to a position corresponding to its dignity and importance.

In those days Hazen and Francis A. Wilson of the *Youth's Companion* were the two bright particular stars in the advertising firmament. They were also very close personal friends. When Hazen went to Boston he always "breakfasted" with Wilson at the St. Botolph, and when Wilson came to New York he "breakfasted" with Hazen at the "Aldine." Mr. Hazen is now chairman of the Board of the great Crowell Publishing Company. Mr. Wilson left the *Companion* many years ago.

The serenity of the Big Three in the magazine field was rudely disturbed at this time by Sam McClure, who essayed to enter this field with a magazine much cheaper than had ever before been attempted. The success of George Newnes, in London, with the "Strand", a sixpenny monthly, first directed attention to the possibilities of a popular priced magazine on this side. T. B. Browne, a wealthy and prominent advertising agent in London, broached the matter to me on one of his visits and offered to assist in raising the capital. Mr. Browne's sudden and unexpected death shortly afterward ended the negotiations.

McClure, however, was syndicating to the newspapers work of the best English writers and was abundantly supplied with high class material at a price that a cheap magazine could afford to pay. He thereupon entered the field with 15c. as his selling price. It was hard going at first, but Conan Doyle suddenly came to the rescue by the investment of $5,000.00. McClure had never seen so much money at one time before in his life and he immediately found it possible to do a lot of things he couldn't do before. His circulation began to creep up to formidable figures. The late Mr. Munsey had a 25c. monthly and John Brisben Walker owned the Cosmopolitan, also 25c. For a few months no special attention was paid by any of them to the lower price of McClure's. There was no equivalent in our money for the English sixpence which was twelve cents, and the wholesale price demanded by Mr. Farrelly of the American News Co., for a ten-cent publication prohibited any profit for the publisher of a journal at that figure.

Such was the situation when things began to happen.

Mr. Walker suddenly reduced his price to 12½c.—an awkward figure. Mr. Munsey took the flop at once to 10c. He had in the meantime organized his own distributing plant and was in full competition with the American News Co. To meet the situation created by Munsey and which was fraught with great peril to Mr.

Farrelly's hitherto unassailable monopoly, the latter
agreed to handle the Cosmopolitan at a figure satisfactory to Mr. Walker, who promptly lowered his price to
ten cents. McClure also benefited by the concession
made by Farrelly and presently all three were bowling
along merrily and piling up circulation figures that
were causing the Big Three to see things red.

The publishing business is a queer business. Munsey
had a weekly on which he had lavished a fortune. It
refused to budge. Satisfied that he had done everything any man could do, he calmly announced that the
weekly field was dead—its place was taken by the Sunday newspapers—and abandoned The Argosy. Then
along comes Mr. Curtis and starts a weekly, the Saturday Evening Post, which by today's paper I see has a
circulation of over three million and an advertising patronage I am told of over fifteen millions.

Meanwhile all the old time magazines I am speaking
about—the high class as well as the cheap—seem to be
on the scrap heap. They are not even decently printed
and are only ghosts of their former splendor. Even
the Youth's Companion, which in the old days enjoyed
a circulation five or ten times greater than any contemporary has sunk so low that there are none so poor
as to do it reverence.

Richard Watson Gilder was perhaps the best known
among the editors. At least he had the faculty of keeping himself on the front page more frequently. He
enjoyed also the acquaintance of others in the public
eye and managed to shine in the reflected glory of
Grover Cleveland, whose summer home in Buzzard's
Bay adjoined Gilder's. With Joe Jefferson also a near
neighbor, the two managed to be mentioned quite fre-

quently in the news that was constantly telegraphed regarding the movements of the chief executive. He frequently joined Mr. Cleveland and Mr. Jefferson on their fishing excursions but he was a bad sailor and if gossip is to be believed his fishing days with Grover were perilously near martyrdom. His next best friends were Paderewski and St. Gaudens. Yet Gilder will be affectionately recalled—not for his poems—they were junk—but for his really effective service in the cause of American literature and art. Among his public services, his attack and final destruction of the Louisiana Lottery must be placed partly to his credit. Comstock greatly assisted. And his services on the Tenement House Commission resulted in material benefit to a large portion of our community who were helpless in themselves.

Mr. Gilder lived in a rather peculiar but strangely appropriate home on 15th Street. It was originally a stable and as such it stood well back from the street with quite an open space leading to it. Stanford White remodeled it for him. This he garnished with flowers and green stuff. The stable lent itself readily to the few changes demanded by its new use. It resulted in a novel and charming residence. Strangers coming to it the first time were agreeably surprised; for it was probably the first exotic of its kind in New York and the fame of its charm and quaintness travelled far and wide. All of Washington Mews and much of Macdougall Alley, formerly the homes of horses, have now been transformed into dwellings for artists as a result of Gilder's idea. Today an abandoned stable ranks high in the estimation of many householders, but none are to be had for love or money.

GROVER CLEVELAND

It was at Gilder's summer cottage at Buzzard's Bay that E. C. Benedict first met Cleveland, then President, in the nineties. The Commodore, as Mr. Benedict was familiarly known to his friends, told me about it one afternoon in his late home in Connecticut. As it recalled a famous friendship between two eminent personages, his account of his first meeting with Mr. Cleveland is worth repeating.

"I first met Mr. Cleveland," said the Commodore, "at the little town of Marion, Mass., on Buzzard's Bay. My daughter was paying a visit to the family of Richard Watson Gilder and I went ashore to pick her up. There was some sort of a social affair going on among the summer residents and it was held, I think, in an old unused barn. The Clevelands lived in a modest cottage up the street, and there seemed to be a congenial group among the strangers who had gathered there that summer. Besides the Gilders there was L. Clarke Davis, of the *Philadelphia Public Ledger,* and his gifted wife, Mrs. Rebecca Harding Davis; at that time doing much literary work for the *Youth's Companion* in Boston. Their talented young son, Richard Harding Davis, had not yet written "Van Bibber" or a "Soldier of Fortune". He was still, if I remember correctly, a "cub" reporter on the New York Sun. Charles Dana Gibson was also in the party.

"Mrs. Cleveland, then a young bride, was among the friends to whom my daughter presented me, and remarked that she had invited her to go sailing next day on the *Oneida,* an invitation which I cordially endorsed. Toward the middle of the evening two strangers entered, one rather short, but the other a very powerfully built figure, and dressed in a manner somewhat in contrast to the rather summery garments of the others present. The suit had evidently seen much wear, and he wore a dark outing shirt. A soft, nondescript hat was crushed in his hand and his whole aspect denoted to my practiced eye the natural born fisherman. A moment later I was shaking hands with Grover Cleveland. The shorter man was 'Dan' Lamont, at one time private secretary, but then a member of Mr. Cleveland's second cabinet.

We had not talked very long before he discovered that I was a Buffalo boy and, like himself, the son of a Presbyterian minister. There was at once a common ground of fellowship. When I later remarked that all I knew of the three R's was what had been pounded into me through my hands and my jacket by the well-known Doctor Cook, who ran a sort of a private school in Buffalo, his interest in me sensibly increased. We compared many things pertaining to our common bringing up and found, to our delight, that we had both suffered in about the same measure from the severity of the Calvinistic Puritanical atmosphere which had surrounded our boyish days. This began an intimacy that continued without interruption for nearly a quarter of a century and which, to me, was one of the greatest happinesses in my long life.

The straitened circumstances in which we both grew up formed a common bond of sympathy. I recall one of his letters, out of more than three hundred which he wrote me during his life, with particular gratification. In it he sent me what little money he had been able to save up with a request that I do with it as I would with my own. And if I were to mention the meagreness of this sum it would be laughable in contrast with the ridiculous stories that at one time gained credence concerning the vastness of Mr. Cleveland's private fortune.

Cleveland liked nothing better on earth than a day's fishing—a sport he entered into with boyish delight and enthusiasm. Joseph Jefferson and Edwin Booth were often with us, and sometimes Gilder. I am afraid, however, that these last two were martyrs to the cause as both were poor sailors.

The last day we three were together the fish were biting fairly well, and every time Mr. Jefferson's bob would go out of sight he would give a yank, and hook, line, bob and sinker would go skyward. After doing this three or four times Mr. Cleveland, who needed no megaphone to convey his thoughts when aroused, yelled out: 'For God's sake, Jefferson, don't yank them so.' Jefferson turned around in a most injured way and said: 'Well, they yanked me first.' "

Cleveland lived in the house next to Benedict in 56th Street when he came to New York. Benedict owned both. A door was cut through for easy access. When Cleveland wished to avoid callers he would slip through the door to Benedict's and the butler could then truthfully say Mr. Cleveland was not at home.

CORNER OF BROADWAY AND 23RD STREET, 1853

CHAPTER VII.

ADVERTISING

ADVERTISING, which is the backbone of the publishing business, has probably made the greatest strides of all. In the nineties came its first recognition as a really vital factor in business development. Up to that time it had been concerned mainly with the exploitations of patent medicines, nostrums of all sorts and first-class houses looked down upon this form of promotion. Nevertheless Procter & Gamble, after careful consideration, and a study of the subject from all angles, decided to appropriate forty thousand dollars to exploit a new soap that by some fresh discovery in chemicals, would float. Heavy washing was still part of the every day curriculum of the average household, so the market was large. It was obvious that the new nonsinkable soap had many advantages over the one that disappeared the moment it was left to itself. So all the elements for a practical test appeared to be present.

The experiment was a success. Their present appro-

An Illustration by Thure de Thulstrup in Harper's.

Five o'clock te

"
in the Nineties

COUNTESS DE ROGUEMONT AND MR. JAMES HAZEN HYDE
At Bradley-Martin Ball

priation is now about four millions a year. Advertising consequently began to emerge from the odium of its patent medicine days and began to mingle in better society. Now it ranks as one of the learned professions and has become itself one of our leading industries.

Speaking of advertising reminds me of the curious gamble there seems to be in connection with this business and of the funny conclusions that men form in advance regarding the possibility of marketing certain products by this method.

There is that good story told of the late F. W. Ayer, head of the great firm of N. W. Ayer & Son of Philadelphia, one of the most widely known agencies and in the nineties the leading concern of its kind in the world. Mr. Ayer's home was in Camden and many years ago two concerns whose places of business were also in Camden sought his advice regarding the desirability of advertising in connection with their products. One made soup and the other music records—Campbell and Victor Talking Machine, to be exact.

Mr. Ayer had even then made a great success not only as an advertising man but also as a banker and a traction officer. He was conceded to be a leader in all three. Yet he gave it as his sober judgment that while many things could be sold by advertising, there were two that positively could not; one was canned soup and the other canned music!

A note in the papers recording the final settlement of the estate of Oscar J. Gude recalls an interesting figure in the advertising world in the nineties. Gude was working for James Pyle's Pearline when I first made his acquaintance. Pyle decided to cut down his fixed charges and let Gude out. I proffered Gude desk room in my office free of charge and told him to keep after Pyle and add others. He was gravely doubtful of the result at first but was much encouraged to find that his return from Pyle the first month as a free lance was much better than while on the pay roll. His courage increased as the weeks rolled by with a constantly growing income from Pyle instead of a diminishing one. Soon after he added Prescott, of "Rising Sun Stove Polish" fame to his list. This gentleman turned out to be a very important factor in his life.

Gude probably did more to raise painted outdoor advertising to a position of respectability and importance than any one else. He certainly made it a definite factor in advertising. It was he, I believe, who hit upon the idea of building special boards in fixed locations, which were rented yearly or monthly and which were properly cared for. This system quickly placed the entire business of sign advertising on a plane of importance and respectability never dreamed of before. The days of hit and miss methods were over and his business rapidly expanded. Prior to that, Bill stickers and Sign painters were a wild lot. Nothing appealed to their sense of humor so much as to cover up a competitor's work with other paper, or paint a fresh sign over the one just completed by their rival. The fact that in either case, the advertiser paid the bill, added to their hilarity.

Gude's organization was greatly strengthened by the addition of Wm. S. Yerkes of Philadelphia, who merged his interests with Gude in a combination formed in the late nineties. Mr. Yerkes brought great executive ability to the new firm and his excellent judgment in the many problems that were constantly arising played no small part in the great success later achieved by Gude.

Speaking of advertising reminds me of the great esteem in which this profession is held today compared with its former somewhat dubious standing when it was largely monopolized by Pink Pills for Pale People, etc.

What has become of that ravishing damsel with mouth of pearly teeth and lace mantilla who extolled the virtues of Sozodont? Of good old doctor Munyon, who proclaimed with solemn uplifted finger, "There is hope!" of Pyles Pearline which made washday a pleasure, of Sapolio, Soapine, Sweet Caps and Cashmere Bouquet Soap?

That our great town possesses men gifted with business acumen to an inordinate degree is daily exemplified by the sale of the City Hall, Brooklyn Bridge, the Woolworth Building, and other notable structures for trifling sums to the unwary. Notwithstanding repeated exposures of these barefaced swindles, trade in these specialties goes merrily on.

Yet it is rather to inventors that our leadership in commerce, finance and industry is due. A good many excellent ideas however perish for want of capital; others languish for lack of demand. But the enthusiasm of the inventor remains undiminished. Some of the ideas that were patented in the nineties offer an interesting study in sociology, and being absolutely genuine, are worth recording here.

U. S. Patent No. 515,001 is a case in point. In this case the patentee invents a new fishing lure of great possibilities. It is illustrated in the accompanying

A REFLECTION ON FISH

(No Model.)

W. R. LAMB.
FISHING APPARATUS.

No. 515,001.

Patented Feb. 20, 1894.

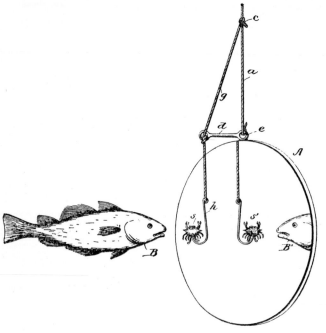

Witnesses.

Charles Hannigan.

E. B. Read

Inventor.

William R Lamb

by Benj Arnold
Atty.

drawing which shows a fish approaching a mirror in
front of which the baited hook dangles. As the inventor
describes it in his claim "The Fish, B, when approaching the bait will see the reflection of himself in the

248

mirror also coming for the reflection of the bait, and
will be made bolder by the supposed companionship,
and more eager to take the bait before his competitor
seizes it. He will lose his caution and take the bait
with a recklessness that greatly increases the chances
of his being caught on the hook".

(No Model.)   2 Sheets—Sh et 1

J. C. BOYLE.
SALUTING DEVICE.

No. 556,248.   Patented Mar. 10, 1896.

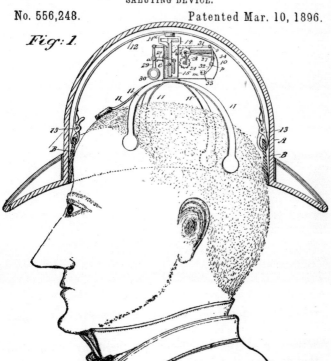

Fig: 1

Patent No. 556,248 is for a saluting device. This
invention relates to a method for "automatically effect-

ing polite salutations by the elevation and rotation of
the hat on the head of the saluting party when said
and without the use of the hands in any manner. This
device raises the hat and bows to the person or persons

(No Model.)

J. MAGUIRE.

WATERPROOF COAT.

No. 273,115. Patented Feb. 27, 1883.

saluted; rotates it and deposits it correctly on the head
of the wearer when he assumes an erect posture; the
actuation of the hat being produced by mechanism
therein concealed." Commuters with both hands full
will find this a wonderful convenience.

Patent No. 273,115 is a device for carrying off water

A NEW RAT TRAP

from a coat by means of a gutter so to speak at the bottom of the garment. When the rain is collected here it runs out through vent E as marked on the drawing, and the gentleman's legs are thus fully protected from water and kept perfectly dry.

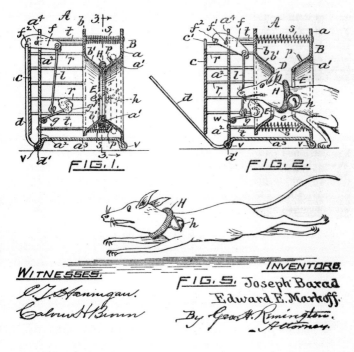

No. 883,611.   PATENTED MAR. 31, 1908.

J. BARAD & E. E. MARKOFF.

DEVICE EMPLOYED FOR EXTERMINATING RATS, MICE, AND OTHER ANIMALS.

APPLICATION FILED DEC. 16, 1907.

FIG. 1.

FIG. 2.

FIG. 5.

WITNESSES:
C. J. Hannigan.
Calvin H. Bunn

INVENTORS.
Joseph Barad
Edward E. Markoff.
By Geo. H. Remington
Attorney.

Patent No. 883,611 is a device for exterminating rats, mice and other animals and is predicated on the well-known fear these rodents experience when any unusual noise confronts them. The inventor's claim reveals such an intimate knowledge of natural history that I copy it in full as related in his application for the patent:

"It is a well-known fact that certain animals, as rats, mice and analogous animals of the rodent class are naturally excessively sly and distrustful, even to members of their own family, although at times working together in harmony, as for example, in carrying off and storing food and articles having considerable weight and bulkiness. It is also known that the sound or tinkling of a bell is, as a rule, very terrifying to animals of the species named, and that if pursued by such sound they will immediately vacate their haunts and homes, never to return.

The object we have in view is to take advantage of the peculiar characteristic or instinct inherent say in the animal class just referred to. To that end we have invented and produced an extremely simple and inexpensive automatic device or mechanism capable when properly positioned and set, of enticing an animal, as a rat, to it, so that when he nibbles or touches the bait the previously set tripping moves, and the annular spring band or collar, having one or more small bells attached to it, will be released simultaneously and the thus freed bell-carrying band, at the same instant contracting around the rat's neck. The 'bell rat' as it may be termed, then in seeking its burrow or colony, announces his coming by the sounds emitted by the bells, thereby frightening the other rats and causing them to flee, thus practically exterminating them in a sure and economical manner. It may be added that the spring-band or collar is not liable to become accidentally lost or slip from the rat's neck, because the adjacent hairs soon become interwoven with the convolutions of the spring to more firmly hold it in place."

OLD SIXTH AVENUE

Sixth Avenue between Fourteenth and Twenty-third Streets,
the great shopping district in the Nineties. Altman, Mc-
Creery, Macy and others were all located here

THE PARLOR OF A SOCIETY LEADER IN THE NINETIES

A Sitting Room in a Fifth Avenue Mansion in the Nineties

The Lounging Room of a Social Leader Showing a Bit of the Turkish Corner

With its scimiters, battle axes, etc., part of the inevitable decoration

AN IDEA FOR LINDY

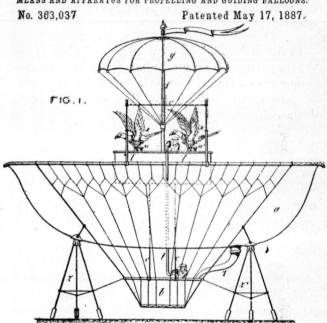

(No Model.   2 Sheets—Sheet 1

C. R. E. WULFF.

MEANS AND APPARATUS FOR PROPELLING AND GUIDING BALLOONS.

No. 363,037   Patented May 17, 1887.

FIG. 1.

Patent No. 363,037.

This was brought out about the time Prof. Langley met with such disaster in his first air ship. This inventor did not bother to imitate birds—he employed the birds themselves. Nor did he employ motors—the birds were to supply the power. He does, however, admit that "he does not claim a device for holding birds that are to carry and hold suspended a car, or other aerial vehicle." "Birds have not," he naïvely admits, "the power to do this for any reasonable length of time." His claim rests on the harnessed birds who are to be tickled into flying. The air set in motion by their wings is to provide buoyancy for the parachute and the pilot pulls the harness in the direction in which the birds are to fly. The birds he recommends as best suited for this purpose are eagles, vultures, condors, etc.

That will be all for today. Copies of these patents may be obtained from the United States Patent Office; enclose ten cents with your letter and order by number, as given above. That is how they were obtained for this article.

FOOT OF 49TH STREET, 1883

CHAPTER VIII.

A GOLDEN AGE IN WALL STREET

THE Nineties in Wall Street will never be forgotten. The flow of gold seemed inexhaustible. Millionaires by the score were created overnight. All sorts and kinds of flotations became possible. If you had any kind of a scheme that would yield Wall Street three or four thousand per cent without risking any of its own money you were sure at least of a respectful hearing.

To a very great extent the position of Wall Street had a reasonable basis. McKinley had been elected; the gold standard was secure and the highest kind of a tariff kept foreign competition at a respectful distance. A proper course of treatment would eliminate competition at home. All that remained was to parcel out the country's industries to the right people and all would go merry as a marriage bell.

The mind is staggered at the enormous fortunes created on paper within the next few years. Paltry sums like ten or twenty millions were no longer mentioned. The first hundred million dollar corporation did, of course, receive its meed of praise but was speedily relegated to its proper place on the five and ten cent counter. Thousands of millions began to be talked about and finally when the Senior Morgan accomplished this unheard of and undreamed of achievement, the whole world rang with its plaudits and Mr. Morgan was acclaimed the Midas of the Golden Nineties, before whom Kings and Queens paled into insignificance.

I first met Mr. Morgan as the result of a trivial incident. I had picked up an old photograph of St. George's Chapel, in Beekman Street, before it moved uptown. Knowing that Mr. Morgan had been married in it and was still one of its wardens, I wrote him of my find and offered either to give it to him or sell it for the cost of making a copy for myself, about three dollars. In response to my note I received a telephone message to be at his office the following day at two o'clock.

Upon receiving my card Mr. Morgan nodded to the others with him at the time, which evidently was a signal for them to withdraw. Our business concluded, he looked over some other prints of old New York I had with me. When we came to a picture of the old Everett House in Union Square, he exclaimed, "Why that was the first site selected for St. George's when we thought of moving uptown. I was one of the committee and we had almost decided to purchase the plot, which ran back to 18th Street, for twenty-five thousand dollars. As we were on our way downtown we happened to meet Mrs. Stuyvesant. When she learned what we were about to do she said, 'You don't need to spend any money for such a purpose. Come over to Stuyvesant Square and I'll give you all the land you need.' And", he added grimly, "that's the time our church lost a million dollars".

One picture suggested another and he became greatly interested in my project to revive the old Manuals of Valentine. Something was said about Henry Morgan the Pirate; my astonishment can better be imagined than described when he told me that the famous buccaneer was an ancestor of his. It was not till some days afterwards that I suddenly recalled that all his yachts—four of them—were named *"Corsair"*, and his remark came back to me with a wholly different significance. It was a strange experience. He was evidently more deeply interested in old New York than I realized at the time, as he walked all the way to the door with me, his hand resting affectionately on my shoulder. The next day he was summoned to Washington before the Pujo Committee. I never saw him again.

Mr. Morgan was a splendid specimen physically. He was above the average height and powerfully built. His shoulders were massive. He wore a hat that no one could wear by mistake because it would descend to the shoulders of the average man. His eyes were easily the most striking feature of his whole figure. They burned with an intensity that I never saw in any human face before. They seemed to pierce your very soul. No man could look into them and utter an untruth. I saw him once from across the street. Someone had evidently called his name; he turned and halted. At the distance his face was indistinct but there was no mistaking those blazing eyes. You would know them in a million.

No life of Mr. Morgan has yet been published. Mr. Satterlee started one, but it seems to have died a'bornin'. It is something that ought to be done. George F. Baker could do it, but Mr. Baker is now eighty-seven and it is a task much beyond his strength, I fear. Judge Gary has done a little for a Philadelphia publication, but it is merely to correct what he thinks is a Morgan tradition that is growing up and growing in the wrong direction.

In the Nineties the Senior Morgan reached, I think, the pinnacle of his career. He had blazed the way for the entrance of banking capital into industry, a function hitherto reserved only for railroads or other enterprises on which a monopoly was a prerequisite for any financing of a banking nature. While the final steps attending the forming of the first billion dollar combination—the Steel Trust—did not quite fall into the Nineties, most of the steps leading up to that consummation were perfected in this decade and so may be properly included in this period.

The biographer who will correctly estimate Mr. Morgan's position in the closing years of the 19th century has a task of considerable proportions ahead of him. While he may not have created conditions, he certainly knew how to make the most of them and he was absolutely honest in his belief that the money of the country was safer in his hands than if left lying around for others to take a whack at it. Neither did it occur to him that there was anything wrong with a system that made such a situation possible. That he was a despot he did not deny. He qualified it by the adjective "benevolent". And he was sincere in his belief that his despotism was a good thing for the country.

There were numerous occasions when he acted solely and wholly for the public good. I remember one time when a money stringency made an issue of New York City bonds practically unsalable. Metz was Comptroller then. He explained the situation to Mr. Morgan. Without a moment's hesitation he told Metz to announce that J. P. Morgan & Co., would take the entire issue at the price he quoted. "I don't want them, Metz," he remarked, "but I think that will help you out." It did. All Mr. Morgan had to take was eight millions out of fifty and these he disposed of readily.

Wherever the Government was concerned, Mr. Morgan was more than anxious to do his share. He stopped the export of gold during the Cleveland administration at a time the enormous withdrawals threatened a general prostration of business. His services during the great panic of 1907 are well remembered and that famous meeting called at his suggestion ranks as one of the most courageous stands ever taken by any man in the face of such threatened disaster. It is probable that the consensus of opinion will accord him a high place as a constructor and builder and that time will soften the asperities that may have been provoked by conditions of which few of us have any intimate knowledge. Take him all in all we shall not see his like again.

GEORGE F. BAKER

No doubt the closest friend Mr. Morgan had was George F. Baker. When Mr. Baker dropped into the library the night before Morgan sailed, never to return, the older man took occasion to express the great pleasure he had experienced in his friendship with him all these years. He turned to the others in the party and commended Mr. Baker to their good affections. "If I am not here", he said, "and you need advice, go to Mr. Baker. He has never failed me yet". That was the last meeting of the two old friends. Not long after Morgan died in the city of the Cæsars.

His old home, on the corner of Madison Avenue and 37th Street, has been torn down. I doubt whether the son would ever have consented to this, had it not been to make room for the library which he knew would be in keeping with the senior's wishes. As a symbol of his love for old New York, this wonderful library is a magnificent expression and a worthy monument.

Mr. George F. Baker, Morgan's friend, is the last of the Mohicans. Of all that dazzling group who made financial history in the Nineties,—Stillman, Frick, Rogers, Hill, Schiff, Harriman, he alone remains. At eighty-seven years of age, his wisdom and experience entitle him to be called the Sage of Wall Street. In private life he is the First National Bank.

Brought up in the Morgan school, Mr. Baker early discovered the value of silence. His first and, I believe, his only public speech was made at a dinner a year or two ago that was given for somebody or something, but which resolved itself into a love feast for Mr. Baker. It was upon that memorable occasion that he broke the silence of many years, and even in this his remarks

An illustration by Thure de Thulstrup in Harper's Weekly.

W

The New York Yacht Club land

ET

Twenty-sixth Street, East River

were brief and could hardly be dignified by what is generally understood as a "speech".

Both outside and inside the First National, Mr. Baker has stood for character, for solid judgment, and as a great upbuilder of the United States. Mr. Baker's financial interests have not been so diversified as those of J. Pierpont Morgan. He has been identified almost wholly with the United States; in fact, it will surprise a great many people in Wall Street if Mr. Baker's holdings should show securities of any company beyond the three-mile limit. The United States, apparently, has been good enough for Mr. Baker's investments.

Within recent years Mr. Baker's public benefactions have been on a lavish scale. His gift of Baker Field to Columbia University, and a school of Business to Harvard being among the most notable. Each year the list of his philanthropies expand.

This expansive period in American development brought several picturesque figures into the limelight. One of the most colorful of all was undoubtedly Edward Henry Harriman, savior of the Union Pacific. The story of this strenuous life, of the herculean accomplishments of this son of a country minister makes for one of the most interesting romances in the annals of our national life. It is related of him that on his first call on Kuhn, Loeb & Co., after having been unsuccessful with Morgan, his interview brought no encouragement. "I guess I am not in good shape today, otherwise I could make you see it", and with that remark he left their offices. The next time he called he must have been in fine fettle, as after that Jacob Schiff convinced his partners that the scheme was sound and Kuhn, Loeb & Co., entered the field as contenders in the railroad world against the all-powerful firm of J. P. Morgan & Co. In later years, this struggle took on titanic proportions in the contest with James J. Hill for mastery of the Pacific. The famous Northern Pacific corner was one of the results of that struggle and before Hill and Harriman could adjust their differences the entire financial world was seriously threatened.

Out of these bloody days of rapine, murder and sudden death came a new era in Wall Street, largely through the establishment of the Federal Reserve Bank and government control of railroads.

The theory that a despot, however benevolent he might be, should control all the capital had suffered a severe shock. The human element was still too strong in the individual and an impersonal machine was substituted.

If Mr. Baker enjoyed for many years the reputation of a Sphinx, what shall be said of Mr. Arthur Curtiss James, who has not yet broken a silence of more than forty years? It is probably no exaggeration to say that of all the really big men in the world of finance, Mr. James is perhaps the most retiring and the most self-effacing of them all. Occasionally some slight paragraph strays into the newspapers that he is the largest individual owner of railroad shares in the country for one thing—but rarely does one read a full account of this man's extraordinary activities in the many different fields in which he plays an active part.

Little is said of the great private firm of Phelps, Dodge & Co., of which he is the chief owner. In Boston, the papers keep one tolerably well informed of the great

Calumet & Hecla Copper Mine, the richest yet discovered, but has little to say of Phelps, Dodge & Co.,
who are the sole selling agents of this Golconda or of
the fact that Phelps, Dodge & Co. control a large part
of the copper output of the entire country.

What is more important to Mr. James is the fact that
he possesses the only Master Navigator's Certificate in
the New York Yacht Club and that he is called by his
intimates Commodore by virtue of his tenure in that
office of the Yacht Club. His auxiliary steam yacht
Aloha is an old-time three-masted square rigger. And
it is her owner's delight to drop the smokestack out of
sight, stop the engines and sail her under a full spread
of canvas. In his recent trip around the world in the
Aloha the log book carefully records the number of
knots sailed under steam and the same under sail. The
comparison is eloquent testimony to the love of this
genuine deep-sea sailor to the delights of life on an ocean
wave.

Few prominent men in Wall Street are so successful
in hiding their identity to the general public as is Mr.
James. There are no authorized interviews on questions
of the day given out by Mr. James, though his views on
almost any topic would be read with avidity. His public
spiritedness, his public and private benefactions are on
an imposing scale but are rarely mentioned. To those
on the inner circle of high finance the name is one to
conjure by. Mr. Baker has made one public speech, Mr.
James none. So he is one lap ahead of his friend for the
laurels of the Sphinx.

Another spectacular figure of these times was John
W. Gates—"Bet-you-a-million-Gates," as he was popu-

larly called. His partner, John F. Harris, now of Harris, Winthrop & Co., tells me no more erroneous impression of the real man ever persisted than the newspaper creation of Gates.

"A just, sane and accurate story of John W. Gates might mention casually some incidents of his gambling operations, but he founded companies of great size which endured and are now in a highly prosperous condition. He did a great deal for the industry of this country and he was a true captain of commerce.

There was a certain foam and froth and perhaps folly in his life as in all men's, but that side as compared to his great administrative ability was insignificant. He had as comprehensive, alert and analytical mind as anyone with whom I ever came in contact, and every corporation with which he was connected profited by that ability.

That Gates was a man of extraordinary business acumen is readily acknowledged by those who knew him. An incident which goes to prove this was his offer to Lord Cowdrey to buy his Mexican oil properties for fifteen millions. Gates died pending the final negotiations and his successors decided to forego their option. Cowdrey willingly assented to a release and when the last papers were signed, promptly disposed of the same property, but this time for seventy-five millions to a Belgian Syndicate. In less than one year the new owners received over forty millions in profit and since then have accumulated a surplus far in excess of the original investment. This is only one instance cited by Mr. Harris of his friend's uncanny vision in locating unsuspected sources of wealth.

Mr. Gates flouted conventionality. It was "Hello

Jake," "Hello Henry," meaning Mr. Jacob Schiff and Mr. E. H. Harriman. While this is not exactly a criminal offense it served to create a dislike of Mr. Gates and brought him much harmful publicity. It totally obscured the many lovable traits by which he was endeared to his intimate friends. They speak of him as a man of generous impulses, frequently extending material aid to old and less fortunate friends, and possessing a nature wholly at variance with the popular conception.

Of the brilliant young leaders of finance today such as the junior Morgan, Chas. D. Mitchell, Thomas Cochrane, Clarence Dillon, Charles Steele, Thomas Lamont, Dwight Morrow and half a dozen others, not one of them was on the horizon in the nineties with the exception of Mr. Morgan, who was then more closely identified with the Lombard Street than with Wall.

STUYVESANT'S PEAR TREE, COR. 3RD AVENUE AND 12TH STREET

CHAPTER IX.

PASSING OF THE LIVERY STABLE
INTRODUCTION OF GOLF

THE amazing rewards of the prize ring today must embitter the declining days of the slugger of yesteryear who fought in the "sporting" clubs that were engendered by the Horton law, which was the first legal sanction that the noble art ever received in New York. It was then that the voice of Joe Humphries was heard

274

in the land, announcing "Kid" O'Brien, *nee* Lubinsky, vs. "Battling" Brophy *nee* Sirocco, "both members of this club", this last being an assurance that the social and legal amenities were being observed.

The old Broadway Athletic Club, near Waverly Place, was one of the most prominent of these early cradles of legalized assault and battery. The "Tar Babies", "Harlem Coffee Coolers" and assorted "Kids" and "Battlers" of later renown fought there for what would now be regarded as cigarette money by the "big business" of the prize ring. The absurd pumped up reputations, the enormous commercial ramifications, the "publicity" departments, the "movie rights", the "sporting writers", the preposterous earnings, the paternal State partnership in a traffic once hounded from pillar to post, and its inevitable political implications, were all fostered in the little clubs of the nineties.

Some of these clubs held forth in unlikely places. One of them I remember upstairs in the old "White Elephant" on Broadway at 31st Street, a dangerous trap in case of fire. Another was in a disguised stable on 42nd Street on what is now the site of the Rialto Theatre. There were no cameras, no speculators, no managerial "Napoleons", no State percentage, nothing but knockouts and blood. Those were the happy days.

The close of the century marked also the passing of that time honored institution, the livery stable, which was in some respects the prototype of today's garage. Perhaps Mike, the hostler, was not quite so rapacious as the mechanician to whose tender mercies one entrusts one's benzine buggy. Of course patient Dobbin could never tell of skimped oats except by a lack of spirit when driven out, but as a rule he was fairly used.

THE OLD LIVERY STABLE

A good part of livery stable income was acquired from Sunday "buggy rides". A girl whose "mash" took her for a Sunday tour to Coney Island or a Bronx road-house had a "live one", even if the nag which drew them performed a similar service during the administration of Rutherford B. Hayes. An average charge for this luxury was $4, exclusive of a quarter to the hostler.

Sunday night was a busy one with the stablekeeper, who made it a point to be on hand to redeem his flock from the tender mercies of the amateur whips to whom they had been consigned. A stock comment was, "You've druv this hoss purty hard, young man". This observation was often a just one. It required no license to drive a horse and there was scarcely a male extant who would admit the least incapacity in "handling the ribbons" over the greatest equine star that ever showed its paces on the Harlem Speedway.

Livery stables were even more numerous than garages today. They were on almost every other block and apparently all built upon the same plan. There was always a weather vane perched on top surmounted by a wooden horse. The entrance to the stable was via an inclined platform with ribs across it to give the horse a purchase when he negotiated a landing. In some mysterious manner this platform was always wet and slippery for some reason or other and this wooden bar was a necessity.

The office was always a very diminutive affair, usually in the left hand corner as you entered. It generally contained a small base burner in winter and always had a lot of whips, horse blankets, fly nets, etc., stowed aloft. There was room for one man com-

Drawn from life by V. Gribayedoff.

J. PIERPONT MORGAN, SR.

In his office about the time of the Steel Corporation merger

THE FIFTIETH ANNIVERSARY OF THE FOUNDING OF THE NEW YORK YACHT CLUB

The toast in the Model Room

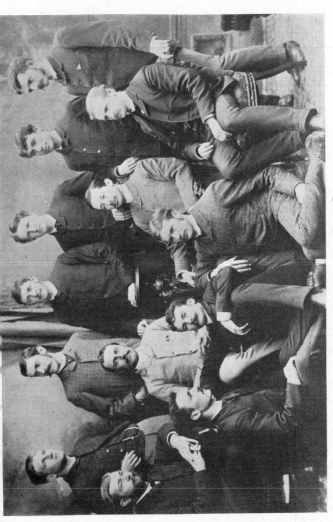

THE JOHNS HOPKINS GLEE CLUB

Top row, second from left, Woodrow Wilson, then writing historical articles; next Albert Shaw, well-known editor, "Review of Reviews." Taken at Johns Hopkins University

From a Painting by Benjamin Constant.

JAY GOULD, WHO DIED IN 1892

fortably, but it usually held three or four. The windows facing the street were never cleaned.

There were always a few broken down grooms hanging around and a veterinary surgeon's sign was always in evidence. In fact no livery stable was genuine without it. Some men could always be found there Sundays and holidays. What they did or how they existed no one knew. But they were part of the setting.

Among our prominent local families there are two that figure conspicuously in the affairs of the nineties, of whom I must say a passing word. These were "The Seven Sutherland Sisters" and "The Six Little Tailors", or as a sub-title "The Six Jacobs Brothers". The Seven Sisters sold a preparation to encourage the growth of hair. The Six Jacobs sold wearing apparel of tricots, corkscrew and bird's-eye worsted, diagonals and other archaic fabrics—perfect fit guaranteed.

The Seven Sisters were on view in crude advertising cuts in the papers, and also in the flesh in Sixth Avenue shop windows. Each of the Seven had a prodigious mane that fell like a cascade, nearly to the ground. The nostrum they sold was presumably calculated to reproduce this phenomenon on the head of each and every purchaser of the same. How far this radiant hope was realized I am unable to state, but I never noticed any diminution in the number of nude scalps in the front rows of "leg shows" during the "crowning glory" days of the hirsute Seven.

Another "blessing on the head" that was widely acclaimed was the "electric hair brush". This was in the category to which belonged the "electric belt" and the "electric insole" which were declared therapeutic agents and were the forerunners of the various "vibrators" of more recent memory. Among other external remedies was the "rheumatism ring" which sold for $5. It was merely an iron finger ring which was regarded with superstitious awe by its wearers. At the prevailing price of old stove lids, it will readily be discerned that its vendors made a tidy profit in the huge sale that this miraculous article commanded.

The word "home town" had hardly come into the parlance of the New Yorker thirty years ago. A New Yorker's home town was New York, the vast majority of its dwellers, outside of the foreign colonies, being natives of Manhattan Island, except that by chance, it happened to be Brooklyn or Jersey City. The only indication of a non-indigenous element in the American population were the annual dinners of the New England Society, the Southern Society, etc., whose nostalgic reunions were addressed by prominent after dinner orators, who condoled with their audiences over the absence of certain provincial delights, which in their secret hearts most of them were anxious to shove still further into oblivion. How delightful it was to remind a well-fed banker at a Delmonico banquet, smoking a Havana perfecto, of stone bruises, poison ivy, chores, wood-splitting, freezing attic bedrooms, with basins of ice for ablutions, linsey-woolsy clothes, backwoods cooking, burnt corn coffee, mumps, home haircuts, chapped hands, and all other seasonable bucolic joys. Ah! those were the happy days, but these were bully nights "with fair round belly, with good capon lined".

The period also marked the decline of after-dinner speaking as an art of its own kind. The special exemplars of this form of entertainment were Chauncey

M. Depew and General Horace Porter, whose dinners at home were a negligible ceremony, by reason of their absence to attend the festive board of some public banquet room. The newspapers used to report these post-prandial utterances in extenso, as it was not necessary to "kill" news matter to accommodate advertising.

These great dinners were plethoric in their menus, canvas back ducks and terrapin (the former now under a legal ban) being usually the most exploited delicacies. Each course had its own appropriate wine, from hock and oysters to cognac and coffee. Of course, the rounders at these affairs indulged sparingly in their bounties, but the tyros usually found themselves in the spring with one foot lifted on a cushion, or taking the waters at Carlsbad, Saratoga or French Lick.

Golf was just about making its appearance as a panacea for these indulgences. Tennis was a "dude's" game, and only a few cranks went hiking for health. The tramp was still the chief biped that enjoyed nature afoot. Indoor gymnastics were proportionately much more pursued than at present. The sport shops abounded in rowing-machines, weight-lifting machines, trapezes, horizontal bars, and all the paraphernalia of the Turn-Verein, which the Germans had introduced years before.

Fencing had many devotees among the upper classes of society, and among stage professionals. The romantic and classic drama called for a good deal of sword-play and all the principal stars of the stage were more or less adept with the foils. The principal teacher in the art of thrust and parry in New York was Regis Senac, in whose salon in the Broadway Theatre Building, one might encounter d'Artagnan or Romeo, or

Hamlet brushing up with the professor, in a bout with the foils. Senac was also instructor at the New York Athletic Club. He was an ex-officer of the *Chasseurs d'Afrique* who had set up an establishment in New York in the Seventies when the rage for everything French was much more pronounced than it was later. He was a typical *Beau Sabreur* in appearance and many distinguished lights of society and the stage will remember the genial *maitre* who taught them the swift turn of the wrist, and helped otherwise to reduce an *embonpoint* that was stretching the lines of beauty.

One of the most distinguished assemblages that has ever gathered in New York was present at the Metropolitan Opera House on the night of April 10, 1891, to celebrate the fiftieth anniversary of the founding of the New York Tribune. Among the speakers from the stage were William McKinley, Charles A. Dana, George William Curtis and Chauncey M. Depew. The house was filled with the elite of the Republican Party, from Vice-President Morton to the Collector of the Port, with a sprinkling of not a few distinguished Democrats.

Horace Greeley was the posthumous hero of the occasion and his famous slogan "Go West, Young Man!" was responded to by Roswell Horr, a statesman from Michigan, who spent a half hour discoursing on the animal, vegetable and mineral resources of that fabulous region, interspersed with geographical information as to how many times the State of Rhode Island could be packed into the smallest County of Arkansas without overlapping the jurisdiction of the neighboring sheriff. All the old familiar rhetoric of the "Star of Empire" was employed in this deadly bally-hoo and many an owner of upper Broadway real estate in the audience felt impelled to trade his holdings for a few thousand square miles of Texas prairie.

Most amusing was Charles A. Dana, the redoubtable editor of the *Sun* and former associate of Horace Greeley. Among his remarks was the following very pertinent comment on a question of large public concern today:

"He was a man of almost no education—indeed, of no education at all, except what he had acquired for himself. The worst school that a man can be sent to, and the worst of all for a man of genius, is what is called a self-education. There is no greater fortune for a man of extraordinary talent than to be thrown into contact with other youths in the conflicts of study and in the struggle for superiority in the school and in the college. That was denied to Mr. Greeley. He knew no language but his own; but of that he possessed the most extraordinary mastery. His wit and his humor flowed out in idiomatic forms of expression that were surprising and delightful, and that remained in the mind forever. When I first was connected with him he would not have any notice taken of the theatre. He began by refusing to print theatrical advertisements (laughter). He would not allow horse racing to be reported.

"But one day there was a horse race of enormous interest. It was the great race between Boston and Fashion, which occurred along about 1842 or 1843, if I recollect rightly. It was a great conflict between the North and the South—a sort of premonition of that enormous and dreadful conflict which later covered the land with devastation and sorrow. Well, this was a horse race in which the whole public was interested, because it was not only a horse race, but it was also to a certain extent a political event; and everybody about the office felt that it ought to be reported. Finally the man who was to report it, or who ought to report it, went to Mr. Greeley and said, 'Mr. Greeley, we ought to report that horse race. It will not do for *The Tribune* to appear day after tomorrow without any account of that event in which the whole public mind is absorbed'.

" 'Well', said Horace, 'I don't know'. Finally, said he, 'I guess you will have to do it, we have to report hangings anyway.' "

But what caused the most uproarious mirth of all Mr. Dana's remarks was his assertion that the personal antagonisms of the American press were obsolete. This innocent remark was enjoyed immensely by an audience who were still having their breakfasts enlivened by the bludgeonings and rapier thrusts of Mr. Dana's *Sun* and Mr. Pulitzer's *World*.

One of the examples of Mr. Dana's unconscious humor was, about this time, daily imprinted upon the first page of the earlier editions of his *Evening Sun*. It was a label running "Read Our Sporting Extra for Complete Record of Wall Street Happenings". Mr. Dana was probably not the first man to recognize an analogy between the aims of the Stock Exchange and that of the race course.

Among the remarks of the Hon. Chauncey M. Depew, the following reference to the *Tribune's* dramatic department has a peculiar interest in view of the slipshod school of dramatic criticism that has developed since:

"Vitiated tastes and depraved appetites, ephemeral applause and unstinted praise for anything from nudity to inanity, which crowded the house have all tended to demoralize managers and degrade the stage. Here again *The Tribune* had its own, and a purely original and sturdily American standard of art. If it was pervaded by a Puritan flavor, it was the Puritanism of Milton, modified by the traditions of Shakespeare and Sheridan. It demanded purity of purpose, elegance of expression, a visible touch of genius, and an interpretation upon the models, and close to the best ideals of the stage. The undisputed chief of this school is William Winter".

The following is the kind of dramatic review that did *not* appear in the *Tribune*:

(By "Con" in Variety).

Get a load of the flossy stage names the janes in this opera have picked. It's a Mutual sponsored by Williams & Jordan and in addition has a novelty that nobody will ever cop unless another producer finds himself with a Bowery set on his hands and nothing to fit it.

Williams & Jordan didn't let it bother them any, for they trotted out a chorus in ante-bellum costumes for a minute and alibied it with a program note, "New York in the Early '90s."

However, nobody from the Theater Guild saw it and the customers registered it was all okay with them by applauding the number.

Rather an attractive chorus cavorted out upon the twin runways several times and never failed to grind to returns. While the girls don't seem to bother much about calories there were no trick shapes visible, and they looked well on each occasion in their various changes.

And Mlle. Fifi, the Oriental dancer, back after a long vacation, hasn't lost an ounce and didn't lose a customer, although she was spotted way down near the finale. Feefe gives them what they want and how. She has a hop on her fast one that none of the principals can match. Under black Chantilly lace Feefe led the exotic league and hit .400 without using a rabbit ball.

Summing up, Williams & Jordan have assembled a good Mutual show and one that should gather many pennies around the wheel.

The ethics of modern newspaper advertising would have been a great astonishment to the late James Gordon Bennett, whose *"New York Herald"* enlightened the public on the merits of clairvoyants, palmists, astrologers and sundry purveyors of occult learning. Its "Personal" column was also famous as an intermediary in matrimony, not to mention less permanent attachments. As an example of this column's advertising let me quote the following.

"Refined gentleman, $200,000, beautiful home, but lonely, will make home happiest place on earth to kind wife."

"Secretary (28) to multimillionaire, eligible to best society so constituted as to make any woman supremely happy, desires marriage but will consider no one not refined, educated and wealthy."

"Horse Show, Saturday, box 35, left corner, youngest lady accompanied old man Madison car, kindly grant interview, gentleman she repeatedly noticed."

"Attorney of distinction (bachelor, author) seeks stately woman of culture, independent, matrimonially inclined."

"Lillie—am obliged to work; shall go as a corset model, no longer in the chorus."

"The acquaintance of young lady of refinement and means is desired by young man having noble ends to attain; none but strong personalities need answer."

One of the *causes célèbre* of our period was the Laidlaw vs. Sage trial in which Joseph H. Choate represented the plaintiff and Colonel James the defendant. It was contended that Sage had used Laidlaw as a shield when a murderous crank attempted to blow up

A de Thulstrup drawing in Harper's Weekly.

Waiting for carriages in

lobby of the Metropolitan

Sage's office, and succeeded in himself departing in pieces. Regardless of the specific merits of the case, Laidlaw had the sympathy of the community, for he had been seriously injured in the explosion and the ordinary promptings of humanity might have moved the renowned old Wall Street curmudgeon to salve his wounds with a substantial solace. But old "puts and calls" ran true to form, hence a few blistering hours in the witness chair under Choate's barrage.

Choate's summing up was a most impressive one. He began by reading from a book—not a law book as might have been expected, but the story of Dives and Lazarus. It was a dramatic gesture and had its effect. Laidlaw was awarded $40,000 damages. A second trial reduced the sum to $25,000, and I believe further litigation resulted in a compromise.

Sage asked someone if it were true that Choate had been appointed Ambassador to London, and when assured of the fact, raised his hand in supplication and murmured, "God save the Queen!"

We were slowly but surely ceasing to decorate our walls with chromos given free at the corner grocery with each purchase of a pound of tea. There was a store on Nassau Street, near Fulton, which still stood high in the art world, and many of its choicest productions were still popular in the best families. Its show window proved a great attraction to the average errand boy. No matter how much of a hurry he was supposed to be in, he couldn't resist the temptation to linger here a minute or two. It was the shop of Currier & Ives.

One thing is certain. They knew how to display their wares. The window was low—it almost reached to the ground and the glass was large French plate, with no sashes to obstruct the view. All sorts of gaudy pictures were tastefully arranged in this window and they held the passer-by spellbound. The subjects and sizes covered every possible demand.

Strange to relate, the pictures that were most popular then, are regarded as the least desirable today. To my mind the series entitled *"The Darktown Fire Brigade"* were the most laughable things I had ever seen. The coons were everlastingly turning the hose accidentally on each other, or a great big wench weighing about five hundred pounds would jump out of a window and be in the act of landing upon the most diminutive member of the brigade. Then other household impedimenta would be descending upon various other gallant fire eaters till the whole scene was side splitting in its effect.

This same group of darkies would be shown playing billiards. It was a close match and the title was *"Two to go"*. The darkey in the picture was shown as intensely absorbed in his effort to win the game. His huge eyes almost popped out of their sockets. The companion picture was entitled *"Got 'em both!"* and showed the cue had slipped and hit about a dozen onlookers, and a free fight was in the offing. It was very funny. These pictures were always sold in pairs and I imagine enjoyed a fair circulation. The *"Darktown"* series had about a dozen subjects.

The high prices now obtainable for some of the Currier & Ives prints is due solely to the fact that their prints have ceased to be merely lithographs, and have entered that higher spiritual state known as "Americana." There were other pictures portraying hunting and fishing scenes, camping and other outdoor sports made as early as the 50's and 60's. These Currier & Ives prints reproduce faithfully the costumes, accessories, and background of that period. Accuracy was absolutely the first essential in the drawing of these prints; the customer was as well informed on the subject as the artist and would reject a faked or amateurist reproduction of his favorite sport. They have therefore unquestioned authenticity. And that is what the collector pays for in a Currier & Ives print.

The rapid advance in value of these pictures has been one of the surprises of the auction room. One described as a railroad junction brought $800. Others of a similar character, in proportion. Their clipper ship pictures which were priced in the old Nassau Street window at $1.00 each, now command more than two hundred times that amount. Miscellaneous rural views share in the general prosperity.

It will be interesting to note the trend of prices. Their output was undoubtedly of impressive proportions. Yet for many years they were looked upon as crude specimens fit only for the junk heap. A whole bundle of them would frequently be sold for a dollar at different auction sales and they were in general disrepute. During this period, destruction must have reduced the floating supply very materially. Yet high prices have a strange tendency to bring forth unsuspected sources of supply. There must be plenty of them around but the country hay seed is no longer the yokel he used to be regarding antiques. The day of real bargains, I fear, has largely vanished. Currier & Ives prints have gone to join that other "Vanished American" the cigar store Indian. Try to pick up one of the latter on your travels next summer and see what will happen. The Indians themselves will let out a war whoop if they don't bring their weight in gold.

Some idea of the extent of their activities may be gathered from the vast field they covered. Items of news such as shipwrecks, fires, disasters of all kinds sufficiently large to engage public interest were included as part of their output. Their finest work, however, is in sporting scenes, the wonderful clipper ships of the "roaring forties," and railroads. In addition there were no end of sentimental subjects, political portraits and rural scenes. They were in pictures what the Rogers groups were in statuary and no American home with any pretensions to culture was without either.

The firm was exceedingly prosperous in the '60s and '70s. That was about the zenith of their career. After that it became increasingly difficult to compete with the advancing improvement in the graphic arts, which enabled weeklies and monthlies to publish illustrations of current events, a field hitherto practically their own. When *"Puck"* and *"Judge"* appeared, both printed by lithography and in colors, the end was definitely in sight. Early in the nineties this old firm gave up the struggle and disappeared from view leaving behind them, however, a reputation which they never dreamed would preserve their names as part of the incunabula of a great country in its adolescent days.

Negro longshoremen and roustabouts are now found in great numbers on our river front, but in the early Nineties they were still a novelty. The first to find out that the colored man's brawn was peculiarly fitted for this class of labor were the National and the Old Dominion lines, which on the failure of the Knights of Labor's great strike to control the shipping of the port, gave employment to negroes in large numbers. Many of these had been roustabouts on the Mississippi cotton wharves and could handle 400-pound bales without great inconvenience. They brought their levee songs with them. One of them was a famous old timer called "Limber Jim", which had about thirty stanzas, of which these are samples:

"A jaybird sitting on a hick'ry limb
He winked at me, an' I winked at him;
I up wid a rock and hit him on de shin
Says he, 'Young man, doan you do dat agin.'

Oh! Limber Jim—Shiloh.
Talk it agin—Shiloh
Walk in, my lub—Shiloh
You turtle dove—Shiloh.

I went to Mary's house, Mary was in bed

She opened de winder an' she poked out her head
An' she say 'No nigger's gwine ter marry me.'
Such a gittin' up-stairs I nebber did see.

Eighteen pennies dey wah hidden in a fence
De Cynthiana gals haint got no sense
Foh ev'ry time dey go from home
Dey comb dey ha'r wid a big jawbone."

Another roustabout song had this in it:

"Shawnee town am a-burnin' down
Who tole you so?
Shawnee town am a-burnin' down
Lord, is dat so?
How de debbil d'ye 'spect me to hold her
Way down below;
Dere ain't no skin on any shoulder
Who tole you so?
Shawnee town am a-burnin' down
Who tole you so?
Shawnee town am a-burnin' down
Lord, is dat so?

De pilot t'rough de pipe he git de firemen de news
Dey couldn't make a fire foh de heatin' of de flues,
De Cap'n on de b'iler deck a-scratchin' ob his head
An' yellin at the roustabout to heave de starboard lead.

> Shawneetown, etc.

I come down de mountain
An' she come down de lane
An' all dat I could say to her
Was good bye, 'Liza Jane.
> Good bye, 'Liza Jane
> Oh, farewell, 'Liza Jane
> Oh, do not t'row yo'self away
> I'se comin' back again.

Shawnee town am a-burnin' down
> Who tole you so?
Shawnee town am a-burnin' down
> Lord, is dat so?"

In 1898 the Afro-American had not yet found his chief habitat in our fair city in the distant regions of Harlem. The northern outpost of our colored colony was in that declivity west of Amsterdam Avenue and north of 59th Street, now known as San Juan Hill. This district was rapidly depopulating the classic shades of Thompson Street and lower Seventh Avenue when the Spanish-American War broke out, and it was an incident in its hostilities that gave the region the honorary title it has since retained.

The 71st New York Infantry was ordered to advance on an enemy position during the Battle of San Juan Hill. The order was ill-advised, the regiment being composed of raw, unseasoned boys who had never smelled powder, and the situation was something of an ambush. The 71st was rapidly being cut to pieces, when a regiment of colored regulars was rushed to their support. The black warriors, unmindful of the nullification in certain of these United States of the Fifteenth Amendment, made short work of the business, and when the news reached New York, the city rang with plaudits for the saviors of its pet militia at the front. The name "San Juan Hill" by some spontaneous agreement was affixed to the region aforesaid, which since that time has not been without some battles of its own.

The 71st Regiment held a peculiar place in local esteem during the war. The city's "crack" regiment, the Seventh, had volunteered, but learning that they would have to serve under officers of the regular army, instead of their own accustomed commanders, refused to do so. Their action was the occasion of a good deal of acrimonious discussion on both sides. The regiment certainly lost caste by it.

The colored warrior of '98 did not lack his bard as the following, despite its facetious vein, proves:

"I quit my job and went to war to serve my country right
But a rifle ain't the weapon dat I use when in a fight;
My weapon is a razor in de light or in de dark
'Cause when you strike your enemy you're bound to leave
    your mark.
Colonel Roosevelt's Rough Riders were always in the
    brunt,
But if the war had been wid razors, tough coons would
    have been in front.
Smokeless powder had me nervous, I'd a did some real
    warm service,
If they'd only fought wid razors in de war.

Chorus

If they'd only fought wid razors in de war,
I'd certainly spilled a lot of Spanish gore;

TORCH LIGHT PARADES

> I know a gun shoots fast an' loud
> But a razor's the real thing in a crowd
> I can handle it better than a forty-four,
> If they'd only fought wid razors in de war,
> I'd certainly carved dem Spaniards to de core;
> Dewey took Manila dat is true, but I'd a took Havana too
> If they'd only fought wid razors in de war."

All this genuine old time Southern atmosphere seems to have disappeared from the colored race as we now know it in New York. The sophisticated denizens of Harlem's night club life recall little that suggests the darkey of ante-bellum days or recall the delightful characters portrayed in the songs of Stephen Foster.

The close of the century also saw the passing of that peculiarly American institution, the political parade. Of course there are still some reminiscences of these in the little local parades that yet bring out the band-wagon. But the enormous processions of partisans made memorable by the Business Men's Parade for Cleveland and the Sound Money Parade for McKinley are of the past. Politics are more Machiavellian nowadays, and the flaring kerosene torch no longer serves to enlighten the intelligent voter on the issues of the day. The aforesaid Sound Money Parade drew out an enormous army of Republican patriots trembling for the nation in the face of the Free Silver agitation and the 16 to 1 slogan. The campaign of '92 also involved the country's welfare in the question of High Tariff or Free Trade. The issues of the campaign were mainly economic, although the Democrats pointed the accusing finger at the corruption of the Harrison Administration and the Cleveland slogan was "Turn the Rascals Out". Campaign songs of the period reflect the issues with a

OLD FULTON MARKET

Ancient New York market rights when the Fulton Street
market men occupied the whole street on Thursday mornings

Fog-Bound on the East River

Impatient passengers going ashore in small boats from a Boston steamer anchored near Hell Gate

"Up the Hudson"

The Mary Powell, "Queen of the Hudson" for nearly half a century, and a great favorite with old New Yorkers

good deal of pungency. The Republicans sang the following among other marching ditties.

"The prophet of Gray Gables and the Sage of Buzzards'
   Bay
Had better go a-fishing in the good old fashioned way
The nation's sons will turn him down upon election day
      As we go marching on.

      Glory! shout the glad Hosanna
      Glory! Ben of Indiana
      Glory! Glory, Hallelujah!
         As we go marching on."

      "Mary had a little lamb
       She sheared the wool to spin it;
       Grover took the tariff off
       And then she had to skin it."

"Let the British Lion roar his free-trade thunder out
 And growl at reciprocity while Dave and Grover shout
 Their billion dollar war cry, 'We will keep the rascals
      out."

CHAPTER X.

COMING OF BIG HOTELS, LOBSTER PALACES, ETC.—BUSINESS ARCHITECTURE

NEW YORK has always been noted for the wide variety of its architecture. Its buildings have never been subjected to the municipal restrictions of Paris, or the strong traditional tendencies of London and they, therefore, reflect with a singular force the dominant fads and fancies in construction of their times. The Nineties were distinctly the age of the Italian Renaissance. Nearly all the early skyscrapers were in this style. The Gothic, so strikingly used in the Woolworth Building, was undreamed of. Indeed, its use in this city, in its entire history, with few exceptions, has been until a very recent date, exclusively ecclesiastical. The architects of the early skyscrapers, fearful that their fifteen and twenty stories might dismay the onlooker, endeavored to break up the impression of height by the horizontal line, not knowing that their true theme was

ARCHITECTURE IN WASHINGTON HEIGHTS IN THE EARLY NINETIES

the towering perpendicular of the Gothic. It is to the Renaissance that we owe the absurd cornices and friezes, far out of sight, on many of our first skyscrapers.

In other types of architecture there was the same avoidance of the problem of a native, or at least a traditional style; a style adapted if need be from exotic sources but not a slavish imitation. The Italian palazzos of Mr. Stanford White, vide the Metropolitan Club, and the Spanish Giralda of the late Madison Square Garden might be very handsome and elegant ornaments to our streets, but they had no roots in our architectural past, nor suggestions for the future. Mr. James Gordon Bennett's "Palace of the Doges" on Herald Square had one advantage: that it seemed eminently suited to its triangular site, its rhythmic arrangement of pillars being singularly effective in its situation. But its dainty elegance hardly suggested the home of a metropolitan newspaper, and a repository for "personals and help wanted."

In domestic architecture, the show place of the metropolis was, of course, "Millionaires Row" on the eastern fringe of Central Park. This in its early stages was devoted to the French châteaux of the Astors and other superabundant householders. The Georgian revival along this luxurious lane is rather an affair of the present century. It was hastened, I should say, by that superlative folly, the Clark mansion, the crowning example of a belated Forty-niner's idea of a Nob Hill palace transplanted to the eastern shore. There were certain statistics given out when this prodigy was completed, regarding the number of pounds of solid bronze in its fittings, the tons of copper on its roof, the blocks of hewn marble in its myriad bath tubs, the miles of electric wire in its chandeliers and other entertaining et ceteras of a tired miner's homestead on Fifth Avenue. I believe this structure was declared fireproof, burglar proof and bomb proof, and that nothing could enter without permission, except microbes. All this data filled pages of the Sunday supplements, to be eagerly absorbed by the habitues of Bowery lodging-houses, who figured on their margins, the possible profits of buying Anaconda at $2 a share, instead of backing mud-horses at the winter tracks. There is no doubt that when a "he-man, with red blood in his veins, from the great open spaces, where men are men", *ad lib*. hits New York, with collateral securities, he can make the home of the last of the Knickerbockers look like a hot-dog shed on a detour.

In municipal architecture of this period, the name of Horgan and Slattery reigns supreme. This eminent firm of architects favored of the powers that be, had a full set of books relating to their craft, and when they were commissioned to draw plans for a fire-engine house they had no difficulty at all in producing a wing of the palace of Versailles that even the fire horses were delighted with. Their police-stations, replicas of villas on Lake Como, always made Italian criminals who were brought in, shed tears of homesickness and beg to be deported. Their garbage incinerators were adaptations of the Casino at Monte Carlo, and their Blackwell's Island workhouse evoked the unstinted admiration of every deck hand on the Astoria ferryboats. Their hospitals were gay without being vulgar, and their jails were discreetly ornate without being flamboyant.

But the *chef d'oeuvre* of the official architecture of

the time, was that monument of ineptitude, the Criminal Courts Building on Centre Street. This structure was probably designed with the aid of some discarded plans for a magnificent Turkish Bath, for it has all the characteristics of such an institution, including a huge marble pit in the central hall that might be used for a tank. Its corridors, galleries and stairways run riot with twisted ironwork, interspersed with bronze dragons, griffins, sphinxes and other mythological fauna. On the pedestals of the lamps, appears the conspicuous legend "Mitchell, Vance Co." A contemporary observed: "It is to be hoped that the company was not guilty of the depraved art in bronze on the landing, consisting of a nude youth with flattened Dante features, who raises one hand upward as if in terrible warning against worse horrors in the galleries above. It may be that the intention was to impress criminals with the uselessness of striving to exist longer in a city capable of accepting such atrocities. After seeing them, the average crook rightly concluded that the barest dungeon may well seem a relief."

This punitive structure was built on the site of the old Collect Pond. At frequent intervals cracks and crevices appear in its masonry and hurry calls are sent out to the Department of Public Works to jack up the tons of trumpery gimcracks that distinguish it. Perhaps there are some demon Dutchmen in the pond below, who are relieving their outraged feelings by pulling at the foundations of the intruder over their ancient fishing grounds. Only the old Post Office in City Hall Park offers a more conspicuous object for obliteration.

HOLLAND HOUSE AND THE PLAZA

Hotels

It was also an era of great hotel building, which began with the erection, late in the Eighties, of the first Plaza Hotel, a monumental, spacious and comfortable house which was the first of the modern group at the southeast corner of the Park, only recently outmoded. For a number of years the city had languished in the matter of houses of public entertainment. The inflammable old Windsor, Fifth Avenue, Brunswick and Hoffman House, all antediluvian structures, were its chief caravansaries and the butter and egg men from the West were beginning to draw invidious comparisons with the ultra-modern Auditorium in Chicago, the West in Minneapolis, the Hollenden in Cleveland, and other new and splendiferous hostelries in the then booming middle section. The challenge was soon met by a series of gilded super-taverns with enough onyx, Carara marble and precious metal to make the proprietor of the Palmer House barber shop, which had 800 silver dollars sunk into its mosaic floor, weep with chagrin.

First, and most restrained in decorative exuberance, was the Holland House, some of whose apartments were reproductions of rooms in Lord Holland's famous London mansion in which the early Victorian wits and gallants used to foregather. Then came the Savoy, whose builders pooh-poohed Lord Holland's economy in golden interior decoration and called upon the mines of Ophir to embellish its appointments. Then Wm. Waldorf Astor wanted to know why the family hadn't built any hotels since the famous old stone box down at City Hall and gave order for a German Renaissance

palace with bronze chandeliers set in a ceiling finer than
that of any movie house on Times Square. This was the
New Netherlands, which had a very precarious early
career before the last bleating goat on the upper Fifth
Avenue ·rocks was turned into chamois gloves.

Meanwhile, Mrs. Goelet, jealous for the fame of
Broadway as the seat of hotel empire, built the Imperial
with the goldenest lobby in which drummer's yarns
were swapped, ever known. Whereupon a green and
sickly hue o'ercast the features of William Waldorf
Astor and with a true Astorian gesture he called upon
the mighty Hardenbergh to construct a hostelry that
would make the Imperial look like a dog kennel.

John Jacob Astor was not on the most friendly terms
with his cousin W. W. and when the Waldorf began to
rise to the south of the former's mansion at 34th Street
he felt the neighborhood was running down. There
was to be a glorified tavern adjoining, and just across
the way the famous old marble ice-box built by A. T.
Stewart, in the style of the Second Empire, was leased
to the Manhattan Club. In its window sat Tammany
politicians hob-nobbing with broad-clothed bulwarks
of the Solid South over Manhattan cocktails, and blow-
ing the smoke of Henry Clay perfectos toward the
frescoed ceiling in a futile effort to turn a stone
refrigerator into a human habitation. There was
Judge Truax telling Henry Watterson how many
bottles of Medoc '69 reposed in the catacombs under-
neath; and Henry giving the Judge a recipe for mint
julep that made the judicial bosom heave like a movie
star's, and eye glisten like a bridegroom's. The Waldorf began to fill up with recently manicured iron
workers from Pittsburgh, loggers from Duluth, copper

T. Suffern Tailer   S. S. Howland

The men who made the Horse Show a success in the Nineties

WATER POLO AT THE OLD MANHATTAN ATHLETIC CLUB

THE FUNERAL OF GENERAL SHERMAN

For many years our most popular citizen, passing through Madison Square

RECRUITING IN UNION SQUARE FOR THE SPANISH-AMERICAN WAR

miners from Michigan, brewers from Milwaukee and St. Louis, and other gentry, who thought a cotillion was something to eat, but who could sign checks with numbers on them as long as a Santa Fe freight train.

The Waldorf was a big success and emissaries of the W. W.'s approached the camp of the J. J.'s with propositions to extend the premises. The negotiations resulted in the mammoth Waldorf-Astoria, the premier hotel of the golden Nineties, and still a notable institution. The elder Mrs. Astor packed her black velvet dress and pearl necklace in a suitcase and rode in her brougham up to the new Renaissance chateau at 65th Street, away from the politicians and the hat shops and art stores that were beginning to let plate glass windows into private house basements; and from the gambling houses with bronze barricades in their vestibules and collections of old masters on their walls.

The advent of the Waldorf-Astoria marked the partial eclipse of the famous Delmonico's, still at 26th Street. Its gorgeous ball room accommodated larger crowds than the exclusive confines of the renowned old restaurant, and its lofty public rooms, including the celebrated "Peacock Row" afforded a *mise en scène* not to be neglected.

The renowned Inspector Williams, of Tenderloin fame, was a candidate for legislative office in 1895. He, like Devery, was a picturesque figure with a turn for epigram. He was opposed by certain politicians because of his police record. To a reporter who asked if he intended to withdraw, he replied:

"You've heard of Jumbo? Well, harness Jumbo with straps, and hitch him onto me with chains and you couldn't drag me out of the race."

"BILL" DEVERY, CHIEF OF POLICE

"They say because I own a little three-story brick house that I'm crookeder than Pearl Street. They call me 'Clubber Williams.' I was good enough and big enough to club folks when there was a dangerous row on, but in times of peace they denounce me for it. It's the way of the world. Stones are always thrown at the best tree in the orchard. You don't find any dents in the crab apples."

The Inspector concluded by remarking that if the enforcement of the Sunday law was carried to its logical conclusion there wouldn't be a street car running in the city. He also anticipated the Eighteenth Amendment by thirty years in remarking, "There's no moral law against a drink, and you can't force a man not to do that which he don't think a great moral sin."

Perhaps the most picturesque figure involved in the reform movement that began with Dr. Parkhurst's campaign against the Tammany administration, and the Lexow inquiry that resulted from it, was "Bill" Devery, characterized by Mayor Van Wyck as "the best Chief of Police New York ever had". Although Devery defaulted in actually achieving this laudable distinction, there is no doubt that his vernacular and a certain rude common sense that prompted it, made him the most talked about office-holder in the local government of his time.

Mr. Devery's usual preamble to a State pronunciamento was the phrase "Touchin' on and appertainin' to". This rhetorical formula appeared regularly in the newspapers as a prelude to certain sage observations on police, politics and social order that edified and amused their readers. One of Devery's aphorisms "touchin' on and appertainin' to" the men under his command was

318

that historic declaration, worthy of perpetuation in bronze over the door of Headquarters, "A policeman has got a right to have some sense".

"I removed McCloskey from the Detective Bureau because he got too chesty. Titus will do better than McCloskey did, unless he gets the 'handsome' habit, and tries to wear a beaten track to the tailor's shop", was another characteristic utterance.

Speaking of the activities of Wm. Travers Jerome, then on the bench, Devery said:

"He's like the rhinoceros up in the park. Every time he goes down under the water he comes up with a gulp, and blows it all out over everybody".

There were few subjects that escaped his attention. His philosophy covered all subjects:

"When you dig a political grave, dig a deep one. It's a most disgustin' sight to see one of them dead ones kickin' the sod aside and crowdin' in with the live ones".

"The people are goin' to nail that Croker outfit, one by one, till they're all against the wall with their hides dryin' ".

"Three or four years ago Roosevelt started out to smash all the trusts but some ward-man gave him the tip and he closed up".

To his cohorts on the way to the Democratic Convention at Saratoga he advanced this counsel:

"If you boys get there cryin' for bromo-seltzer and ice water somebody's likely to come back to New York and gossip about you. No decent man will take more than a quart, unless he absolutely needs it as a medicine".

Animadverting on his successor in office, he remarked: "The present Police Department is a chop-suey administration".

As Deputy Police Commissioner, Devery presided at the trials of police misdemeanants and the *obiter dicta* delivered from his seat of office was as good as a play. To a citizen who complained that an officer had refused to arrest a woman on his charge, Devery said, "It takes two to do the solicitin', a lady and a gentleman. The lady won't solicit if you don't make goo-goo eyes. If you hadn't been making goo-goo eyes she wouldn't have troubled you. Anyway, I guess you were excited. Call the next case."

In the case of a policeman charged with firing a revolver at a prisoner, Devery said, "Twenty days' pay for not hittin' him. Next time you hit him". To a policeman charged with intoxication while on duty, he said, "If you wanted to go on a bum, why didn't you get a surgeon to give you a sick leave for a couple o' days? Anyone would 'a' done it".

While on the subject of police, I must not overlook that famous legal fiction the "Raines Law Sandwich". This mysterious form of nourishment was prescribed by law to be the concomitant, and sworn ally, of every glass of beer legally served on a Sunday within the precincts of every first-class city in the sovereign State of New York. According to law, liquor could be served on a Sunday, only in hotels, with a meal, and as the Supreme Court in its wisdom had declared that a sandwich constituted a meal, it became, *ipso facto,* the most widely circulated pabulum in all the Sundays of its existence. I say "circulated" because the Raines Law Sandwich was never consumed. It went the rounds of the so-called diners, eyed suspiciously, con-

temptuously or curiously as a relic of medieval legisla-
tion. It attained an adamantine quality that would
have fitted it for a constituent part of a fortress, while
retaining the outward semblance of an article of food.
Arctic explorers studied its possibilities as a substitute
for pemican. Chemists assayed it with a view to de-
termining whether it was animal, vegetable or mineral,
and a rat, excluded from other nourishment, starved to
death in its company.

Consistent with our gilded era came the "lobster
palaces" of Long Acre Square. These resplendent resorts were the successors of the old oyster houses that
used to satisfy the simpler tastes of an earlier age. The
old-time theatregoer used to regale himself and his consort with a plate of "half shells" and toby of cream ale,
of delicious memory. The oyster-house was more
notable for the excellence of its fare than for its interior
decorations. As time passed, however, there was a demand for a more diversified menu and more sumptuous environment. Such resorts as Burns's and Jack
Dunstan's responded to it as in an earlier era O'Neill's
and Bristol's and Dorlon's had done a mile or so to
the southward.

In the early nineties the Astor estate had on their
hands the vacated premises of the Flandrau Carriage
Company on Broadway, just north of 42nd Street.
There were no eager clamorers for it, as 42nd Street
was then regarded as a kind of dead-line to active business. The building long remained idle until the Astors
entered into negotiations with the Shanley brothers,
who had served a novitiate in restaurants further downtown, for its tenancy. For the new tenants, the Astors
made lavish expenditures on the structure—gilding,

321

chandeliers, luxurious carpets, elegant fittings—all without stint, and the first "lobster palace", as it was afterward dubbed, was opened.

It was an immediate success. The playgoers, demimonde, "wine buyers", the "sports", the stock brokers, and the tired business men trooped across the 42nd Street car tracks that were once symbolic of a barbed wire fence to indulge in the "Fish", "Game", "Oysters" and "Chops" that were emblazoned in bronze on the outer walls and to enjoy the orchestra, one of the first introduced into New York's restaurants. Strangers flocked there to see the new centre of gay life, and altogether it became an institution. Although the Olympia, two blocks farther up was a more spectacular affair, Shanley's was really the first trail blazer of this new centre of night life.

The success of Shanley's did not remain unnoticed among possible rivals and it was not long before Rector, the Chicago restaurateur, opened another resort on the block above, under the sign of a luminous green dragon, that was also an early landmark. Later on was erected the Pabst Hotel on the south end of what is now the *"Times"* building flatiron. This was perhaps the narrowest structure devoted to hotel purposes in the city. Its first boniface was Jimmy Reagan, later to manage the Hotel Knickerbocker on the opposite corner, pleasantly remembered as headquarters of the country club, presided over by Max Parrish's *Old King Cole*.

None of these resorts attracted the gastronomes that haunted the aromatic halls of Delmonico's, the Brunswick or the other houses of early renown. The race of gourmets was passing, game was becoming scarce, the canvas back and the terrapin on the way out, wines no longer had their McAllisters, Sam Wards, Truaxes *et al.,* to discourse learnedly on their bouquets and the epicure was no longer abroad.

BAR TENDING AS A PROFESSION

It was just about the beginning of this era that marked the decadence of the Bowery as a thoroughfare of international celebrity. Charley Hoyt's ditty of *"The Bowery"* was its swan-song. McGlory's; Owney Geohagen's "Slide"; McGurk's "Suicide Hall" were on their last legs. The saloons and barrooms were all changing into "Cafes" and "Wine Rooms". One could still see relics of earlier days at Harry Johnson's "Little Jumbo" saloon near Grand Street, which had a sign before the door dating back to the time when a bartender had to serve an apprenticeship of several years. The bulk of the trade was then in mixed drinks, the drinks that carried the fame of American beverages around the world. Bartenders had black moustaches with waxed ends in those delectable days, and wore ornamental elastics on their sleeves to keep their cuffs from getting into the drinks. The sign, aforesaid, was a pyramid about four feet high. On the sides were the names of about one hundred mixed drinks. The pyramid tapered from the long-named mixed drink at the bottom to the short ones like "gin fizz" having fewer letters nearer the top. Oh, that this pyramid were as those of the Pharaohs, of aye enduring stone! And the legends thereon. Let me muse over them, as fond memory brings their glowing letters once more into view. Many of them are classics of concoctional nomenclature and as a faithful historian I must endeavor to reproduce one side of this pyramid to a generation that knows not the "Little Jumbo".

GIN FIZZ
RAINBOW
EGG NOGG
ALABAZAM
GIN RICKEY
ROYAL FIZZ
MINT JULEP
SHANDYGAFF
TOM & JERRY
TOM COLLINS
POUSSE CAFE
BRAIN-DUSTER
CLARET PUNCH
WHISKEY SOUR
BRANDY TODDY
HAPPY MOMENT
WHISKEY SLING
PORT SANGAREE
CATAWBA PUNCH
SHERRY COBBLER
ABSINTHE FRAPPE
HANNIBAL HAMLIN
SITTING-BULL FIZZ
MANHATTAN COOLER
NEW ORLEANS PUNCH
MANHATTAN COCKTAIL

A bartender in those days was a combination of artist and scientist, who was looked upon with some awe by mere statesmen, bankers and leaders in other professions. To know just how many dashes of lemon to introduce into a Manhattan Cooler was no small accomplishment. Great friendships have sprung up therefrom between white jackets and their steady

Steamship "St. Paul" Goes Ashore off Long Branch

THE FIRST OF NEW YORK'S LOBSTER PALACES
Shanley's at extreme right and Rector's in center. 1890.

The Old Time Melodrama "Under the Gaslight"

One of the first offers of Augustin Daly

patrons. A bartender who knew the exact proportions of a Supreme Court Judge's tipple might expect any favor from His Honor, short of causing the latter's impeachment.

It was the Horse Show that brought the most brilliant assemblage to the Waldorf-Astoria of early days. The social world and its apers and gapers jammed its dining rooms and cafes to repletion. George Boldt, who had heretofore been a minor hotel personage, now became a great metropolitan figure, and his head waiter "Oscar", a despot, to whom millionaires truckled, and on whom haughty dames, with heraldic devices on their broughams, fawned. In those days it was necessary to combine cash, diplomacy and social position for a central table at a Waldorf's Horse Show supper. There were no cover charges for all and sundry, and only the elite had a chance to bask under the chrysanthemums that embowered the gorgeous public rooms of the hotel.

It was just about this time, too, that the chrysanthemum was introduced to New York society. It was a great rage, even men wearing it as a boutonniere in their blue kersey overcoats. The yellow chrysanthemum was the floral symbol of the Princeton football team and the Polo Grounds were alive with it at the great Thanksgiving Day games, which first gave the football its present vogue amongst the public.

The Horse Show revolutionized our local attitude in equine affairs. Prior to its advent, the trotting horse was king. All the big bugs of finance and society had their fast trotters and sulkies, and the trotter and pacer was *the* American contribution to the equine species. But with the Horse Show a new cult arose. Now all the talk was about hackney cobs, polo ponies and hunters. It was no longer speed that was demanded, but stamina, form and smartness. People who never before saw a horse take a hurdle now watched performers negotiate a five-bar gate. English experts were imported to judge the entries, and the arena was dotted with ruddy faced grooms in whipcord from British stables. The Horse Show also brought in its train certain chevaliers d'industrie who found unique pickings here. Typical of these was the notorious Baron Greenbaum, whose knowledge of horseflesh gained as a stable-boy in the Emperor of Austria's stables, placed him in the good graces of the wealthy novices of the Show, who submitted docilely to an unmerciful plucking by the pseudo-Baron until a term on Blackwells Island put a period to his activities. Others of the same ilk found the Horse Show a climacteric to careers usually begun as hostlers in the stables and riding schools of Warsaw, Vienna and points east. Indeed the Horse Show had as many camp-followers, fakers and sharpers as any "big tent" circus in the "sticks".

Among the cruelties that used to be practiced on horses one of the most atrocious was docking their tails. It was considered ultra-fashionable by the progenitors of the same people who are slaughtering off our fur-bearing animals, to drive horses with mutilated tails. It was a misdemeanor punishable by a year in prison or $500 fine, or both, to maim a horse in this fashion, but there was no law covering the possession of the unfortunate animal, therefore he was not an uncommon sight on the streets and in the parks.

The Society for the Prevention of Cruelty to Animals under its president, John P. Haynes, however, took

vigorous measures to suppress this practice. It offered
a standing reward of $100 for the arrest and convic-
tion, or for simply the information that would lead to
the same, of anybody docking a horse's tail. Among
the convictions obtained was one against the groom of
a Hungarian Count, well known at the Horse Show.

According to the officers of the S. P. C. A., women
encouraged the docking of horses' tails more than men.
One of the officers said—"The custom is dying out in
England. The Prince of Wales denounced the crop-
ping of dog's ears and tails, and it is no longer the
fashion to crop them. It is thought that it will be
only a question of time when he will pronounce against
dock-tailed horses." The late J. A. Mitchell was also
a savage fighter against this custom and the pages of
Life fairly sizzled with the scorching pictures printed
against this abhorrent practice.

Horse racing occupied a far more important place in
sport in America than it does today. The opening of
the racing season in New York was an event of almost
national interest. It marked the development of the
chrysalis of winter racing on dubious tracks into the
brilliant butterfly of legitimate sport participated in by
leading men of all classes. The Brooklyn Handicap
opened the season. It was run at the Gravesend Race
Track, owned by the Dwyer Brothers, successful
Brooklyn butchers. During the summer, racing moved
to Sheepshead Bay, Monmouth Park and Morris Park.
All manner of vehicles were used to transport the enthusiasts to the tracks, besides the regular railroad
lines. Fashionable tandems and dog-carts, family carriages, hired hacks in various stages of decay, and ultra-
fashionable brakes and buckboards came over the same

road with their occupants bent on the same objects, the seeing of sport and the making of money, for all the tracks had bookmaking rings, and fortunes changed hands on big race days.

One of the great sporting events of a period much devoted to equine affairs was the Salvator-Tenny match race at Sheepshead Bay. Tenny was one of the romantic phenomena of the turf, having been picked up as a yearling, for a few dollars by David Tenny Pulsifer and developed into a great race-horse. Salvator, the Man o' War of his time, was just a nose too good for him, however, and brought home the bacon, in one of the most exciting races in the history of the local turf. The poet-laureate of this occasion was Ella Wheeler Wilcox, whose "How Salvator Won" was a standby of the contemporary "recitationist":

"There's a roar from the crowd like the ocean in storm
  As close to my saddle leaps Tenny's great form
  One more mighty plunge, and with knee, limb and hand
  I lift my horse first by a nose past the stand;
  We are under the string now—the great race is done
  And Salvator, Salvator, Salvator won!

  Cheer! hoar headed patriarchs; cheer loud, I say
  'Tis the race of the century witnessed today!
  Though ye live twice the space that allotted to men
  You never will see such a grand race again
  Let the shouts of the populace roar like the surf,
  For Salvator, Salvator, King of the turf!"

This lethal balderdash shared the honors of epic song at "surprise" parties with "The Charge of the Light Brigade", "Casey at the Bat" and "The Face on the Barroom Floor". There was one phrase, however, now current in sporting parlance, that the golden Nineties was spared—"the greatest race horse of all time", "the greatest boxer of all time", and the greatest this, that and the other of "all time". This phrase is ineffably silly to an old-timer, who has seen champions come and go. Even the lyric Ella limited her classic to the span of a century.

There were two spectacular figures on the turf in the Nineties, who succeeded to the aureole of "plunger" that had been worn in the previous decade by the famous "Plunger Walton". These were "Pittsburgh Phil" and Riley Grannan, who used to be pointed out to awe-stricken admirers as the big bettors of the turf. Pittsburgh Phil's real name was George W. Smith, and his early career had been as a brush-maker in Pittsburgh. He was remarkable for the imperturbability with which he won or lost enormous wagers. This superhuman control over his emotions probably cost him his life, for he died at an early age and it was said that his shattered nervous system hastened his end.

Riley Grannan had been an elevator boy in a St. Louis hotel at four dollars a week. Within a few years he had wagered as high as seventy thousand dollars on a single race. He made book in the famous match race between Domino and Henry of Navarre, and gave 6 to 10 against Domino, the favorite. He took in sixty-five thousand dollars of the public's money and stood to pay out one hundred and five thousand if Domino won. He then went the round of the betting ring and placed thirty thousand dollars on Henry of Navarre against forty-two thousand. But there was a dead heat, and in the division that followed the young plunger was nineteen thousand dollars ahead, and not nearly as satisfied as if he had lost. Pittsburgh Phil kept his money, but Riley Grannan vindicated the dictum of Davis, the big English bookmaker, who remarked on Walton's winnings, "It makes no difference, it will all come back to us." And so it did.

CHAPTER XI.
TROTTING HORSES.—FLEETWOOD PARK. PASSING OF CARRIAGES, ETC.

THE equivalent of the space now occupied by automobile advertising in the papers was in the nineties given over to horse dealers, carriage and harness manufacturers. East 24th Street, near the old Bull's Head Hotel, on Third Avenue, was a great horse trading centre in those days, as was also Broadway and Seventh Avenue from Longacre Square to Central Park. The Brewster carriage factory and Flandrau's were in the latter region. These were the last days of such ads as—

"ELEGANT CARRIAGES OF THE BEST CLASS
Suspension Victorias, Cabriolets, Coupe, T. Carts, Mail Phaetons, Stanhope Gigs, Two-Wheelers, Landaulets, Rockaways, Surreys, Dos-a-Dos, Buckboards, Vis-a-vis, Spiders, Depot Wagons, Broughams,"
to mention only a few vehicles of which there were as many varieties as there are pickles.

Macy used to have a department for harness and saddlery where were sold "road harness", "coach harness", "physicians' harness, silver mounted", "riding and driving whips", "crops", "saddles" and "horse clothing".

How curious this all sounds today with our "step on it," "blowouts," "carburetor trouble," "all six" and other mechanistic terms of the modern driver. How curious this jargon would sound to the old-time horseman.

The passing of horseflesh from the city's streets has been in certain respects a desirable consummation. Horses suffered terribly when they were almost the sole means of vehicular transportation on surface roads, not alone at the hands of avaricious and inhuman masters, but also owing to the extremes of climate. Their struggles through snow and on icy pavements is too well known to require historic witness, while the sweltering summer sun took toll of many equine victims of stupidity and greed.

Among the many thousands of horses that did service in pre-motor days there were several well-cared for and noteworthy types. The police horses were always the pride of the mounted squad, as were the fire engine horses only recently banished to less strenuous fields. Among commercial quadrupeds the finest to be seen were the magnificent Percherons that were used principally by the beer brewers to haul the great wagons loaded with casks. These massive and splendid animals were very expensive, costing upward of one thousand dollars each to purchase. Most of them were iron-gray, with flowing manes and tails. They have completely vanished from the town now, and may almost be classed with the pre-historic monsters of scientific research.

The year of 1897 saw the closing of Fleetwood Park trotting track, which stood in rural serenity for many years, in the area now between 165th and 167th Streets and Webster and Sherman Avenues. Many famous trotting cracks showed their paces on this one-mile course, including *"Goldsmith Maid"*, *"Dexter"* and *"Maud S"*. Robert Bonner had his stable in the vicinity, and often

W. T. Smedley in Harper's Weekly.

The supper room of the Waldorf sp

ow

'or this purpose during Horse Show

held the reins over *"Maud S."* in a spin around the course as did W. H. Vanderbilt with *"Early Rose"* and *"Aldine"*. The course was leased by the Gentlemen's Driving Club, its members including such famous roadsters as Bonner, Jerome, Vanderbilt, Frank Work, George Law, Jay Gould, John D. and William Rockefeller and others.

During its last days Fleetwood Park resounded to the cheers of the trotting fans (and a more rabid lot were never known) watching some record-breaking performance of *"Nancy Hanks"*, *"Directum"* or *"Stamboul"*, under the veteran guidance of "Bud" Doble or John M. Gears, both not long since passed to the happy trotting tracks where perhaps some celestial *"Maud S."* or *"Simol"* is forever going the rounds of the "Maud Circuit".

Almost in the style of a best seller of detective fiction was the Guldensuppe case, which provided an absorbing, if somewhat sordid criminal narrative in real life in 1897. The dismembered torso and limbs of a powerfully built man about thirty-five years old were discovered that summer floating in the East River, the separate parts wrapped in cheap oilcloth of a kind commonly used in the poorer class of kitchens. Owing to the absence of a head, the chances of identification of the remains were regarded by the police as exceedingly remote, and their efforts were concentrated on tracing the history of the oilcloth. Inquiries among dealers revealed the manufacturer of this particular type of oilcloth, and as it was of a pattern not in great demand, the hunt, after a few small retailers had been investigated, finally culminated in a shop in Astoria where it was ascertained the oilcloth had been sold to an unknown stout German woman, and there the trail ended.

341

With what must have been regarded by the perpetrators of the deed as a curious example of the irony of fate, it transpired that inquiries had been set on foot for a masseur named Guldensuppe employed in the Murray Hill Baths on Forty-second Street, who had been missing for several days. A description of the body being broadcast, a number of his co-workers, after viewing the remains, readily identified them as those of Guldensuppe, his associates being quite familiar with his stripped figure after his four years' employment in the Baths. It later developed that the cunning device of encasing the head in plaster of Paris and dropping it in the East River had been employed to forestall the possibility of an identification.

The scent was now hot, and it led to the apartments on Ninth Avenue of Mrs. Nack, a married lady, and midwife, where Guldensuppe had been a lodger and incidentally a paramour. Mrs. Nack was so lavish in her favors as to disregard the traditional stage dramatist's "triangle", and enlarge the geometrical figure to that of a quadrangle, of which the added corner was occupied by a dupe named Martin Thorn who, as a rival for the affections of Mrs. Nack, had incurred a number of beatings from the massive Guldensuppe and cherished a burning hatred towards him. The lady, it appeared, had also been the recipient of similar attentions from the occasionally peeved bath rubber and finding them intolerable, connived with Thorn for his rival's removal. Herr Nack, the husband, appears to have been a negligible quantity. The surviving members of this menage were arrested, and Mrs. Nack being identified as the purchaser of the oilcloth, it behooved her to avert·the extreme limit of the law by turning

State's evidence against Thorn and revealing how she had lured her inconvenient lover to a house in Woodside, Long Island, where Thorn had shot him and then dismembered the body, after which they both had disposed of the ghastly relics at different points in the river. This testimony had the effect of seating Thorn in the electric chair, and gaining for Mrs. Nack a twenty-year sentence. The newspapers, some years ago, recorded her release, a chastened and repentant sinner.

The case reflected great credit on the Detective Bureau, then under the very capable Captain Stephen O'Brien. The police department had undergone a severe raking over in the recent Lexow Investigation and under the reform administration of Mayor Strong were on their mettle to prove that their ancient efficiency had been restored under the commissionership of Theodore Roosevelt and his confreres.

Another murder even more fiendish and cruel was the heartless poisoning of young Helen Potts, a mere slip of a girl, student in a school for young ladies by Carlyle Harris, a young medical student to whom she had been secretly married.

At the time of her death there seemed no suspicion of foul play and but for the subsequent discovery of this marriage the murderer might have gone unshrined of his crime.

Helen occasionally suffered from slight headaches, and to relieve this annoyance Harris prescribed six capsules which were compounded at a reputable drug store and contained only quinine and 1-6 grain of morphine. At least five of them did. The sixth had enough morphine in it to kill a dozen persons. He told Helen to take them, one each night, before going to bed and to talk to no one after taking them. He then left the city for a few days.

When the sixth capsule was reached the effect was immediate and the seriousness of Helen's condition caused medical help to be hurriedly summoned. In the face of an unmistakable case of lethal poisoning, the doctors were puzzled to account for such a condition as a result of a capsule containing only 1-6 grain morphine, admittedly harmless. Harris was summoned as the name "C. W. Harris, Student," appeared on the prescription and told of his connection with the case, which seemed innocent enough. His utter indifference to the dying agonies of a young girl, with whom he was supposed to be deeply in love, disgusting as it was, did not, of course, warrant the physicians in accusing him of murder. Helen was buried a few days after. Carlyle was absent, fearing that he might "break down." It was a nine days' wonder and was practically forgotten when the circumstance of his secret marriage to Helen was suddenly discovered by a *World* reporter a few months later among the records at the City Hall.

Public interest in Harris suddenly took a menacing turn. The district attorney arranged for an autopsy of Helen's body. Morphine was discovered in deadly quantities, but no quinine as was in the original form in five capsules. Young Harris at once appeared before the authorities, and with a candor at once disarming, announced that anything he could do to aid in clearing up what the police called a mystery he would be glad to do. After a slight delay, the district attorney accepted the public-spirited offer of young Harris, but not in the same friendly spirit. He had been indicted by the grand jury on a charge of first degree murder.

William T. Jerome, who was afterwards to achieve quite a spectacular and sensational career as District Attorney, appeared for the defense. Francis L. Wellman was the prosecutor. Dr. Allan McLane Hamilton, who performed the autopsy, refers feelingly in his memoirs to this pathetic event. He gave the particulars of his investigation to the jury.

Harris' defense suddenly began to crumble. As one damning fact after another was brought to light—one line of defense after another riddled and demolished—the appearance of Jerome suddenly became alarming. Perhaps a belated realization of how completely he had been hoodwinked by his client was slowly seeping into his consciousness, and when the verdict of "Guilty!" was rendered, he collapsed utterly. Wellman must have been strongly affected also, as he again and again returns in his published works to the scenes and incidents of this trial. Of all his experiences in court the climax of this extraordinary murder trial was evidently the most spectacular and dramatic moment of them all.

Harris died with a lie on his lips. He stoutly protested his innocence. Yet the Court of Appeals upheld the verdict; Governor Flower, having access to still other and more convincing testimony than was permitted the jury—including unpublished remarks of Helen to her closest friends—refused to commute the sentence.

During the trial it was proven that Harris was by no means the saint his friends claimed he was. His secret life was unspeakably cruel and immoral testimony was adduced showing that he had suggested other nefarious schemes which had not been carried out, mainly by reason of his failure in the present case.

Poison murders are all marked by a devilish cunning that promises every success. But they invariably overlook some apparently innocent trifle which proves their undoing. In the Harris case it was the secret marriage. That furnished the clue for the motive. And his execution followed.

The East River front, following the example of Sutton Place, is gradually resuming its rank as a habitat of the gentry which it had a century or more ago when the Astors, the Gracies and the Schermerhorns graced its shores with their summer mansions. Among the reclamations in order is that recently in process in the neighborhood of Corcoran's Roost, which thirty years ago still flourished, but is now part of Tudor City.

The specific centre of this delectable region was a ramshackle tenement at No. 317 East 40th Street, the residence of John Corcoran, the founder of the Corcoran dynasty. Corcoran first settled on the aboriginal rocks of the neighborhood, and established squatter's sovereignty by building a shanty out of driftwood from the river. Here he reared a family, and as the family increased the shanty expanded. In time Corcoran acquired enough money to go into the trucking business, for though a tough citizen he was not a loafer or idler. As his sons grew up they married into the families of the neighboring squatters and the result was an autocracy of Corcorans that established a reign of law and disorder, both of their own making all through 40th Street to the East River.

In the Nineties the original Corcoran was a patriarch

and came to be known as "Genteel" Jamie Corcoran, a
bit of delicate satire which he resented by breaking the
head of "Liver" Slade, who first gave him the name,
with an iron bar. But the name stuck and Corcoran
was often so addressed from a distance.

The favorite mode of warfare against the hereditary
enemies of the Roost—the police—was by the descent
of bricks from its roofs. The stiff police helmets then
worn were designed with such a contingency in view
and prevented undue mortality among the wearers. A
German policeman caused the first breach in the Corcoran despotism. When he first came on beat the
scandalized residents sent a message to the police station:

"Take the Dutch ———— off the bate. He will get
kilt if he stays." A member of the clan "Pickled"
Corcoran, so called for obvious reasons, was shot by the
resolute cop in self defense, and after numerous other
encounters with attendant lacerations, suffered mainly
by the local belligerents, the indignity of a "furriner"
as supervisor of the district was perforce tolerated.

The elder Corcoran's last appearance before a Magis-
trate was in 1897, when he appeared as witness in a
case of illegal registration. Corcoran insisted on shaking hands with the justice, and making a speech.

"I'm 78 years old", he said, "and I've been at the
Roost forty-eight years, come St. Patrick's day. I'm
Corcoran, of Corcoran's Roost, and time was when it
was in the papers every week. But it's very respectable
now, yer anner. It's full three years"—he sighed regretfully—"since so much as half a brick's been t'rown
out of me windies".

The problem of the slum tenement which is at present so acutely before us, was attacked with some vigor during the nineties. As I have before remarked, most of the small East Side parks were the result of the intelligent action of the authorities in the attempt to ameliorate the lot of the slum dweller. Mulberry Bend Park, one of these, occupies the site of the notorious "Five Points", an early classic among New York infernal regions. Another celebrated locality was Mackerelville, which passed out in the Nineties. It was around Avenue A, south of 14th Street and was in its time the home of the Irishmen who peddled fish from wagons about town. They lived side by side, not always amicably with the rag and bottle men whose bells years ago were far more in evidence than now-a-days. Some of the precursors of modern Lenox Avenue also became fragrant memories then, among them Bleecker Street's "Burnt Rag", "Black and Tan" and "House of Blazes" and "Niggar Alley" on Thompson Street.

The upper West side, until our time, boasted of "Hell's Kitchen" on 39th Street, "The Gap" on 28th Street, which contained a savory slum called "The Tub of Blood". There was something of "Shantytown" still left, in our decade, notably along Central Park West and when the Majestic Hotel at 72nd Street was built it adjoined a rural acre on which reposed a squatter's shanty with the usual appendage of styes, coops and other shelters for domestic fauna.

Few people have any idea how the advance of sanitary measures has contributed to the remarkable growth of New York in the last thirty years. The enormous skyscrapers, the huge tenements, and the almost inhuman congestion now prevalent would be impossible

The Dog Dealer. A Familiar Sight in the Nineties

The Columbian Celebration, 1892. Military Parade on Fifth Avenue

COLUMBIAN CELEBRATION. PONTIFICAL HIGH MASS AT SAINT PATRICK'S CATHEDRAL

WHERE THE TURKISH CIGARETTE CRAZE ORIGINATED

The Syrian Colony in lower Washington Street now wholly given over to Armenians.

without the plumbing, sewerage, water pressure, etc., of modern times. Pasteurization of milk, filtration of water, and the common use of disinfectants in the household are all parts of the growth of the last three decades. The ravages of diphtheria, croup, cholera-infantum and other scourges of childhood have been almost completely nullified by the scientific discoveries during that period. Before then there was an almost incredible neglect of the tenement house population. The physical examination of the child, now part of the public school function—I understand—was unknown. Dirty slates and sponges were part of the educational process, and the average pupil was a superb germ-carrier.

The prosperous New Yorker seated on a seashore verandah, during the heated term, was regaled by the illustrated weeklies with pictorial representations of "Tenement House Dwellers Seeking Relief on the Roofs", "The Recent Hot Wave on the East Side", and other comfortable spectacles. Touched by pity he immediately sends a check for $5 to the "Free Ice Fund" of the *Herald* newspaper and settles back in his porch chair to enjoy the pictures of the "Steamboat Explosion on the Hudson Lines", or the "Mad Dog Scare on Oak Street". The evening paper aforesaid used to print columns of harrowing descriptions of the "homes" of some of the recipients of the free ice, and these cool crystals represented practically their only domestic luxury.

In the early decades of the nineteenth century, New York's supreme disregard of public sanitation brought upon the city occasional epidemics of a decimating character. The open drains, the cesspools, the swill-clogged gutters, the peregrinating pigs, poultry and other domestic fauna which astonished the foreign observer, all favored the visitation of plagues from the tropics and the Orient of a terrifying nature. These were only mitigated by New York's admirable situation on the ocean and at the confluence of broad rivers. As the city outgrew these barbarous conditions, and a vigorous Board of Health took control of its hygienic destinies, these old plagues were forgotten or became legendary, and its only menace of this type of contagion was from incoming ships. Certain signs persisted however, reminiscent of the jolly old days of blood-letting, boluses, allopathic doses, "night air", closed windows, etc., in the nostrums commonly sold in the "Deutsche Apotheke" or "Pharmacie Française" whose colored globes were beacons to the sufferer from common or garden "bellyache". The "Sun Cholera Mixture" was one of these, and there was no lack of competitive panaceas liberally compounded with opium or its derivatives, such as laudanum or morphine. In fact, one could purchase ten cents worth of laudanum and with parts of Jamaica ginger, alcohol, peppermint, oil of cloves, mustard, or other "warming" ingredient, compound a home-made remedy that would stupefy the most recalcitrant intestine.

The New Yorker felt himself well guarded by a vigilant quarantine against foreign epidemics and it was with a considerable shock that a recrudescence of an old-time "cholera scare" assailed him.

In 1892 New York had a cholera scare similar to those which had earlier in the city's history been sporadic visitors. This latest menace was brought over by the immigrant ship *"Moravia"* from Hamburg, and was characterized by that ship's doctor as "Cholerine" which is the first stage of the true Asiatic article. Inasmuch as twenty-two people had died on the ten-day voyage to New York, the ship was ordered to the lower bay for quarantine. "Hardly the oldest inhabitant remembers such a sight as is now presented off the quarantine station, near Fort Wadsworth", said a contemporary. "A whole fleet of European steamers, and some from southern ports as well, awaiting the inspection of health officers, is lying at anchor off the wooded heights of Staten Island". Another plague ship was the *"Scandia"* which reported thirty-two deaths during the voyage.

The efforts to stamp out the pest on the infected ships were marked, of course, by great inconvenience to the passengers. The cabin passengers on the crack liner *"Normannia"*, on which nothing untoward had been reported, were subjected to great discomfort, owing to the inability of the authorities either to permit the vessel to pass up to the city or to remove the passengers from it. After a good deal of difficulty provision was made for them through the generosity of J. P. Morgan who purchased the abandoned steamer *"Stonington"* and placed it at the disposal of the health authorities and the *"Normannia's"* passengers were transferred to her. Queer fellow this Morgan; he seemed to be the only man in New York who could keep his head in a panic be it cholera or Wall Street.

Meanwhile the State authorities had purchased Fire Island for $210,000, including a large summer hotel with a capacity of one thousand persons, and proposed to maroon the incoming passengers there. Violent opposition was manifested by the citizens of Islip and Bay Shore who, gathering to the number of one thousand, many of them armed, prevented by force the landing of the *"Normannia's"* passengers from the steamboat *"Cepheus"*, which, the *"Stonington"* proving unseaworthy, was employed to transfer them to the island. In this inhuman proceeding the citizens were aided by an injunction granted by Judge Barnard, restraining the Governor and health authorities from landing persons from an infected ship on Fire Island. All efforts to appease the mob proved for two days unavailing, the passengers on the *"Cepheus"* meanwhile suffering every imaginable horror, being not only overcrowded but without proper food and unable to sleep. Finally, Governor Flower ordered two regiments of the National Guard and the Naval Reserve to go to the scene of the disturbance and on the same day Judge Barnard's injunction was revoked and the passengers released from their confinement and landed on the island, where after a day or two they were permitted to depart for their homes.

The World's Fair in commemoration of the Discovery of America was the subject of an acrimonious contest between New York and Chicago for the seat of its location. It was thought for a long time that New York's claim was indisputable and its victory certain. So certain, in fact, that a large unoccupied section of land just north of Central Park was tentatively chosen as the site for the Fair and a boom in real estate resulted that when Chicago was finally chosen, brought many adventurous "realtors" to grief.

The loss of the Fair to New York was the result of political machinations in Congress. The Republicans were in no mood to let the fat pickings that were certain to accrue fall into the hands of Tammany—the real estate contracts, the building grafts, the amusement concessions and all the multitudinous items of possible profit. The cry was then, as it is today "Anything to beat Tammany."

The peculiar American faculty of haphazard enterprise was responsible for the delay of nearly a year in opening the World's Fair in Chicago. An odd reminiscence of this delay is seen in what is known as the Columbian half dollar minted by the government. This was first put out in 1892 and carries a premium, but on account of the postponement of the opening it was again minted the following year in large numbers as a World Fair souvenir and is still occasionally encountered in circulation.

New York's Columbian celebration, however, came off on time and was attended with some very spectacular features. Perhaps the most interesting of these was the rendezvous of the squadrons of nearly all the European navies on the Hudson, and the land parade of their crews and marines on Fifth Avenue. It was in this latter that the native had what was probably his first view of the regulation Prussian "goose-step" done by professionals, as the German contingent marched by to the strains of the "Wacht am Rhein". Very picturesque too were the tars of the British quota, in their broad brimmed straw hats, looking for all the world like the "shiver my timbers" salts of the Dibdin —T. P. Cooke—"Black Eyed Susan"—vintages.

The World's Fair also resulted in a considerable reduction in the running time of trains between New York and Chicago. Previously, a flat twenty-four hour schedule had been accounted the best possible for the distance, but a few months before the fair opened the New York Central Railroad put on its famous "Empire State Express", which, with the usual modesty of our railroads, it labelled "the fastest train in the world", a somewhat equivocal statement, considering the fact that there were at least a score of trains in England and France running on a faster schedule although, perhaps, for a shorter distance.

The "Empire State Express", however, proved so practicable and popular, and was moreover such an advertising stunt, that when the Fair opened another "crack" train was put on the line, called "The Exposition Flyer", which ran to Chicago in twenty hours, and was the precursor of the present "Limited" now so popular. The "Flyer" ran throughout the period of the Fair, and the management attempted to continue it thereafter as a regular train, but in the then condition of American railroading it was regarded as a somewhat hazardous *tour de force* of transportation and the service was discontinued. The next attempt to better the twenty-four hour time was some years later, when an eighteen-hour train was put on, which proved too hair raising and the present schedule was adopted, which remains to this day.

Curiously enough most of the patronage of these fast trains comes from people whose time is of no particular value. An hour or two longer on the journey would make not the slightest difference. But to preserve the appearance of being important, the ten dollar extra fare seems cheap. It's these same people who rarely eat breakfast on the train unless it is behind time and they are sure of a rebate.

CHAPTER XII.

GROWTH OF OUTLYING DISTRICTS.—THE HOT DOG ARRIVES.—BOHEMIA

A GREAT deal of territory now solidly built up in rows of apartments and small dwelling houses, was still given over, thirty-five years ago, to rural delights. In fact, the Sea Beach Railway, from Bay Ridge to Coney Island, referred in its advertising to the charming scenery along its route. The Brooklyn shore of New York Bay was still the haunt of the picnicker and holiday maker. The Gravesend Race Track brought large numbers of the latter to Bath Beach and the neighboring hamlets such as Bensonhurst, Ulmer Park, etc. Sheepshead Bay's marine attractions were also potent magnets to the excursionist. On Long Island Sound there were a number of pleasure resorts, now only memories, where steamboats used to land thousands of city dwellers for a day's outing; Glen Island, exploited by John A. Starin, was the chief of these, being served by its own fleet of steamboats. Its "Kleine Deutschland", its zoo, and its clambakes will be remembered by old timers. It is now part of New Rochelle's public park system. Oriental Grove where all the Brooklyn

Sunday school picnics went as well as political organizations from the East Side was particularly well known. Sea Cliff was a popular resort for a very orderly class of picknickers and City Island was a great fishing centre. On the Hudson, Alpine Grove, Dudley's Grove and Iona Island were attractive to large numbers of steamboat excursionists, who found their sylvan pleasures a welcome recreation.

Dudley's Grove was just north of Yonkers and is now Glenwood. Part of Wm. Boyce Thompson's famous Plant Research Institute is on part of the old grove. There was a song composed in its honor *"Up At Dudley's Grove"*, the chorus of which was:

> She played the concertina as through
> the woods we'd rove;
> I was all alone with Kitty McGlynn
> up at Dudley's Grove.

I think the small hotel attached to it was run by the people who owned the Fifth Avenue. Nothing now remains of this old pleasure ground. A trolley runs through the centre and trim little suburban dwellings line both sides of Warburton Avenue which is the name of the street that bisects the old grove.

Most of these excursions started or made a stop at Jewell's Wharf next to the Fulton Ferry in Brooklyn. This was one of the most celebrated jumping off places in our local history. All the Coney Island excursions and Rockaway boats stopped at Jewell's Wharf and its name appeared in countless thousands of advertisements. It finally became the Pennsylvania Annex Ferry.

There was as yet no hint of such places as Bear Mountain Park. That might have been in the Cana-

Thulstrup in Harper's Weekly.

A Hook and La

dian Rockies as far as distance and accessibility were concerned. And the Palisades for miles were as wild and primeval as any other wilderness with the exception of one of two small landing places opposite Yonkers. The whole idea of day excursions on the nearby waters seems to have entirely ceased. Meyer's Barges, and Starin's tugs have also gone where the woodbine twineth. Yet they were both great institutions in those days.

The present great vogue for college football had its inception early in the nineties, with the Thanksgiving Day game in New York as its high spot. It was customary for a number of years for swarms of the collegians and their devotees to take possession of the hotel and amusement centres at this particular time and indulge in by no means subdued merriment. Restaurant brawls were quite in order and the old Bowery tactics of the "flying wedge" became an unwonted feature of Tenderloin eating houses. Disorder broke out in the theatres, and occasionally the curtain had to be rung down. Finally the shopkeepers began to complain of depredations among their sign-boards and other movable appurtenances, and it began to be recognized that the college rowdy was only a slum rowdy dressed up. Finally the police took the matter in hand and the liberal use of the ever potent nightstick supplemented by stiff fines in the courts abated the nuisance. In this connection I may say that with all its faults of administration this city has hardly ever seen a better state of public order and security than in the golden nineties.

The trolley lines also gave a great impetus to Coney Island and brought the first influx of those enormous holiday crowds that have since resorted there. The ease with which it was reached marked the decline of many other less accessible resorts which had hitherto flourished. The groves on the Hudson, Glen Island and other pleasant beaches on the Sound where pick-nickers used to resort in great numbers, now relapsed into their pristine somnolence. Long Branch, in the Seventies and Eighties, a seaside metropolis, now lost caste, and its great clapboard hotels, and ditto gambling casinos, showed woeful need of new tenpenny nails and fresh paint.

This new accessibility not only profited Coney Island as a holiday resort, but also made it a week-day recreational centre. Thousands of business men took an afternoon off in hot weather to run down for a surf bath, a dinner, and a cool evening at the shore. The Manhattan Beach Hotel found a new source of patronage besides its permanent guests, and the crowd that used to flock over from Sheepshead Bay during the racing reason. The Brighton Beach Hotel, which had gone into decay for some years, now began to brush up, and what with fresh paint, fragrant gardens, and band concerts, again began to attract a well dressed throng; also augmented by the Brighton Beach races.

With the inclusion of the "Island" in Greater New York came a large modification of the rowdyism and tin horn gambling that had held considerable sway there. Orders came from Manhattan headquarters to "Clean up". Before the consolidation of the boroughs, the Island had been in the hands of the McKane clique and the local constabulary was a mere tool of a riparian despotism almost as absolute as the Prince of Monaco's. With all its faults, however, the old Coney Island was never the sink of iniquity that sensational writers have described it. It was the nearest ocean resort to the teeming millions of a great city, and it always drew a large majority of decent pleasure-seekers to its then clean and revivifying sands. It was early noted for its cosmopolitanism and democracy. Where other resorts had their great preponderance of Germans or Irish or other aliens, at Coney Island they all mingled, and among them not a few of the social elect of native persuasion.

It may almost seem a preposterous statement, but it is nevertheless a fact that thirty odd years ago the winter population of the town of Gravesend, which included besides that hamlet, Coney Island, King's Highway, Sheepshead Bay and intermediate villages, was less than 7,000. This was mainly composed of caretakers, employees of the three race tracks within its borders, dive keepers and their dependents. This sequestered dominion was almost as independent, politically, as the noted republics of San Marino or Andorra, but had as its overlord John Y. McKane, renowned as the "Czar of Coney Island", who as a minor boss shone in the reflected light of Croker, McLaughlin, McCarren, *et al*.

Mr. McKane ruled with a high hand. The steamboat companies, the amusement concessionaries, the bath house men, in fact all deriving profit from Coney Island and its environs, kowtowed to him and to his viceroy "Bob" Sutherland, and for a time all went merry as a marriage bell. But along with power came pride and McKane had the temerity to defy Supreme Court injunctions in relation to notorious irregularities in the election of 1893. This brought Judge Gaynor down upon him with such effect that McKane rounded out his career with a six-year sentence to State's prison. This was the beginning of Gaynor's political renown in the greater city and led to his election as Mayor, in which capacity he proved one of the most able, sensible, and well endowed executives the city has ever had.

During the heated term the wharves and piers of the river front were largely resorted to during these intolerable periods. There was much more of this kind of space available than there is today, when the commerce of the port has practically preempted the entire Manhattan shore line. Nearly all the river front parks were developments of the Nineties, Coenties Park, Corlear's Hook, East River, Carl Schurz, St. Gabriel's, Striker's, as were many inland, such as Seward, Hamilton Fish, Mulberry Bend, to mention only those in the lower city.

The boon of the seashore was much more uncommon to the poor than in our five-cent subway days. Before the trolley lines began to penetrate Coney Island, the cheapest fare to that resort was forty cents. The all-water route was fifty, which after the trolley competition began to be felt was reduced to twenty-five. A laborer with a brood of small children found the delights of an excursion under those terms almost prohibitive, except as a special treat. There were compensations, however. Vast stretches of beach were unoccupied by concessions, and a family could picnic on the sands, without crowding and without cost. Even a sea bath could be obtained for as little as fifteen cents, which included a bathing suit of fast color bed ticking, and no objection was raised if pater or mater crowded their little dressing booths with their offspring, also enjoying the embraces of Neptune, in home-made garments, of miscellaneous antecedents.

The decline of Long Branch, which for years had shared with Saratoga Springs the fame of being the premier summer resort of the country, was coincidental with the decay of that upstate spa. Some of the old-time flavor of "The Branch" still was manifest in the early nineties in the gambling clubs that kept the ball rolling and provided an attraction for the old stagers who would have felt lost without an evening's play at Phil Daly's Pennsylvania Club, the Ocean Club, or at John Daly's establishment. These resorts were kept running with as much eclat as ever, although with increased restrictions in the matter of patronage. The same handsome equipment, soft carpets, bright chandeliers and buffet suppers were in evidence. But Long Branch was no longer the national institution it had been; its patronage was now almost entirely local, and when the New Jersey legislature passed laws striking at open gaming it received its final quietus and lapsed into its present status as a pleasant but undistinguished seacoast town.

Since the palmy days of the old clipper ships, and the not so palmy ones of the disastrous Collins Line of steamers, it had been the dream of many enthusiasts to see the American flag streaming over the taffrail of an Atlantic liner. This dream was realized in 1893 when the old Inman Line was reorganized under the title of the "American Line", and, applying for registry under the Stars and Stripes, the first steps toward a rejuvenated American merchant marine was signalized by President Harrison raising the flag on board the steamship *"New York"* amid great jubilation.

One of the conditions of the government subsidy that prompted this movement was that the line should build two more ships in American shipyards and accordingly the Cramps of Philadelphia were commissioned to construct these, and two years later the *"St. Louis"*, followed shortly afterwards by the *"St. Paul"* were launched. Their interior fittings resembled somewhat those of our coast liners, being rather devoid of the lavish ornamentation of the greyhounds of the foreign lines. Their large social halls and pipe organs were novel features, and the boats soon became popular units of the Atlantic ferry. During the Spanish-American War they were withdrawn from mercantile service and did duty as scout cruisers under the names of *"Yale"* and *"Harvard"*. The American line was soon after absorbed by the International Mercantile Marine. During the Great War the *"St. Louis"* and *"St. Paul"* fell upon parlous days and became little better than tramp steamers.

It was about the period of the World's Fair that a somewhat novel element became part of New York's foreign population. This was the Syrian vanguard of the now well known colony just northwest of the Battery. It was the period of the "Armenian Atrocities" which became a commonplace of newspaper headlines. The famous Midway "Hoochee-Koochie" or *danse du ventre,* which probably drew more people to the Fair than any other attraction, artistic or scientific, lent its name to the transplanted sector of the Near East in New York, for with that sensitiveness to local idiosyncrasies that guides police philologists, it was dubbed the "Hoochee Koochee precinct".

From this colony was born the enormous Turkish

and Egyptian cigarette business that "satisfies" people who "would walk a mile to buy a Sahara". Certain humble cigarette rollers of lower Washington Street have since climbed to dizzy heights of opulence convinced that "such popularity must be deserved". Before their time ninety-five per cent of American cigarettes were composed of Virginia tobacco. *"Sweet Caporal"*, *"Virginia Brights"*, *"Richmond Gems"*, *"Duke's Cameo"*, *"Duke's Best"* were the legends on most cigarette boxes. The few cigarettes of Levant tobaccoes sold in New York were imported makes, and high-priced, smoked only by connoisseurs. There was also a small trade in Cuban cigarettes, mostly in demand by the Latin Americans of the University Place District.

There was very fierce competition among the cigarette men in those days and the rival firms turned out an enormous amount of advertising material in the shape of small colored cards of every possible subject under the sun, including actresses in tights, fishes, flags, medals, wild animals, domestic animals, flaura and fauna of the whole world. These were inserted in the box containing the cigarettes. They spent huge fortunes in this direction and several lithographers attained a high reputation for the quality of work which they produced in this direction.

I believe it was a man named Allen who first thought of a combination of the cigarette manufacturers. Allen printed a paper which dealt largely with the trade marks used by the various manufacturers. It was not an unusual thing for one firm to adopt, innocently or otherwise, the name of a brand that was registered by a competitor, but not in use. When a rival had built up some

371

business on this new brand, the original owner would then set up a howl and claim that he had been greatly injured by such infringement.

This led to a great deal of expensive and unnecessary laws-suits among the various firms and Allen used his good offices in many instances to effect amicable arrangements in such disputes. In this way he became personally acquainted with the leading manufacturers and when he proposed a consolidation of all the cigarette interests the idea carried more weight than if it had originated through some other channel.

Allen was left out in the combination and I think afterwards sued for a large sum, which I think was settled out of court. At all events the American Tobacco Company was shortly afterwards formed as a result of his idea and the leading cigarette manufacturers came into the deal.

James B. Duke, who died recently, left forty-six million to a university in his own town and that was probably less than a third of his wealth. This was only one of the many multi-millionaires created by this organization. The story of this combination is a long one and very interesting, but it must be postponed for another time.

The city was infested with gambling houses as a result of the political corruption of the times. Houses like Canfield's, Daly's, "Shang" Draper's, Kelly's, and Davis' flourished with only occasional interruptions by police raids. An institution that was almost an obsession among the colored population was the policy shop. This was a form of lottery which extorted even pennies from its devotees. While the Louisiana lottery was still

THE GREAT JOHN L.

In his rôle of Temperance Lecturer in the latter years of
his life

Dr. William T. Bull

One of our best known surgeons in the Nineties

ONE OF MR. BRADY'S STARS IN THE NINETIES

unforbidden by Federal law, the policy shop winning numbers were taken from its lists, but after its ban by the Government the policy shops had so called drawings of their own. Business was transacted in rear rooms of cigar-stores, candy-stores, etc., of the poorest type, the darky superstitions regarding "gigs", "horses", "straddles", "saddles", "Christmas", "4-11-44" (a big drawing), were so complex and weird as to constitute a sort of voodooism. "Hunches" and dreams were relied on as guides. Necromancers were consulted, and impromptu trance mediums held forth for small rewards in the neighborhoods of the policy shops. The overlord of the policy shop system was the celebrated Al Adams, who acquired a large fortune in the business, and whose reputation as a family man, and attendance at church, were nullified by his incarceration, late in life, in the penitentiary on Blackwell's Island.

Until early in the nineties there still existed in New York what was probably the best known gambling house in the country, old "818" Broadway. This was in its heyday the headquarters of John Morrissey, pugilist, adventurer, gambler, and finally Member of Congress. In the nineties it was run by Lucius Appleby, of bookmaking fame, and by Gus Abel. It was the resort to which country people, curious to see a grand gambling establishment were generally taken. An old negro who had acted in that capacity since the house opened was doorkeeper and he had a remarkable memory for faces. At 12 o'clock every night a sumptuous supper was served, including wines, to all present, without charge. The only creature comfort that one could pay for in the house was cigars, which cost a white check, 25 cents, each. One could wager anything from this white check to $250. The average play varied between $5 and $25. People visiting the house "to see what it was like", seldom departed without making a wager of $5 or $10 for the experience, and to acknowledge the great courtesy shown. There was a bank roll of about a quarter of a million at "818" not against the average player, but against some high roller like Ed. Walcott, Pat Sheedy or Dink Davis, of whom the last two, it was said, caused the faro dealers to "turn the box", at "818" more frequently than any other players of their time.

The Long Branch gambling clubs were merely summer annexes of the winter games in New York. John Daly's had its town clientele at 39 West 29th Street. John was celebrated as a "square gambler" and his house was noted for its elegance and the quality of its viands and wines, which rivalled Delmonico's.

Phil Daly's rooms were on the corner of Sixth Avenue and 31st Street where he ran what was known as a "tight game". One of his partners was Al Adams of policy shop fame.

Charley Reed held forth at 5 West 24th Street. One of his partners was Albert Spencer, owner of the Saratoga Club and of the Saratoga Racing Association and reputed the wealthiest gambler of his time. His art collection sold at the American Art Galleries for $90,-000. A big price for those days.

There used to be a number of "day games", downtown, best known of which were Joe Doyle's, "Bud" Kirby's and Pete Downing's. Small gamesters abounded, running what were known as "kindergartens", and "sweat" games—a crooked "piker's" game— were not uncommon.

CHARGING FOR PARK CHAIRS

The old palmy day sports that ran the big games have had no successors. They had a code of ethics, which though it may have been dictated by policy, gained them the confidence of thousands among those who liked to "buck the tiger", many of them business men of all classes. They are no kin, nor do they bear the least resemblance to the "crooked gambler" of today.

In those far off idyllic days when our city parks were sporadic havens of rest and quiet enjoyment; when there were still green lawns and flourishing, umbrageous trees; when the turf of these oases did not resemble an unoccupied building lot, and when orderly, well behaved persons still resorted to them to while away a pleasant hour, it occurred to an enterprising citizen named Spate that perhaps some of these aforesaid persons might be willing to pay a small stipend for a reserved chair in the parks, and especially at the evening concerts given at some of them. The notion meeting with the favor of the authorities, Mr. Spate proceeded to locate his chairs in favorable situations, under the control of agents, instructed to collect 10 cents each for their use.

Immediately there arose a hubbub such as no park had ever seen since the statue of George the Third was pulled down by a mob in Bowling Green. Liberty, fraternity and equality were declared outraged by the Weary Willies, Ragged Roberts, and Dusty Rhodes who used to inspire the romances of O. Henry when he lived among the "Four Million". Other indignant upholders of democratic principles voiced their sentiments in the press, while some took possession of the chairs and refused to pay for the accommodation. Fights were frequent, arrests were made by the police, but the accused were discharged by the magistrates and finally it was realized that the new system was not alone unpopular, but illegal. Mr. Spate, thereupon folded up his chairs, like the Arabs their tents, and silently stole away, leaving the parks once more in their wonted quiet, the abode of the staunch upholders of their ancient liberties.

Until the Spanish-American War brought together thousands of irreconcilables, there was a great deal of Civil War talk still current. Politicians used the old rancors as campaign issues. Colonel Waring, himself a Union veteran, brought down the wrath of many of his old comrades in arms by references to some of the office seekers among them as "Grand Army bummers". The theatres had several conspicuous successes among plays of the late "onpleasantness", notably *"Shenandoah"* by Bronson Howard and *"The Heart of Maryland"* by Belasco. Parlor entertainers were still reciting *"Sheridan's Ride"* and *"The Blue and the Gray"*. James Whitcomb Riley's kindly muse was invoked as follows:

> "I was for Union, you agin it.
> 'Pears like to me, each side was winner
> Lookin' at now and all 'at's in it
>   Le's go to dinner.
>
> Le's kind o' jes set down together
> An' do some pardnership forgittin',
> Talk, say, for instance, 'bout the weather
>   Er sompin fittin'.
>
> The War, you know, 's all done and ended,
> And ain't changed no pints o' the compass,
> Both North and South and health's jes' splendid,
>   As 'fore the rumpus.

FALL OF THE GREAT JOHN L.

The old farms and the old plantations
Still occupies th'r old positions,
Le's git back to old situations
    And old ambitions.

Le's let up on this blame, infernal
Tongue lashin' and lap jacket vauntin'
And git back home to the eternal,
    Ca'm we're a wantin'.

Peace kind o' suits my diet
When women does my cookin' for me,
Ther' wasn't overly much pie eat
    Durin' the Army."

Without doubt, the greatest sporting debacle of the period was the downfall of John L. Sullivan from the pedestal of premier pugilist, which he had pre-empted for twelve years. The great "John L.", the "Big Fellow", the "Boston Boy" gone down under the fists of a stripling, with 5 to 1 against him. Not since the Heenan-Sayres match had there been such excitement over a prize fight. People crowded the squares, the hotels, saloons, gambling houses, poolrooms and brokers' offices to get the first news of the modern Waterloo. No one but the "wise money" thought John L. could possibly lose. These, however, saw John's prodigious paunch and the layers of fat festooned over his belt, and took the short end. The result was an earthquake to the gullible public who always play into the hands of the "sporting men". If John L. was licked, anything might happen. The Boston State House, or the Statue of Liberty might tumble down; Russell Sage might buy somebody a drink; Pennsylvania go Democratic; in short, chaos come again. Of course, the fight was celebrated by a bard, as was every event then calculated to stir the poet's ardor. I spare you the opening stanzas, but offer the peroration, in token of its quality:

"But the story you are familiar with, how John was
    whipped at last
 From the very start, in fact, we're told that he was much
    outclassed
 He did not seem himself at all, at no time in the fight
 And somehow he did not have the use of his big awful
    right.
 At the end of twenty-one hard rounds Jim got the victory
 Was proclaimed champion of the world by the gallant
    referee
 To show the hero that he was when Jim the fight had won,
 John said he was glad still we'd have an American
    champion.

Chorus

 John L. has been knocked out! the people all did cry
 Corbett is the champion! how the news did fly.
 And future generations, with wonder and delight
 Will read in hist'ry's pages of the Sullivan-Corbett fight."

This was sung to the classic tune of *"Throw Him Down, McCloskey!"* and there is one detail of the lyric to which I desire to call particular attention, as an early example of the "alibi":

"He did not seem himself at all, at no time in the fight". It seems to me that Mr. Dempsey, who recently honored the Declaration of Independence by assuming a horizontal position on the Sesquicentennial of its adoption, suffered a similar loss of identity. If my fading memory serves me right, Mr. Corbett at Carson City, Mr. Jeffries at Reno, Mr. Johnson at Havana and Mr. Willard at Toledo, all underwent a metamorphosis in which the use of thumb prints might have served to reassure their backers that a "ringer" had not been

382

foisted on them. The old-time ringster had no such Jekyll and Hyde qualities. He was always himself, until he was carried out on a shutter to be bathed in vinegar, when he resembled something else. Mr. Sullivan's long tenure in office had almost petrified his claims and the doting public were nearly ready to believe that something preternatural had been the agency of his downfall.

Among the articles of diet that this period introduced to the popular consumer by far the most permanent and attractive was spaghetti. Although there had been a few Italian eating houses before this time, notably in the neighborhood of the Academy of Music, this type of restaurant did not become ubiquitous until the Nineties, when our Italian fellow citizens began to add a commercial element to the almost exclusively day laboring population it had heretofore contributed to the city's activities. The table d'hote dinner which had been regarded as a rather Bohemian adventure—by virtue of its concomitant bottle of "red ink"—now became a regular institution among our natives. The old time "regular dinner" was gradually abandoned for this new exotic and the "spaghetti joint" flourished exceedingly. The first "quantity production" of spaghetti was produced in a factory on Staten Island. It used to be an article of faith that only Italian handmade spaghetti was fit for human consumption. In fact, it was all that then existed. The machine-made article of Staten Island, which defied detection, shook the foundations of culinary Mulberry and Bleecker Streets, and revolutionized their dietary. Since then the huge canning industries have naturalized this wholesome comestible, and it has been one of the most prominent factors in the gradual decrease of meat eating in this country.

Coincidental with the rise of spaghetti was that of another alien esculent the "hot dog". This was known to the early German residents under the traditional title of "Wiener-wurst". I believe it began its great vogue at Coney Island where it gradually converted the addicts of the entirely native clam chowder to its charms. In the early days of the Island clam chowder was its most toothsome delight. It ranged in price from 15 cents a platter at the Manhattan Beach Hotel to 5 cents near the West End, and at any number of places was offered as free lunch with a schooner of beer.

The "hot dog" when it first made its appearance on the Island was served *au naturel,* coyly ensconced in a roll. Then a *cordon bleu* with a touch of the genius of Brillat-Savarin, embellished it with sauerkraut; this with unlimited mustard completed the conquest of the public. It was a more mobile nourishment than chowder. It could be carried on the march, eaten on the sands between baths, consumed on a carousel, used as a baby's nipple to quiet an obstreperous infant, and had other economic appeals to the summer pleasure seeker.

The poets of Bohemia have long sung lyrics to all and sundry belonging to that delectable region, including its esculents. Thackeray's *"Ballad of Bouillabaisse"* immortalized a soup, but the only sonnet to spaghetti that I can remember is Henry Tyrrel's verses to Maria da Prato, the famed chatelaine of 12th Street:

"How oft, Marie, hostess debonair,
 Have we, gay wanderers in Bohemia's way,
 Gathered at closing of a weary day
 To feast on thy minastra past compare!

Drawing by W. T. Smedley.   From Harper's Weekly.

QUESTIONS OF THE CENSUS TAKER

Thou makest spaghetti and ambrosial fare,
And oh, thy ravioli! Hence we say
Salute! and as staunch admirers may
Pledge thee in Tuscan rose Chianti rare.
The storms of fate and weather beat in vain
Around the walls that comradeship enclose,
Who haply entereth in thy domain,
Dulness resigneth, care to the four winds throws.
For hid in cold Manhattan though it be,
The place is part of sunny Italy."

I hear a good deal these days about the Bohemian delights of Greenwich Village and the Night Clubs, but somehow or other I miss the familiar names that graced Bohemia in my day.

The city has, of course, always had a Bohemian centre; a gathering place for brilliant wits and followers of the Muses—lovers of art for art's sake. As far back as the fifties a coterie of men of this type were wont to gather at Pfaff's celebrated restaurant—men like Bayard Taylor, William Winter, William Dean Howells, Richard Realph, A. C. Wheeler, and a host of others. But I think it can be said that Bohemia first became crystallized in Gotham when one Jauss opened a *table d'hôte* on Sixth Avenue, near Twenty-sixth Street, some time in the eighties. Barring the food, which was detestable, the place had a good deal of the Latin-quarter flavor. The *menu* was written in French, and the waiters answered you in the same language. The presence of actresses out of work and "grisettes"—I think this is what they loved to hear themselves called—and the general *désinvolture* of the guests, as a whole, brought to mind some of the students' eating-houses of the Rue Jacob or the Boulevard St. Michel. Despite the food and a growing tendency on the landlord's part not to give credit beyond certain reasonable limits, the place flourished for several years, during which time its portals were darkened by geniuses of every stripe. Maurice Barrymore, Wilton Lackaye, Augustus Thomas, Edward Henley, Laura Burt, Daisy Temple, Mabel Morris, Ray Douglass, Bertha Colby, poor Selina Dolaro in the last stages of her malady, Nettie Lyford, and many more constituted the theatrical contingent. The journalists' and artists' list of names was a lengthy one, and comprised among others James Creelman, the war correspondent; "Billy" Walsh, editor of *Lippincott's Magazine* and literary sponsor of Amelie Rives; W. E. S. Fales, lawyer and poet, exuding perspiration and geniality at all seasons of the year; Paul Potter, already the proud author of "The City Directory," foreshadowing so many subsequent theatrical successes; George R. Halm, whose presence, as was once remarked, lent an air of stately dignity to all proceedings; Captain de Mandeville, known as the "Knight of the Iron Wrist" (with a record of fifteen hundred handshakes an hour) ; Henry Guy Carleton, the playwright; and last but not least, poor Jack Moran, the gentle warbler of dainty sonnets, whom even a hacking cough and the spectre of approaching dissolution could not detain from these reunions.

The true spirit of Bohemia characterized the evenings at Jauss's, and the presence of a Philistine was scarcely ever tolerated, unless, indeed, he paid a generous liquid tribute to the genii of the place; for albeit the practice of "wine-opening" is the most serious offense on the calendar of Bohemia when indulged in by a member of the fraternity, there is no rule forbidding his sharing in the fruits of such depravity on the part of a Philistine.

Unfortunately for Jauss, these "terrible examples" were not sufficiently frequent to compensate him for losses in other directions, and one fine day the habitués found their gathering place in the hands of workmen, transferring it into a vulgar, every-day liquor-store.

Upon the disappearance of Jauss', another similar establishment which had already gained a reputation for better food came into the spotlight. This was Maria's, on Twenty-second Street near Sixth Avenue, and to this new rendezvous the old crowd repaired. Dozens of new-comers joined the old group and soon Maria's was the talk of the town. "Spaghetti hour" at Maria's became famous and her chicken dinners brought everybody who was anybody. George B. Luks, the painter, Jim Ford, the dramatic critic, Fayles Coward, afterward leader of "The Strollers", George Sheldon of Salma-gundi, "Chimmie Fadden" Charley Reinhart, Pete Dailey, Oliver Herford, Valerien Gribayedoff, Amos Cummings, Dan Kellogg, Walt Macdougall, "Chip" Bel-lew and a score of other playwrights, actors, artists and well-known characters from every calling, made the nights at Maria's something to be long remembered. "Mickey Finn", singing "Slattery's Baby", would bring down the house. Music and monologues contributed by the guests themselves imparted a spirit of gayety and pleasure that I have never recognized in these denatured joints in the Village where painted mottoes on the walls take the place of the brilliant repartee that was the charm of Maria's. However, we are living in another age and it is hard to assume a spirit of *bon homme* and good fellowship toward utter strangers on nothing but Canada Dry or Sarsaparilla.

GREATER (?) NEW YORK

When Greater New York was an accomplished fact we stretched out so many miles into rural lands that the following lines on another similar expansion could have been applied to New York with equal justice.

The shades of night were falling fast
As o'er a Kansas prairie passed
A youth of presence gaunt and thin,
But vast the shoes he travels in
He'd driven ninety miles that day
Nor seen a shed where he could stay
"Oh, where am I?" at last he groaned
A passing stranger softly moaned
                              "Chicago!"

He sped through fields of luscious wheat
Untrod for months by human feet
He roamed o'er pastures never mown
Through forest wild and overgrown
He forded rivers still unnamed
Saw dusky redskins yet untamed
"Where am I now?" he wildly cried
An Indian maiden sadly sighed
                              "Chicago!"

Still on he sped nor stopped to gaze
Upon the waving fields of maize
Up rocky slopes he madly flew
Up peaks where naught but lichens grew
Land of eternal snow and hail
And read there, "City lots for sale."
"What place is this?" he wildly howled
A hungry grizzly fiercely growled
                              "Chicago!"

CHAPTER XIII.

SCHOOL DAYS.—END OF OLD NEW YORK

Mary had a little lamb
Its fleece was white as snow,
She never heard of Henry Ford
Or even of his flivver.

THE great interest shown by the entire country in
Mr. Ford's preservation of the old school house at
Sterling, Mass., in which Mary's little lamb first appeared, suggests that the recollections of our own school
days might recall something of interest to the readers
of these memoirs.

The public schools of New York City forty years ago
were by no means the magnificent institutions that they
are today. Writing of good old Grove Street No. 3, which
was visited by Lafayette a hundred years ago and has
never gotten over it, my young friend Dr. I. Wyman
Drummond gives me this vivid description:

"From a sanitary point this old school was certainly
the limit. Back of the teacher's chair, against the wall
was a closet, 7 feet high, 10 feet wide and about 18
inches deep. It had sliding doors, on the face of which

was the blackboard. In this closet was hung all the coats and hats of the thirty or forty boys in the class. Imagine the steaming mess, especially on rainy days! Worse still, all the lunch boxes were piled up on each other on the floor of the closet. They added their own particular aroma to the clothes, and what came out of the closet from 9 to 12 was aplenty. In those days teachers never opened class room windows. The lunch box was about the size of a small loaf of bread, hinged cover, lacquered black, and made of tin. They were all alike and to identify them the boys scratched their names on them through the lacquer. At noon time a monitor dug them out of the closet and distributed them. Then, when the thirty or forty boys opened them it added quite a bit to the already choked arena."

Notwithstanding these unfavorable surroundings, the fact still remains that, some of our best and really worth while citizens matriculated from old No. 3 and the list of her distinguished sons is a long one. Among them is the present leader of Tammany Hall, Hon. George W. Olvany, Charles R. Lamb, designer of the Dewey Arch; Senator Quinn, who succeeded Mayor Walker in the State Senate; the late Postmaster, Edward D. Morgan; the present Sheriff, Charles W. Culkin; everybody's friend, the Hon. John W. Voorhis, Grand Sachem of the Tammany Society, and Dr. Thomas H. Darlington, of the Health Department. Of others who are more nationally known were: Schuyler Colfax, Vice-President under Grant; Rear Admiral George W. Melville, of Arctic fame; Major George W. De Bevoise, of Hawkins Zouaves and Everett P. Wheeler.

Any number of prominent financiers could be included like Henry R. Carse of the Hanover National Bank; Andrews of the Chase National, Hebbard of the Guaranty Trust; Heeley of the Farmers Loan, or Heinerick of the East River Bank. Then there was Congressman Wm. W. Cohen, who defeated Ogden Mills; Judge Caffrey, Police Inspectors Quinn and Howard; and Captains Rourke and Scoble. The complete roster would read like a social register book. The school has an alumni association named after the last and best beloved principal, D. B. V. Sutherland.

Another famous down-town school was old No. 35 on 13th Street near 6th Avenue. The fame of its principal, Thomas Hunter, brought boys from all parts of the city to No. 35. The alumni have formed an association named after their old prexy—The Thomas Hunter Association.

This elementary school afterwards became a graduate training school for women teachers under Doctor Hunter and was the beginning of our Normal College. When the old building on 13th Street was abandoned for the present site on Park Avenue the name of Hunter was added to Normal College in honor of the old principal of No. 35, who had done so much for the education of women teachers and is now known as Hunter Normal College.

No. 35 school has also a long list of distinguished pupils. I cannot name them all but here are a few still living: Ex-Secretary Charles E. Hughes, heads the list.; the Rev. Franklin B. Dwight, Princeton University; Clarkson Cowl, of G. A. Hearn & Sons; the Rev. Dr. Deems, Dr. I. Wyman Drummond, chairman, F. W. Devoe-Raynolds Co.

James F. Drake, the learned dealer in rare books

and accomplished bibliophile. The Right Reverend Bishop Darlington, of Harrisburg, Pa. Maurice Bouvier, Hayward Cleveland, Hanford Crawford, Rev. Edward M. Deems, Eben E. Olcott, of the Albany Day Line; Theodore H. Price, Simon F. Rothschild, of Abraham & Straus; Samuel Untermyer, Barton K. Weeks, Marcus M. Marks, William D. Guthrie, are only a few that I know out of the many members of the Hunter Association. Once a year they meet at a dinner and recall old times.

There are quite a number of the old schools whose pupils have kept alive memories of the old days by the organization of Alumni Associations. No. 2, old Henry Street, No. 20 in East 20th Street, No. 40 in East 26th Street are only a few.

Judge Otto Rosalsky is an old No. 2 graduate. Arthur M. Lamport, of the Lamport & Holt Line; Dr. William L. Ettinger, Superintendent, Board of Education; also Hon. John F. Ahearn. In No. 40 we find our musical friend Dr. Frank Damrosch and General George W. Wingate. George Goethals, builder of the Panama Canal, and Abe Hummel came from No. 15; Surrogate Foley and Professor Mario Cosenza from No. 14, and from DeWitt Clinton High came Dudley Field Malone, attorney for Gertrude Ederle; the two Hart boys, Harold and Percy, executive managers of Cammeyer's; Justice Salvatore A. Cotillo, of the Supreme Court; Alexander Eiseman, of the Freedman-Eiseman Radio Corporation; Louis Untermeyer, the poet; Raymond E. Jones, 1st Vice-President Bank of Manhattan Company; S. Jay Kaufman, writer; Vincent J. Frank, Frank Towing Company.

"TRAFFIC"

This scene never varies much no matter what the decade. New York has always had its traffic jam and probably always will

The "Spaghetti Hour" at Maria's

HENRY MORGENTHAU, MAJ.-GEN. O'RYAN

From No. 131 came Hon. Judge Levy, of the Children's Court, and Congressman William Sirovich.

The demand for higher education was not so large nor so general in the Nineties as it has become in recent years and the old "Free Academy," that ancient church-like structure on the corner of Lexington Avenue and 23rd Street was amply large enough to accommodate the demand. In 1861, this title was changed to the College of the City of New York though the old name is still occasionally used in referring to the down-town structure. The City College today is a gigantic institution, numbering in all its activities an attendance of over twenty-three thousand pupils.

The graduates of our City College probably occupy more positions in our Judiciary Courts than all our other colleges combined. In about every walk in life there are eminent names who come from the City College. The astronomer at Yale University is one, Frank Schlesinger; several are professors in Columbia and Fordham, while scientists, authors, doctors, lawyers, editors, architects, engineers, diplomats, etc., are too numerous to mention. The beautiful Roosevelt Memorial addition to the Museum of Natural History was designed by John Russell Pope. Henry Morgenthau gained a world-wide reputation in diplomacy; the great lawyer, Stroock, attorney for R. H. Macy and United Cigars; the distinguished educator, Edward C. Zabriskie, principal of Washington Irving High; Rabbi Wise, Supreme Court Justices Taylor and Mahoney, Major General John F. O'Ryan, Montague Glass, Alexander M. Bing, the builder; Upton Sinclair, Senator Robert F. Wagner, S. Stanwood Menken, the lawyer, are merely representative of thousands equally entitled to honorable mention. There is no other equally large institution of higher learning supported by municipal funds in any city in the world. As the flowering of our entire public school system, the College of the City of New York, is the outward and visible sign of the unquestioned success of the system in spite of its lack of absolute perfection.

The rather backward physical condition of public schools in the 90's was responsible for a rather large number of private schools that flourished in that era and which provided New York with a quota of men eminent today in business, in art and science, that is surprisingly large considering the very limited output in comparison with the number in the public schools. Thomas Hastings, architect of the Standard Oil Building, is one of them. He attended Mr. Farrand's school, housed in an old building on the southeast corner of 42nd Street and 6th Avenue, and the boys played on the vacant lots around the old reservoir, which Hastings was destined to remove in after years in order to erect our present Public Library. Mr. Hastings thought one half of the water in the reservoir was hot and the other cold and to this day has never quite gotten over his bitter disappointment when he learned the truth.

His French was bad in school but a four-years' residence in Paris remedied that fault. Upon his return, he unexpectedly met his old French teacher and to the latter's surprise, greeted him in almost faultless French and complimented the old teacher for his excellent instruction, never letting him know what had happened in the interim.

Next year I shall add a chapter on the girls schools and on Hunter Normal College.

END OF OLD NEW YORK

I now come to that tragic moment when the ancient City of New York is wiped off the face of the map. There is something classic and heroic when a city is engulfed by molten lava from a blazing volcano, but when it is simply submerged by Hunter's Point, Newtown Creek, Long Island City, the Rockaways, Canarsie, and the Bronx, there is nothing to write about. We may have added a little to our cubical square miles, but that's about all.

Brooklyn, our dearly beloved sister city which for many years played the part of dormitory to our own and was always neighborly and decent about it, had the bad taste to draw cartoons showing the Tiger crossing the East River Bridge with numerous red light banners in the van. A valiant band of trenchermen behind a breastwork of rubber plants, nobly defending a world of baby carriages in the background, completed the picture. And this was our reward for our magnanimous conduct in finding for her a place in the sun.

Robert Van Wyck was the first Mayor of the Consolidated Cities. Former Mayor William L. Strong made a few platitudinous remarks appropriate to the occasion. In the evening, the Brooklyn Chamber of Commerce held a dinner. There was the customary amount of drivel in the newspapers about "Progress," etc., but that was all. The last days of this modern Pompeii were much like any other.

We now rejoice in the title, "Borough of Manhattan."

*   *   *   *   *   *   *   *   *

With this passing of old New York, my narrative comes to a close. The City is now one hundred and fifty years old. It is three hundred years since the

Dutch first settled on the shores of this island. She has lived under three flags. It may be of interest to portray the background from which New York emerged just a little more than a century ago. It is a picture that staggers the imagination.

December fourteenth, seventeen ninety-nine, saw the death of the great Washington. The opening of the new century a few days later disclosed a country with the burden of an untamed continent resting on the shoulders of less than seven million people, nearly half of whom were slaves. Except upon a narrow stretch of land along the seaboard, the land was uninhabited save by wild animals and still wilder savages. Nowhere beyond this narrow strip could the wants of civilized life be sustained. Communication was by means of virgin paths through forest and frequently impassable by freshets and torrential rains. Commerce was confined to small vessels that made infrequent trips to seaboard towns and the exchange of commodities was irregular and uncertain. The denizens of the deep furnished the oil which lighted the cabins at night. Afloat and ashore disaster beset the traveller at every turn. Comforts there were none, and life was a constant struggle for bare existence.

The imperial city of New York was imperial in name only. Cruel scourges attacked it with relentless regularity, threatening at times its almost total extinction. Water was scarce and much of it undrinkable. It was hawked about the streets in carts and sold by the pennysworth. Plank roads were on one or two of the principal streets, but dirt paths were the rule. Here and there an attempt had been made to improve the condition by cobble stones and brick, but only in occasional sections. The Capitol, which had promised much for the advancement and wealth of New York, after a residence of barely ten months, was removed to Philadelphia. A large section of the burnt-over area of 1776 was still covered with temporary shanties, blacksmith shops and other nondescript buildings that reared themselves on the ashes of the conflagration. Broadway, where the Standard Oil building starts the famous thoroughfare with a magnificence rarely seen even in modern architecture, to Wall Street, was at that time a street of melancholy ruins.

At the close of the Revolution the population of New York had declined to about twelve thousand souls. Newport, whose supremacy as the leading Atlantic seaport had been seriously threatened by the rapid growth of New York before the Revolution, once more breathed freely. Her unrivalled situation at the head of Narragansett Bay was evidently Nature's own guarantee of her enduring eminence. The competition of New York was evidently a passing gesture which had now disappeared forever. None was left to repeat the prediction that New York would ever again rival Newport or even attempt it. Such and so curious are the minds of men. Yet at the close of the century she had left Newport far in the wake, had even overtaken Philadelphia, and with her sixty thousand population was bidding defiance to the untamed wilderness which even then stretched almost to her doors.

Such then, was the aspect of the town which Washington, in his letter to the Common Council accepting the Freedom of the City, designated in the flowery language of the day as the "coming seat of Empire." The curtain descends on the Eighteenth Century on a scene indescribably remote from the splendors contained within the confines of the same city a scant hundred years later.

If her first hundred years was a miracle of progress what shall be said of the second, half of which is still to come? Even as I write, Col. Lindbergh has completed his epoch-marking flight from New York to Paris in less than thirty-four hours. Judging by the progress we made in the half century from 1876, it seems beyond the ken of man to predict what the Imperial City of New York will be within the next fifty years.

My great regret is that I shall not be here to see it.

These random recollections of New York, as I remember it as a boy, the first of which began in number ten of the Manual have enjoyed a measure of popularity far beyond my expectations.

The city began to expand in the Nineties on such a prodigious scale that no condensation or abridgment of its many activities would permit of an adequate recital within the pages of one modest number of the Manual. Much of it must remain, therefore, to be "continued in our next" as the old story paper had it.

With this much by way of explanation I will only add that the present number covers only a few of the first years of the Nineties. The second installment will, I hope, complete the decade.

VALENTINE'S MANUAL

No. 12   JANUARY, 1928   New Series

NOTES BY THE EDITOR

It is not unlikely that this issue of the Manual will
be read by an audience many times greater than any
number yet issued. To most of them the title will have
little or no significance and be more confusing than otherwise. From a popular point of view the word Manual
doubtless suggests a dull prosy compilation of facts and
figures, mainly statistical. This conception, it is needless to add, is something of a handicap and has no
doubt repelled many readers who otherwise would have
been with us from the first number.

One hesitates to tamper, however, with a title that is
known to every booklover, collector and librarian in the
world. In these circles *Valentine's Manual* is a household word. For over half a century it has been known
to them as an official publication of the City of New
York, and its reputation extends wherever books are
known. At a recent auction sale in New York a set of the
old Manuals formerly given away free, brought $840.00,
which means a good deal more at retail.

Nevertheless the general public respond more readily
to the Manual when it is advertised under the title of
its leading article. Thus *New York in the Elegant
Eighties* sold many more copies than if we had advertised it as *Valentine's Manual No. 11; The Last Fifty
Years in New York* better than as *No. 10 of the Man-*

ual, and, *In the Golden Nineties,* than as No. 12. Yet they are one and the same thing.

*   *   *   *   *   *   *   *   *

Many of our new-found friends will be glad to know a little more about the Manual and for that reason we think it will not be without interest at this time to reprint the editorial which appeared in our first issue, just twelve years ago:

Any attempt to revive Valentine's famous Manuals is, of necessity, an undertaking fraught with the liveliest anticipation to all Old New Yorkers, and of more than passing interest to the generation to whom his work is fast becoming merely a romantic tradition.

The present year marks a full half century since the gifted pen of David Thomas Valentine ceased to labor on the work he loved so well. It has also seen the realization of his wildest dream—that New York would some day be the greatest city in the world. And this effort to continue the brilliant record of the "faithful old clerk" is attended with no small amount of apprehension and a due appreciation of the difficulties to be surmounted. For his was the work of the heart as well as of the head.

To those of us who know, and appreciate the worth of these veritable store-houses of antiquarian lore concerning the past of our glorious city, the mere mention of Valentine's Manual conjures up visions of a city with tree embowered streets, little two-and-a-half-story red brick houses with quaint dormer windows, and awnings over most of the stores along Broadway. Our churches were still below Fourteenth Street and Sunday morning in any part of old New York was sure to be crowded with worshipers in goodly numbers; the women in wide hoop-skirts, poke bonnets and dainty little parasols; the men in huge furry beaver hats, fancy waistcoats, brass buttons, etc. Washington Square, St. John's Park, St. Mark's on Stuyvesant Place, and Union Square Park marked the extreme northerly limits of fashionable uptown in Valentine's day. Greenwich vil-

HORSE SHOW

FAR FROM THE MADDING CROWD

The new editorial offices of *Valentine's Manual* at Hastings-on-Hudson. Washington Irving owned this property in 1835, but the house has been materially altered by successive owners. It is only four miles beyond the city limits and looks out upon the Hudson River and the Palisades

lage was still a village only to be visited with trunks for
a two weeks' stay; Chelsea, Harsenville, Bloomingdale,
Manhattanville, Tubby Hook, Ft. Washington, Inwood,
Kingsbridge, were all small settlements on the West side,
quite remote from the city; while Corlears Hook, Manhattan Island, Yorkville, Kip's Bay and Harlem were
scattered on the East. Stage coaches were still the main
means of transportation although street cars were beginning to appear.

But for Valentine, and this is now admitted to have
been his greatest work, many of the characteristics of our
city at this interesting period of its development would
have been lost. "The trash of to-day," historically speaking, "becomes the treasure of to-morrow," and it is to the
pictures, which he preserved for us at a time when their
value was little realized, that we owe him a debt of inestimable value. Photography and wood engraving were
practised to a limited extent, but copper-plate printing was
still the popular method of preserving the work of the
artist. All three methods were still in an expensive stage,
which necessarily restricted their use to works supposedly
of prime importance and precluded their use in the average book of moderate cost. For this reason, few publica-
tions of that period contain illustrations of our city, and
to the Manual we are indebted for the preservation of
street scenes, notable buildings, land marks, maps, etc.,
between 1840 and 1868. All of them have long ago disappeared and but for Mr. Valentine the record would have
been lost irretrievably.

Turning to the issue of 1841-1842, the first under Mr.
Valentine's editorship, we find an insignificant volume
only 3½ by 5 inches in size, containing 186 small pages
and bound in inexpensive board covers.

The frontispiece is the first of the City Maps for
which Mr. Valentine was afterwards to receive so much
credit. This map shows the extent of the city at that time
(1842) and is now an eagerly sought item by New York
collectors. These are followed in later numbers by other
similar productions showing the constant and rapid
growth of the city.

The preface of this volume contains the following signifi-
cant statement:

"It has been thought expedient to enlarge on the
substance of the City Hall Directory by the introduction of added matter, interesting and useful to the
members of the Corporation and others. The contents
and form of this volume have been selected as most
useful and convenient for reference."

The City Hall Directory, to which reference is here
made (and of which the Manuals were the successor), appears upon investigation to have been a small pamphlet
issued by the City Government as far back as 1818. And
this in turn to have been preceded by a similar publication,
which consisted of a couple of leaves or so containing the
names of the Mayor, Alderman, Assistants, and other
officials of the City Government dating back to 1801. The
entire series, starting with this modest leaflet, continuing
with the City Hall Directory and ending with the Manuals, can be seen at the Public Library on Fifth Avenue.
They form an interesting item of municipal effort in this
direction.

At a later date Mr. Valentine included the names of all
school teachers, constables, policeman, junk-dealers, pawn-
brokers (and all other persons who were licensed by the
city), scrub-women, bell-wringers, firemen in charge of fire-
houses owned by the city (the department was volunteer)
and numberless other items which to-day have so expanded
that a work of ten volumes would not include all this material. For instance, the total number of employees of
every kind given in the Manual for 1842 is 427. The permanent number of city employees on the payroll to-day is
never less than about 85,000, and that is constantly increased by temporary additions, which make the daily
average figure considerably over 110,000. In Valentine's
day the constables numbered 34, while our present police
department numbers considerably over 17,000. And so on
it would go all through the list.

A new Manual, therefore, based on the exact lines of the
old would be doomed to failure. But by taking the good

out of the old, and expanding the same material existing
to-day; by preserving the rapid changes that are constantly going on; by collecting and reproducing the "trash"
of to-day; by such means it is possible that a new series
might be produced that would prove of interest to its
present day inhabitants and valuable to the future historian.

Such, then, is the task confronting the present editor.
How near he will realize the just expectations of the
people of New York in this respect remains to be seen.
The present volume is offered as his idea of about what the
new Manuals should be. Such changes as the comments
of his readers suggest and experience dictates, are cordially invited to assist in making the Manual a book in
keeping with the dignity, importance and glory of the
chief City of the new world.

* * * * * * * * *

The revival to which this editorial refers proved a
success and the number you are now reading is the
twelfth in the series.

* * * * * * * * *

The idea behind the manual, at first, was largely sentimental. It has, however, secured such a generous
means of support from the public at large, that it now
seems wise to place the enterprise on a substantial business footing with ample capital to extend and improve
its operations. It will devote its energies exclusively
to literature about New York and its environs.

* * * * * * * * *

For the benefit of these new readers, let me add that
the Manual's readers occasionally banded together for
semi-public service. It founded the Museum of the
City of New York in the Gracie Mansion and erected
the Liberty Pole in City Hall Park. Its main purpose,
however, is to issue one book each year on New York.

413

There are over twelve hundred rare old plates in these sets and any one interested in old New York will be delighted to get them.

The editions were never very large and the recent unexpected demand from a host of new readers has played havoc with our small supply of back numbers. If any of our old subscribers are short one or two issues they should order the missing numbers at once.

We sometimes feel as if we were to New York what the National Geographic Society is to the country at large. With ample funds we would not hesitate to organize exploring parties to penetrate the mysteries of that huge unknown country, darkest Manhattan. The need of a wider and more intimate knowledge of a region inhabited by about ten million persons seems to us ever so much more important than to discover a new brand of niggers in Thibet or Mongolia.

For years we have been trying to finance just one little expedition to photograph what still remains of old New York. The city of fifty years ago will soon be as completely wiped out as if it never existed

Some twenty-five or thirty years ago, when Mr. Archer M. Huntington was interested in this idea, he offered to provide a fund of a hundred thousand dollars to defray the cost of such a collection. Nothing was ever done. The man to whom the project was first submitted killed it at the start by his hostile attitude—said no one was interested in such pictures and it would be a waste of money. Today that is now seen to be an irreparable loss; and every year's neglect adds to this loss.

Mrs. Carnegie has kindly offered to make one of twenty-five to contribute a thousand dollars for such a purpose. The offer cannot be made available till twenty-four others join. While it is not the Manual's place to raise funds for this purpose it would be glad to co-operate in any such movement sponsored by the right people.

Since writing the above, we understand that Mr. J. Clarence Davies is now devoting some attention to this work. Others can help.

Certain lessons have been learned in the course of our experience and one of them is that more frequent contact with our subscribers is desirable than once a year. With this number we therefore add a quarterly journal, which we have named *Salmagundi,* in honor of Washington Irving, who issued a similar publication in the early days of the last century.

Salmagundi will be what its Greek name implies—a little of everything. In the main, however, it will be a continuation of the Manual's activities, with the addition of special articles about the Hudson River and the historic county adjoining us on the north. The city owes its commercial greatness largely to this noble river and we are quite sure that the extension of our field will prove of great interest to our readers. The subscription will be $1.00 per annum.

A complete index of these twelve numbers will be issued next year. Each picture and article will be fully described and a short description of each plate will be given. It will be of great value as reference. A few errors that unavoidably crept in from faulty proof reading, etc., will also be corrected. This volume will take the place of the regular issue for 1929, but will not be numbered.

INDEX

417

INDEX

418

INDEX

INDEX

420

INDEX

INDEX